16__.
Shakespeare and Tang Xianzu's China

1616: Shakespeare and Tang Xianzu's China

Edited by
Tian Yuan Tan,
Paul Edmondson and
Shih-pe Wang

Bloomsbury Arden Shakespeare
An imprint of Bloomsbury Publishing Inc

B L O O M S B U R Y
LONDON · OXFORD · NEW YORK · NEW DELHI · SYDNEY

Bloomsbury Arden Shakespeare

An imprint of Bloomsbury Publishing Plc

Imprint previously known as Arden Shakespeare

50 Bedford Square	1385 Broadway
London	New York
WC1B 3DP	NY 10018
UK	USA

www.bloomsbury.com

BLOOMSBURY, THE ARDEN SHAKESPEARE and the Diana logo are trademarks of Bloomsbury Publishing Plc

First published 2016

British Library Cataloguing in Publication Data

A catalogue record for this book is available from the British Library.

ISBN:	HB:	978-1-4725-8342-0
	PB:	978-1-4725-8341-3
	ePDF:	978-1-4725-8344-4
	ePub:	978-1-4725-8343-7

Library of Congress Cataloging-in-Publication Data

1616 : Shakespeare and Tang Xianzu's China / edited by Tian Yuan Tan, Paul Edmondson, and Shih-pe Wang.
pages cm
Includes bibliographical references and index.
ISBN 978-1-4725-8342-0 (hardback)– ISBN 978-1-4725-8341-3 (paperback)
1. Shakespeare, William, 1564-1616–Appreciation–China. 2. Shakespeare, William, 1564-1616–Criticism and interpretation. 3. Tang, Xianzu, 1550-1616–Criticism and interpretation. 4. English drama–17th century–History and criticism. 5. Chinese drama–Ming dynasty, 1368-1644–History and criticism. 6. Theater–China–History. I. Tan, Tian Yuan, editor. II. Edmondson, Paul, editor. III. Wang, Shih-pe, editor.
PR2971.C6A26 2016
822.3'3–dc23
2015020628

Typeset by Fakenham Prepress Solutions, Fakenham, Norfolk NR21 8NN
Printed and bound in India

CONTENTS

LIST OF
ILLUSTRATIONS

LIST OF
CONTRIBUTORS

1.1

Yongming XU (徐永明) is a professor of Chinese Literature at the Institute of Chinese Classical Literature and Culture at Zhejiang University and visiting scholar at the Harvard-Yenching Institute and the Department of East Asian Languages and Civilizations at Harvard University. His research focuses on Chinese classical literature from the Yuan to Ming dynasties. He has published three authored books, three edited books and four critical editions of ancient texts, including *A Study of Wuzhou Literati from the Yuan to Early Ming* (元代至明初婺州作家群研究), *A Biography of Song Lian (1310–1381)* (文臣之首——宋濂传), *An Anthology of Critical Studies on Tang Xianzu in Western Scholarship* (co-editor, 英语世界的汤显祖研究论著选译), as well as more than forty articles.

1.2

Paul Edmondson is Head of Research and Knowledge for the Shakespeare Birthplace Trust and an Honorary Fellow of the Shakespeare Institute, University of Birmingham. His publications include *Shakespeare: Ideas in Profile*; *Twelfth Night: A Guide to the Text and Its Theatrical Life* and (co-authored with Stanley Wells) *Shakespeare's Sonnets*. He has co-edited *Shakespeare Beyond Doubt: Evidence, Argument, Controversy* and *The Shakespeare Circle: An Alternative Biography* (with Stanley Wells); and *A Year of Shakespeare: Re-living the World Shakespeare Festival* (with Paul Prescott and Erin Sullivan).

2.1

Wei HUA (華瑋) is Professor in the Department of Chinese Language and Literature at the Chinese University of Hong Kong. Her main field of research is classical Chinese drama. She has authored *Ming-Qing xiqu zhong de nüxing shengyin yu lishi jiyi* 明清戲曲中的女性聲音與歷史記憶 (Women's Voices and Historical Memories in Ming-Qing Drama) and *Ming-Qing funü zhi xiqu chuangzuo yu piping* 明清婦女之戲曲創作與批評 (The Dramatic Works and Criticisms by Women of Late Imperial China). She is also the editor of *Tang Xianzu yu Mudan ting* 湯顯祖與牡丹亭 (Tang Xianzu and *The Peony Pavilion*), *Kunqu chun saneryue tian* 崑曲春三二月天 (Kunqu Opera's New Spring Days) and *Caizi Mudanting* 才子牡丹亭 (The Genius's *Peony Pavilion*), a unique commentary on the *Peony Pavilion* by an early Qing married couple. She has also published *An Anthology of Women's Plays in Late Imperial China* (*Ming-Qing funü xiqu ji* 明清婦女戲曲集). Currently she is at work on the representations of Ming history in the classical drama of the Qing.

2.2

Nick Walton is Shakespeare Courses Development Manager at the Shakespeare Birthplace Trust in Stratford-upon-Avon. As Executive Secretary to the International Shakespeare Association he has helped organize World Shakespeare Congresses in Brisbane (2006), Prague (2011) and Stratford/London (2016). He has written introductory material for the Penguin editions of *Timon of Athens* and *Love's Labour's Lost* and wrote the entry on Shakespeare Societies for the *Cambridge World Shakespeare Encyclopaedia*. He contributed chapters to *Directors' Shakespeare* and *The Shakespeare Book* and is co-author of *The Shakespeare Wallbook* series.

3.1

Ayling WANG (王瓊玲) is Professor and Chair of the

Department of Theater Arts, and Vice Dean of the College of Liberal Arts, at the National Sun Yat-sen University, Taiwan. She obtained her doctoral degree at the Department of East Asian Languages and Literatures at Yale University in 1992. She became an assistant researcher at the Academia Sinica (Taipei) in 1993; an associate researcher from 1998 to 2003; and a senior researcher from 2003 to 2013. From 2003 to 2010 she was Acting Director, Deputy Director of the Institute of Chinese Literature and Philosophy, Academia Sinica. From 2008 to 2013, she was also Vice President of the Chiang Ching-kuo Foundation for International Scholarly Exchange (CCKF). Her main areas of research include Chinese drama, Ming-Qing literature and literary theory. She has published nine books on Ming-Qing literature and culture, and more than eighty articles in Chinese, English and Japanese on her areas of interest.

3.2

Helen Cooper was Professor of Medieval and Renaissance English at the University of Cambridge from 2004 to 2014; she holds Emeritus and Honorary Fellowships at University College, Oxford, and a Life Fellowship at Magdalene College, Cambridge. She has particular interests in the cultural continuations across the medieval and early modern periods. Her books include *Pastoral: Mediaeval into Renaissance*; *Oxford Guides to Chaucer: The Canterbury Tales*; *The English Romance in Time: Transforming Motifs from Geoffrey of Monmouth to the Death of Shakespeare*; and *Shakespeare and the Medieval World*.

4.1

Tian Yuan TAN (陳靝沅) is Reader in Chinese Studies at the School of Oriental and African Studies (SOAS), University of London, and the Secretary-General of the European Association for Chinese Studies. His main areas of research include Chinese literary history and historiography, theatre and performance and cross-cultural interactions between China and other countries. He is the author of *Songs of Contentment and Transgression: Discharged Officials and Literati Communities in Sixteenth-Century North China*; *A Critical Edition of the Sanqu Songs by Kang Hai (1475–1541) with Notes and Two Essays*; co-author of *Passion, Romance, and Qing: The World of Emotions and States of Mind in Peony Pavilion*; and the co-editor of *Text, Performance, and Gender in Chinese Literature and Music: Essays in Honor of Wilt Idema* and *An Anthology of Critical Studies on Tang Xianzu in Western Scholarship*.

4.2

Janet Clare is Professor of Renaissance Literature, and Founding Director of the Andrew Marvell Centre for Medieval and Early Modern Studies at the University of Hull. She is the author of *Art Made Tongue-Tied by Authority: Elizabethan and Jacobean Dramatic Censorship*; *Drama of the English Republic, 1649–1660*; *Revenge Tragedies of the Renaissance*. She has published many articles on Renaissance and early modern literature and drama, co-edited the *Journal of Early Modern Studies 2 (Shakespeare and Early Modern Popular Culture)*, and reviewed Shakespeare productions in Ireland for *Shakespeare Survey*. Her most recent work is *Shakespeare's Stage Traffic: Imitation, Borrowing and Competition in Renaissance Theatre*.

5.1

Stephen H. West is Foundation Professor of Chinese at Arizona State University and Professor Emeritus in the Department of East Asian Languages and Cultures at the University of California, Berkeley. With Wilt L. Idema, he recently has edited four collections of Chinese drama: *Monks, Bandits, and Lovers: Eleven Early Chinese Plays*; *Battles, Betrayals, and Brotherhood: Early Chinese Plays on the Three Kingdoms Period*; *The Generals of the Yang Family: Four Early Plays*;

and *The Orphan of Zhao and Other Yuan Plays: The Earliest Known Versions.*

5.2

Jason Scott-Warren is a Reader in Early Modern Literature and Culture at the University of Cambridge, a Fellow of Gonville and Caius College and Director of the Cambridge Centre for Material Texts (http://www.english.cam.ac.uk/cmt). He is the author of *Sir John Harington and the Book as Gift* and *Early Modern English Literature*, and co-editor of *Tudor Drama Before Shakespeare, 1485–1590* (2004). He has published articles in *Historical Journal*, *Huntington Library Quarterly*, *The Library*, *Reformation*, *Review of English Studies*, *Shakespeare Quarterly* and *Studies in Philology*, and in a number of edited collections. He is currently writing a monograph on Richard Stonley, Shakespeare's first documented reader. He is also co-editing *The Oxford Handbook of Renaissance Poetry*, an essay collection entitled *Text, Food and the Early Modern Reader: Eating Words* and a journal special issue on the relationship between text and textiles.

6.1

Patricia Sieber is an Associate Professor in the Department of East Asian Languages and Literatures at the Ohio State University. She is the author of *Theaters of Desire: Authors, Readers, and the Reproduction of Chinese Song-Drama, 1300–2000.* Her work on early modern Chinese song and dramatic culture as well as Sino-European literary relations has most recently appeared in the *Journal of East Asian Publishing and Society*, the *Berkshire Dictionary of Chinese Biography*, the *Journal of Chinese Literature and Culture* and *Representations* among other venues. She serves as the Associate Editor for *East Asian Publishing and Society* and is a member of the editorial boards of the *Journal of Chinese Literature and Culture* and *Contemporary Buddhism*.

6.2

Peter Kirwan is Assistant Professor of Shakespeare and Early Modern Drama at the University of Nottingham, specializing in book history, contemporary performance and early modern dramatic authorship. His monograph, *Shakespeare and the Idea of Apocrypha*, interrogates the formation of the Shakespeare canon. He co-edited with Christie Carson the collection *Shakespeare and the Digital World* and is Associate Editor of *William Shakespeare and Others: Collaborative Plays*. He reviews Shakespeare performance on his blog *The Bardathon* (http://blogs.nottingham.ac.uk/bardathon). He is Book Reviews Editor for *Early Theatre*, Editions and Textual Studies Reviewer for *Shakespeare Survey* and a trustee of the British Shakespeare Association.

7.1

Shih-Pe WANG (汪詩珮) is Associate Professor of Chinese Literature at National Taiwan University. Her major research field is classical Chinese drama with the main focus on Yuan *zaju*, Ming-Qing *chuanqi* and *Kunju*, especially concerning literati's metaphoric writings and the theatrical performance interwoven through actors, audience and critics. She is the author of *The Actors' Performance of Kun Opera in Qianlong and Jiaqing Periods of Qing Dynasty*. Her recent journal articles include: 'The Metaphor of the Literati during the Song-Jin-Yuan Transition: *Wang Can Denglou* as a Case Study' (*Chinese Studies*), 'The Transformation of the Classics and the Invention of Playwriting: From *Jingchaiji* to *Bimuyu*' (*Journal of Chinese Ritual, Theatre and Folklore*), 'A Trio of History, Drama, and Politics: *Zhougong She Zheng* and Zheng Guangzu's Double-minded Playwriting' (*Bulletin of Chinese*) and 'Classics, Reinterpretation, and Masculine Performance: An Alternative and Innovative Route of 1/2Q Theatre' (*Journal of Theater Studies*).

7.2

Anjna Chouhan is Lecturer in Shakespeare Studies at the Shakespeare Birthplace Trust in Stratford-upon-Avon, where she teaches international students and enthusiasts, as well as UK schools and universities. Anjna works on Shakespeare reception and performance in England in the nineteenth century and edited a sourcebook on the Victorian actor-manager Henry Irving, for Pickering and Chatto's *Lives of Shakespearian Actors* series in 2012.

8.1

Mei SUN (孫玫) is a professor in the Department of Chinese Literature at the National Central University in Taiwan. His main field of research is Chinese drama and theatre. He has published five books in Chinese, including *A Study of Xiqu from the Transcultural Perspective* (中國戲曲跨文化研究) and *A Further Study of Xiqu from the Transcultural Perspective* (中國戲曲跨文化再研究), as well as a number of articles in English.

8.2

David Lindley is a professor emeritus of the University of Leeds, where he taught in the School of English. He has worked as an editor of *Court Masques*, *The Tempest* and of eleven masques in the *Cambridge Works of Ben Jonson*. He has a particular interest in the relationships of literature and music in the period, evidenced in his monograph on *Thomas Campion* and his study, *Shakespeare and Music*. An interest in Jacobean court politics led to his study, *The Trials of Frances Howard*. Currently he is working on an edition of Q1 of Shakespeare, *Merry Wives of Windsor* and of the Antonio plays of John Marston.

9.1

Regina Llamas is a lecturer in the Department of East Asian Languages and Cultures at Stanford University. Her current field of research focuses on early southern Chinese drama and dramatic historiography. Her most recent works are 'A Reassessment of the Place of Shamanism in the Origins of Chinese Theater' in *Journal of the Oriental American Society* and *El Licenciado Número Uno, Zhang Xie*.

9.2

Will Tosh is Post-Doctoral Research Fellow at Globe Education, Shakespeare's Globe. He is coordinating the ongoing Indoor Performance Practice Project, which examines the conventions of performance in the candlelit Sam Wanamaker Playhouse. He is the author of *Letters and Friendship in Early Modern England*.

10.1

Xiaoqiao LING (凌筱嶠) is Assistant Professor of Chinese in the School of International Letters and Cultures at Arizona State University. Her main field of interest is late imperial Chinese literature with a focus on performance texts and vernacular fiction. She is currently working on a book manuscript that explores traumatic memories and their transmission across generations during the Manchu conquest of China in the seventeenth century. Her recent publications include: 'Home and Imagined Stage in Ding Yaokang's *Huaren you* (Ramblings with Magicians): The Communal Reading of a Seventeenth-century Play' (*CHINOPERL: Journal of Chinese Oral and Performing Literature*), 'Law, Deities, and Beyond: From the *Sanyan* Stories to *Xingshi yinyuan zhuan*' (*Harvard Journal of Asiatic Studies*) and 'Crafting a Book: *The Sequel to* The Plum in the Golden Vase' (*East Asian Publishing and Society*).

10.2

Kate McLuskie retired from the post of Director of the Shakespeare Institute in 2011. She has taught at the Universities of Kent and Southampton (where she was also Pro-vice-chancellor), Colorado and Massachusetts and the Jamaica Campus of the University of the West Indies. Her publications include *Renaissance Dramatists*, *Dekker and Heywood*, *Professional Dramatists*, *Plays on Women* (with David Bevington), *Shakespeare and Modern Theatre* (with Michael Bristol), *Writers and Their Work: Macbeth* as well as articles in *Shakespeare Survey*, *Renaissance Drama* and other journals. In 2010, she completed an AHRC funded research project called 'Interrogating Cultural Value in 21st Century England: The Case of Shakespeare": the book of the project was published in 2014.

ACKNOWLEDGEMENTS

The conference that inspired this collection of essays was funded by a generous grant from the Chiang Ching-kuo Foundation for International Scholarly Exchange, with additional support from the SOAS Faculty of Languages & Cultures, SOAS China Institute, National Chung Cheng University, and the Shakespeare Birthplace Trust.

In addition to the contributors to this volume, we are grateful to the following scholars and colleagues who helped in various ways to make the conference such a stimulating and successful event: Bernhard Fuehrer, Drew Gerstle, Michel Hockx, Ruru Li, Andrew Lo and Ashley Thorpe. We also thank Jane Savory and Rebecca Trautwein from the SOAS Centres and Programmes Office, as well as Lucrezia Botti and Alastair Ewan Macdonald, both PhD candidates at SOAS, for their assistance in organizing the conference.

FOREWORD

What makes 1616 an important date for the comparison of English and Chinese theatre? Is it because both William Shakespeare (1564–1616) and Tang Xianzu (1550–1616) passed away in this year? Both were playwrights of genius who created works that were immensely popular during their lifetimes and that not only continue to be performed in adaptations and revivals to this very day but also have given rise to veritable academic industries. Or should we focus on the fact that 1616 witnessed the publication of both the first folio edition of the collected work of Ben Jonson (1572–1637), and the deluxe edition of 100 plays from the Yuan dynasty (1260–1368) by Zang Maoxun (1550–1620)? Both these publication projects played a major role in enhancing the literary status of drama as literature, and as such had a lasting impact on the preservation and reception of dramatic texts. Ben Jonson would go on to play a major role in the publication of the folio edition of Shakespeare's work, while Zang Maoxun produced his own edition of the four representative works of Tang Xianzu.

The year 1616 does not mark the first direct contact between English and Chinese theatre. Marco Polo remained silent to all practical purposes on the vibrant theatrical culture he must have encountered in China of the late thirteenth century, and during his wide-roaming ocean travels of the early fifteenth century the Chinese admiral Zheng He never reached the Atlantic, whatever some popular writers may claim to the contrary, so he had no chance to see any mystery play or secular production. The first Europeans to leave descriptions of Chinese dramatic performances were the Portuguese and Spanish visitors of the sixteenth century, but as opera was yet to be invented in Italy, they largely ignored the musical nature of traditional Chinese drama. While in Europe the Jesuits frequently utilized drama in their schools, the Jesuit missionaries who reached China made no attempt to transplant their plays to East Asia. The first English sailors and merchants reached the seas off China in the early years of the seventeenth century, but the Chinese authorities of the Ming dynasty (1368–1644) and the Manchu authorities of the Qing dynasty (1644–1911) were equally wary of these uncouth foreign barbarians and did not buy into their doctrine of free trade – when eventually trade between China and European trading companies was regularized, it was limited to Canton, where foreign merchants were allowed to reside for six months a year but forbidden to learn Chinese.

For the first translation of a Chinese play we have to wait until 1735, when the French translation of Ji Junxiang's (fl. late thirteenth century) *Zhaoshi gu'er* (*The Orphan of Zhao*) was published by the French Jesuit missionary Joseph Henri Marie de Prémare (1666–1736) as *L'Orphelin de la maison Tchao, Tragédie chinoise* in Du Halde's massive and widely read *Description de la Chine*. Despite the fact that Prémare had omitted all the arias from his translation, *The Orphan* was eagerly adopted by Europe. It was retranslated into many languages and adapted into many genres. Voltaire's adaptation of the play as a classicist tragedy in his *L'Orphelin de la Chine* too was widely popular; performed in French or in translation it occupies a special place in European theatre history because it was one of the first influential plays to be performed in 'authentic costume'. For the first direct translation of Chinese plays the British public would have to wait until the early nineteenth century when Sir John Francis Davis (1795–1890) published his renditions. A few decades later, in 1839, Shakespeare's name would be introduced to Chinese intellectuals. The contents of his works would only become accessible to Chinese readers much later, when in 1904 the prolific translator Lin Shu (1852–1924) offered them his retelling of Charles and Mary Lamb's *Tales from Shakespeare* (1807).

European plays were first translated into Chinese in the early years of the twentieth century. The dominant form in which the Chinese of those years encountered Western drama was the realist problem play of the late nineteenth and early twentieth century as exemplified by Ibsen and Shaw. To the surprise of the Chinese, these plays exclusively relied on spoken dialogue and they coined a new word, *huaju* or 'spoken drama', to designate the genre, which came to play a major role in the modern Chinese literature of the 1920s and beyond. From the late thirteenth century when we first can follow the development of Chinese theatre in more detail, traditional Chinese drama always had made full use of the possibilities of music and song. From a Western standpoint it may therefore better be characterized as opera (including all its light manifestations). Technically, all genres of traditional Chinese drama are a kind of ballad opera because the arias are written to pre-existing music. Each genre – the short four-act *zaju* that dominated the stage in the period 1250–1450; the long *chuanqi* of the sixteenth and seventeenth centuries that could run to several tens of scenes; the many kinds of regional opera that came to dominate the stage from the eighteenth century onwards – had its own body of tunes. Traditional Chinese theatre offers us operas without composers, in which the text-writers and actors reign supreme while composers are almost absent.

The absence of direct contact and the chasm separating the two theatrical traditions make any comparison a difficult enterprise. Scholars who have an in-depth knowledge of both English and Chinese theatre of the late sixteenth and early seventeenth centuries are hard to find. This volume therefore offers a new approach by bringing together specialists from both fields. Focusing on selected topics, scholars were paired and asked to reflect on each other's paper, and revise their papers following an exciting meeting in London in June 2014. The result is a collection of essays that are not only original contributions to the study of English and Chinese theatre in themselves but also go a long way to highlight the differences and the commonalities between the two traditions. As such they provide many stepping stones for further comparative research.

Wilt L. Idema, Harvard University

Introduction

This collection of essays engages cross-culturally with how the professional theatre and the art of playwriting had by 1616 reached new heights of accomplishment in late Ming China and Renaissance England. Our central point of reference is 1616, a significant year for Chinese and English theatre. It was marked by the deaths of playwrights Tang Xianzu 湯顯祖 (1550–1616) and William Shakespeare (1564–1616) as well as other momentous developments which changed the impression of drama writing in both countries. Tang and Shakespeare were different kinds of playwrights and we do not seek to draw simple parallels between them. Rather, they become visible markers to help us understand the different yet interestingly comparable and equally vibrant worlds of theatre of China and England around the year 1616.

In focusing on a single year, this project has been inspired by similar approaches adopted by scholars such as Ray Huang in his *1587: A Year of No Significance* on Ming history and James Shapiro's *1599: A Year in the Life of William Shakespeare*. A number of theatrical and literary histories and biographies of playwrights have provided a useful framework for us to trace and take account of the events that took place in 1616. Unlike earlier studies which have tended to focus on a single country and culture, this book is keen to explore what we may learn by placing the theatrical worlds of the two countries and cultures side by side and by discussing one with an awareness of the other. Thomas Christensen's recent work provides a panoramic survey of the global history of 1616, describing it as 'a world of motion'. It is within this broader historical context that our book proposes to direct its attention specifically at the theatrical worlds of China and England in 1616.

The scope of the book is not limited to major playwrights such as Tang Xianzu and Shakespeare, but covers the wider theatrical worlds and the complex networks of writers, playhouses and actors. By placing the study of Chinese and English drama in a comparative and global perspective, these essays review the fields of study and rediscover the worlds that shaped the developments of theatre in China and England in the early seventeenth century. At the same time, the consideration of two cultures stimulates new research methodologies in both traditions.

During the late Ming dynasty (c. 1572–1644), theatre in China experienced its second golden age (the first took place during the Mongol Yuan dynasty in the thirteen and fourteenth centuries). A new form of southern drama known as *chuanqi* gained increasing popularity over its northern counterpart, *zaju*, which was the dominant theatrical form earlier during the Yuan and in the first half of the Ming dynasty. In general, all genres of traditional Chinese drama can be described as musical theatre (or sometimes translated as 'opera') with its heavy reliance on music and songs, but unlike the Western tradition, the writers of Chinese theatre composed their songs to pre-existing tunes. In terms of performance space, while theatres in both early modern England and China took place in multiple milieus including private and public venues as well as the royal court, it appears that the histories of Chinese and English drama have given emphases to different theatrical forms. The height of English Renaissance drama is represented by popular drama in commercial theatres, whereas in China the focus of late Ming drama is usually on the form of 'elite theatre', written by scholarly playwrights for members of their literary circles and performed in their residences usually by private household troupes owned by themselves or their friends. It would be like the English playwrights and companies operating only to perform privately before their theatre patrons or at court. In terms of educational background and social class, one may be tempted to draw a comparison between these Chinese literati playwrights and the University Wits in English theatre. But while the former occupy a central and dominant place in histories of Chinese drama, the same cannot be said for their 'counterparts' in the English tradition. Likewise, the vibrant scene of the commercial theatre in Renaissance England was not found in late Ming China. Even basic keywords such as 'theatre', 'playwright' or 'authorship' are here shown to have different meanings and relevance in the respective theatrical climates. These essays, then, challenge the homogeneous repercussions of the concept of the 'global' and instead focus on particularities and difference, the better to find complementary (and some overlapping) synergies.

Our structure demonstrates the 'dialogic' concept and design that we believe best serves this kind of discussion. In June 2014, at the School of Oriental and African Studies, University of London, we gathered together pairs of scholars working on similar fields and periods, but in two different contexts and within different scholarly traditions. Each took as their point of departure one of ten theatre-related themes, made a presentation from within their own field of expertise and then engaged in open cross-cultural dialogue. Each section of this volume contains versions of the two essays – one from the Chinese theatre perspective and one from the English – revised in the light of the conversations and discussions that took place.

As dialogues often begin with short exchanges, these essays are meant to speak to one another. For many of us who gathered, it was our first introduction to each other's theatrical cultures by experts. We hope that the occasion of the 400th anniversary of the deaths of two of the greatest dramatists will mark the beginnings of future dialogues between our cultures and their respective fields of research.

Tian Yuan Tan, SOAS, University of London
Paul Edmondson, The Shakespeare Birthplace Trust
Shih-pe Wang, National Taiwan University

Note to the reader

Unless stated otherwise, all quotations from Shakespeare are based on the *Arden Shakespeare Complete Works* (Bloomsbury 1998). Spelling from other printed sources has, when appropriate, been silently modernized. All Chinese dates cited have been converted to their equivalent on the Western calendar.

1

Setting the scene: playwrights and localities

What were the 'geographies' of theatre in China and England around 1616? In what ways was theatre linked to specific locales? This pair of papers explores the localities that were significant both to the production of plays by the two major playwrights, Tang and Shakespeare, and also to their living legacies today.

FIGURE 1 *Portrait of Tang Xianzu (1838), copy kept in Tang Xianzu Memorial Hall in Suichang (Zhejiang province). Photo courtesy of Xie Wenjun, Director of the Tang Xianzu Memorial Hall.*

1.1 The backdrop of regional theatre to Tang Xianzu's drama

Yongming Xu

Tang Xianzu 湯顯祖 (1550–1616) was born in Linchuan (Jiangxi province), and throughout his official career and lifetime he lived in Nanjing (Jiangsu province), Xuwen (Guangdong province) and Suichang (Zhejiang province). In the year 1598, he resigned from his position as County Magistrate of Suichang and returned to Linchuan to live out the remainder of his lifetime. The regions covered by Tang's travels for work and pleasure are amongst the most economically developed in the southeast coastal area of China, and they are also locations where dramatic activities were most active and vibrant during this period. Tang's overwhelming achievements in Chinese drama derived from his literary genius and the late Ming trend of anti-*Daoxue* (Learning of the Way) to value sentiment (*qing* 情) and suppress reason (*li* 理).[1] But they also derived from the dramatic environment of the aforementioned areas. This essay attempts to examine Tang Xianzu's dramatic activity throughout his lifetime by positioning his achievements against the backdrop of regional dramatic traditions and their development.

Tang's dramatic activity in Nanjing and the dramatic traditions of Jiangsu province

After Zhu Yuanzhang (1328–98) overthrew the Yuan dynasty (1260–1368) to establish the Ming dynasty (1368–1644), Jinling (Nanjing), recognized as the 'Capital of the Six Dynasties', became its dynastic capital. In 1421, when the

Yongle Emperor (r. 1403–24) relocated the capital to Beijing, Jinling was then renamed Nanjing and often referred to as the southern capital or secondary capital. Nanjing retained many administrative institutions, including the institution responsible for dramatic activities, the southern Office of Music Instruction (*Nan jiaofang si* 南教坊司). Thus, though the national political centre shifted north, the secondary capital Nanjing maintained its importance as the southern political and cultural centre. However, as the secondary capital, the majority of the institutions in Nanjing teemed with sinecures, leaving its official inhabitants much leisure time, which resulted in the flourishing of dramatic entertainment. Throughout the Ming dynasty, Nanjing remained the dramatic centre of Jiangsu province.

In the eleventh year of the Wanli reign (1583), Tang Xianzu successfully passed the imperial examination to become a *jinshi* (presented scholar) at the age of 34. In the following year (1584), he declined to be recruited by Chancellors Shen Shixing 申時行 (1535–1614) and Zhang Siwei 張四維 (1526–85), and instead was appointed chamberlain at the Court of Sacrificial Worship in Nanjing. In 1588, he was appointed the deputy governor of the Supervisorate of Imperial Instructions, and in the following year he was transferred to the Bureau of Ceremonies governed by the Board of Rites as chief of staff. In 1591, Tang Xianzu submitted his famous 'Memorial to Impeach the Ministers and Supervisors' (*Lun fuchen kechen shu* 論輔臣科臣疏), upsetting the upper authorities, and was demoted to the position of clerk in Xuwen county of Guangdong province. He had spent a total of seven years in Nanjing from the time of his appointment to his demotion. During this period, he engaged in close association with other playwrights such as Zhang Fengyi 張鳳翼 (1527–1613) and Zhang Xianyi 張獻翼 (1534–1604) – brothers from Changzhou – Zang Maoxun 臧懋循 (1550–1621) from Huzhou (Zhejiang) and Mei Dingzuo 梅鼎祚 (1549–1615) from Xuancheng (Anhui). Regarding Tang's relationship with Shen Jing 沈璟 (1553–1610), the leader of the Wujiang School (School of Poetic Metre), Xu Shuofang observed that 'though they might have met (when Shen Jing passed through Nanjing), any relationships between the two were distant'.[2]

Undoubtedly, during his seven years living as a Nanjing official, the dramatic milieu of Nanjing and, indeed, the whole Jiangsu area significantly impacted upon Tang's theatrical composition. Tang's creation of the *chuanqi* drama *The Purple Hairpin* (*Zichai ji* 紫釵記) in 1587 during his residence in Nanjing was a revision of his unfinished early work *The Purple Flute* (*Zixiao ji*). Moreover, his contact with the monk Zhenke 真可 (1544–1604, monastic name Daguan 達觀) also greatly altered his outlook on life and the world.[3] Around the turn of the year from 1590 to 1591, Tang Xianzu met monk Zhenke in the mansion of Zou Yuanbiao 鄒元標 (1551–1624), the military councillor of the Nanjing Board of Punishment. Under Zhenke's influence, Tang embraced a certain kind of religious rite called 'Accepting the record' (*shouji* 受記) to convert to Buddhism. Monk Zhenke even gave Tang a monastic name, Cunxu 寸虛. *The Southern Bough* (*Nanke ji* 南柯記), a play composed by Tang Xianzu in his twilight years, was replete with Buddhist culture that can be traced back to his encounter with Monk Zhenke.[4]

The influence of Tang's short stay in Guangdong upon his dramas

Tang Xianzu was demoted to the position of clerk in Xuwen (Guangdong) in May 1591, and was transferred as District Magistrate of Suichang (Zhejiang) in March 1593. So, discounting the journey time, Tang only spent slightly over a year in the Guangzhou region. So short was the time span that Tang had little chance to work on his dramatic creations or participate in dramatic activity, nor was he much influenced by the local dramatic culture. None the less, in masterpieces like *Peony Pavilion* (*Mudan ting* 牡丹亭) and *Record of*

Handan (*Handan ji* 邯鄲記) composed late in life, we can clearly trace the influence of his stay in Guangdong.

Take *Peony Pavilion* for example: the drama clearly shows the influence of Tang's meetings with Matteo Ricci (1552–1610) in Zhaoqing and Macao, as well as with other missionaries and foreign merchants. The short story 'Record of Du Liniang' from which the drama was adapted originally did not contain any mention of Guangdong customs. It was clear that Tang took his memories of this region and wove them into the drama. During his travels, Tang passed through Shaozhou and Zhaoqing, places where Matteo Ricci lived for years whilst pursuing his religious mission. And even though Tang made no reference to missionaries in his poems written in Shaozhou, it does not mean he was oblivious of the local Catholic churches or had not visited them. 'During his travels after being demoted to Guandong, he deliberately made a detour to visit Macao and it may be assumed that he visited foreign firms (hongs) and met with foreign merchants'.[5] Xu Shuofang suggested that the 'Temple near Xiangshan Bay' in Scene 21 of *Peony Pavilion* was a reference to the São Paulo Jesuit Church in Macao.[6] Other scholars have argued against this position as São Paulo had not been established. However, judging from the scene's spoken dialogue: 'I'm the head monk of the Treasure Temple near Xiangshan Bay, Guangzhou Prefecture. This temple was built by the "foreign devils" [foreigners] to welcome the officials of appraising treasure', the temple is evidently a foreign-built church, though not necessarily the São Paulo Church.

Furthermore, the hero of *Peony Pavilion*, Liu Mengmei, was re-imagined as a poverty-stricken *xiucai* (one who passed the imperial examination at the county level) student from Lingnan, which was a departure from the original character – the son of a prefectural magistrate. All of this demonstrates the mark Guangzhou left upon the author. Another demonstration is found in Scene 25 of *The Record of Handan*, where the hero, Lu Sheng, is demoted to Hainan Island, and the drama also makes references to the 'black devils' (*heigui* 黑鬼)

there, both of which probably stem from Tang Xianzu's visit to Hainan Island, whilst in Xuwen.

Tang's activity in Suichang and the theatrical culture of Zhejiang region

During the late Ming dynasty, Zhejiang produced thriving dramatic performances, numerous playwrights and prolific works, making its dramatic activity as prosperous as Suzhou. Hangzhou had been the capital of the southern Song dynasty (1127–1279) and for a time the political, economic and cultural centre of the country. After the fall of the Song dynasty in 1279, many northern playwrights working in the *zaju* 雜劇 (literally, variety drama) genre moved south to Hangzhou, accelerating the development of *zaju* in Hangzhou. Around the same time as the Jin and Yuan period *zaju* emerged, an early form of southern drama known as *nanxi* 南戲 also originated in Yongjia (modern Wenzhou, Zhejiang). In addition, *The Lute* (*Pipa ji* 琵琶記), an important transitional work from the southern Song *nanxi* to the Ming dynasty *chuanqi*, was written by Gao Ming 高明 (c. 1305–71) from Rui'an in Zhejiang province.

Two of the 'Four Great Dramatic Melodies' (*sida shengqiang* 四大聲腔) of the Ming dynasty were created in Zhejiang: the Haiyan tune and the Yuyao tune. After these two characteristic melodies were formed, they quickly spread to surrounding provinces. Apart from those two melodies, the Yiwu tune and the Hangzhou tune also originated in Zhejiang. Some characteristic melodies from other provinces, for example, the Yiyang tune, the Kunshan tune, the Leping tune, the Huizhou tune, the Qingyang tune and the Siping tune, were also popular in Zhejiang during this time. Distinguished playwrights from Zhejiang in the mid-to-late Ming dynasty included: Shi Pan 史槃 (1531–1630), Chen Yujiao 陳與郊 (1544–1611), Xu Wei 徐渭 (1521–93), Ye Xianzu 葉憲祖 (fl. 1620s), Tu Long 屠隆 (1542–1605), Zhou Chaojun 周朝俊 (fl. late sixteenth century), Lü Tiancheng 呂天成 (1580–1618), Wang Jide 王驥德 (1540–1622), Bu Shichen 卜世臣 (fl. 1610s), Gao Lian 高濂 (c.1527–c.1603), Shan Ben 單本 (1562–1636), Chen Ruyuan 陳汝元 (1572–1629), Meng Chengshun 孟稱舜 (c.1600–after 1655), Ling Mengchu 凌濛初 (1580–1644), Mao Wei 茅維 (n.d.), Zhuo Renyue 卓人月 (1606–39) and Xu Shijun 徐士俊 (1602–81).

Tang Xianzu's dramatic activity in Suichang was manifested in the following ways. First, in his association with contemporaneous playwrights such as Tu Long, Sun Rufa 孫如法 and Lü Yusheng 呂玉繩 (1560–?). Tu Long was from Yin county of Ningbo province, and he and Tang had stayed in touch through letters whilst Tang was in Nanjing. After Tang Xianzu was transferred to Suichang as District Magistrate, Tu Long visited him there once, giving much pleasure to the lonely Tang, as recorded in one of his poems.[7] Two playwrights from Shaoxing, Sun Rufa and Lü Yusheng had both become *jinshi* in the same year (1583) as Tang Xianzu. Sun was famous for his mastery of the principles of drama. In the spring of 1596, Tang wrote two poems to Sun and Lü which expressed his contentment at his relaxed and carefree lifestyle in Suichang. In autumn of the same year, Tang went to Shaoxing to settle the land tax on his farmland in Suichang and met Sun. Over the course of their meeting, they discussed Wang Jide's *chuanqi* play *Poem on the Red Leaf* (*Tihong ji* 題紅記). This play was mentioned in Scene 10 of Tang's *Peony Pavilion*. Tang also enquired about Wang's opinion of his then only published drama, *The Purple Flute*. Sun told him that Wang Jide had been deeply impressed by the author's talent, but had been mildly critical of the principles of this drama. Tang had hoped to seek advice in person from Wang, but this was never possible as Wang was travelling. As Xu Shuofang commented, 'although Tang Xianzu and Wang Jide never got to meet each other, their mutual respect is worth consideration'.[8]

Second, being an official for five years in Suichang also had an impact upon Tang's writing of *Peony Pavilion*. Scholars still debate whether this play was actually composed in Suichang or in Tang's hometown Linchuan. In the Ming edition of *Peony Pavilion*, the inscription reads: 'Inscribed by Qingyuan daoren (i.e. Tang Xianzu) during the Wuxu year of the Wanli reign (1598)'. In March of that year, Tang resigned from his position and went back to Linchuan; *Peony Pavilion* was finished by the autumn of the same year. Scholars from Suichang insist that *Peony Pavilion* was composed in Suichang, but since the drama was published in the autumn of 1598, Xu Shuofang argues that it was created in Linchuan.[9] However, Tang's experience of running the government in Suichang can definitely be traced in *Peony Pavilion*. For example, Scene 8 'Speed the Plough' depicts the pleasant scenery of Du Bao and the Prefect of Nan'an Prefecture inspecting the farms, which was a real-life imitation of Tang's experience of inspecting farms in Suichang. During the scene, Du Bao arrives to inspect the farms in Qingle county. The villagers were glad to have Prefect Du in office for three years, for he was kind and honest and promoted virtue and condemned corruption and evil practices. While he was in office, rules and regulations were established in all the villages, local organizations were set up, public granaries and village schools were organized: he was a true blessing for the villagers. Whilst on a tour to inspect the farms, all the villagers come to greet him in the official pavilion. Du Bao praises: 'A pretty spot and well named Qingle, "Pure Joy"'. And then the villagers and official sing together:

> To see the pure lines of hills,
> the pure stream waters,
> one would fancy oneself
> on 'the fabled road to Shaoxing'.
> And all the sky white clouds of spring.

> What is pure is the heart of our governor
> and the conduct of his officers
> so that the farmer, no cause to take to court
> spends his day singing.[10]

Monk Zhenke had a great ambition to convert Tang to Buddhism. So he sailed from Hangzhou to Longyou county, and then tramped over hill and dale, trekking all the way into Suichang. At Chijing Ridge 赤津岭, 60 *li* (1 *li* = 500 metres) from Suichang, he composed a verse: 'Tang in Suichang, Tang in Suichang, chooses the mountain village over plain county. Up the hills and down the dales, he has worn me out with sweaty clothes.'[11] Fifteen *li* from Suichang was the famous Tangshan Temple, where Guanxiu 贯休 (832–912), the late Tang Master Chanyue, once meditated. Monk Zhenke tried to enlighten Tang Xianzu with the religious legend of Guanxiu's imitation of the Eighteen Arhats. Though Monk Zhenke ultimately failed to convert Tang, his influence was an important factor in Tang's retreat from bureaucracy and his abandonment of officialdom.

Tang's dramatic activities in Jiangxi region

Tang Xianzu was undoubtedly the most outstanding playwright in Jiangxi. His first drama, *The Purple Flute*, was composed when Tang lived in Linchuan, aged around 30. He composed it to the Yihuang tune which was very popular in his hometown. Three of Tang Xianzu's four plays collectively known as the 'Four Dreams', namely, *Peony Pavilion*, *The Southern Bough* and *Record of Handan*, were created and published within three years of his resigning from officialdom in Suichang. *Peony Pavilion* tells the story of Du Liniang and Liu Mengmei falling in love in a dream. Their love – surpassing life and death, space and time – resulted in a strong counter-attack from neo-Confucianism and feudal ethics, and the publication of *Peony Pavilion* exerted great influence on young women for generations to come. Two famous cases during Tang's lifetime concerned two young women, Feng Xiaoqing from Hangzhou and Yu Niang from Loujiang, Jiangsu. After reading *Peony Pavilion* both of them eventually died after going through long periods of sorrow, self-pity and depression.[12]

After Tang completed *Peony Pavilion*, Monk Zhenke twice visited Linchuan in an attempt to convert Tang to the Buddhist religion. After his first visit, Monk Zhenke wrote Tang a rather lengthy and philosophical letter and updated Tang's monastic name from Cunxu (1-inch void) to Guangxu (wide void). In the letter, he wrote: 'Heaven and Earth are the greatest of that which is tangible, and Emptiness is the greatest of the intangible. Heaven and Earth is to the universe from which it was born a cloud in the sky; what Emptiness is to the Great Awakening, is like a bubble in the ocean.'[13] Apparently Monk Zhenke still hoped that Tang would realize the futility of earthliness and achieve epiphany in the Emptiness. Under the influence of Zhenke's ideology, Tang wrote the *chuanqi* plays, *The Southern Bough* and *Record of Handan*. *The Southern Bough* was adapted from a Tang dynasty classical tale titled 'The Story of the Governor of Nanke'. It vividly chronicled the life of Chunyu Fen, who evolves from a student with political ambitions to an honest and upright official and finally degenerates to become a corrupted soul in bureaucracy. *Record of Handan* was completed the following year. It was adapted from another Tang classical tale titled 'The Story of the Pillow', which tells the story of hero Lu Sheng's dream, in which he witnessed the vicissitudes of feudal officialdom. This dreamt life directly exposes the ugliness of feudal bureaucracy, its politics rife with strife and its life full of debauchery. These latter two of the 'Four Dreams' presented the author's complete repudiation of the pursuit of fame and fortune, and also used Buddhist and Taoist thinking to probe the question of man's destiny in life.

Whilst in his hometown, Tang Xianzu not only wrote the aforementioned monumental works of drama, but he also penned one of the most important essays on dramatic theory in pre-modern China, 'Epigraph for the Theatre God Master Qingyuan in the Yihuang County Temple' (*Yihuang xian xishen Qingyuan shi miao ji* 宜黃縣戲神清源師廟記).[14] This essay is an exposition of dramatic theory that encompasses the origins of drama, the relationship between drama and reality, the social function of drama and theories on the artistic self-cultivation of drama performers. It constitutes a founding work in theories on the art of directing in Chinese drama.

After he renounced official life and retired to his hometown, Tang Xianzu maintained his relationships with playwrights like Mei Dingzuo, Zou Diguang, Lü Yusheng and Sun Rufa. After Tang finished the draft of *Peony Pavilion*, he gave several copies of the manuscript to his friends. Mei Dingzuo got a copy from Lü Yusheng and planned to write a preface for the drama. He wrote to Tang to arrange a meeting in Nanjing the following year. However, in the dispute between Tang Xianzu and Shen Jing, Mei was also suspected of siding with Shen by praising him and criticizing Tang.[15] Zou Diguang 鄒迪光 (1550–1626) was from Wuxi, where he spent his time gardening and commissioning troupes and performances after he abandoned officialdom. There were several troupes in his residence, all of which performed *kunqu* dramas, including performances of Tang's *The Purple Hairpin* and *Peony Pavilion*. Zou wrote a biography of Tang Xianzu, which Tang responded to with a letter saying he was 'pleased at first and then moved to tears'.[16] Other playwrights such as Pan Zhiheng 潘之恒 (1556–1622), Zheng Zhiwen 鄭之文 (?–1645), Wang Yufeng 王玉峰 (n.d.) and Zhang Dafu 張大復 (1554–1630) all stayed in touch with Tang Xianzu to some extent: some as nodding acquaintances, some through correspondence, and some had their works prefaced by Tang.

Geographically speaking, the distribution of Chinese *chuanqi* playwrights clustered in southeast areas like Anhui, Jiangsu, Jiangxi and Zhejiang, and the performances in these areas were also the most thriving. Tang Xianzu was blessed to have travelled and lived in these areas where he was able to communicate with excellent playwrights and enjoy many different kinds of dramatic performances. This exceptional dramatic milieu had nothing but positive effects upon his dramatic compositions. With this unique life experience, his remarkable talent and upright integrity and the late Ming romantic trend to 'value sentiment and suppress reason', the way was paved for him to become the most prominent playwright in the late Ming period.

Notes

1   For an introduction to the playwright and his dramas in the context of late Ming China, see also Isabella Falaschi, 'Tang Xianzu, *The Peony Pavilion*, and *Qing*', in Tian Yuan Tan and Paolo Santangelo (eds), *Passion, Romance, and Qing: The World of Emotions and States of Mind in Peony Pavilion* (Leiden: Brill, 2014), pp. 1–43.

2   Xu Shuofang, *Tang Xianzu pingzhuan* (Nanjing: Nanjing daxue chubanshe, 1993), p. 61.

3   Ibid., p. 71.

4   Xu Shuofang, *Lun Tang Xianzu ji qita* (Shanghai: Shanghai guji chubanshe, 1983), p. 4.

5   Xu, *Tang Xianzu pingzhuan*, p. 86.

6   Ibid.

7   Xu Shuofang (ed.), *Tang Xianzu quanji* (Beijing: Beijing guji chubanshe, 1999), p. 491.

8   Xu, *Tang Xianzu pingzhuan*, p. 108.

9   Ibid., p. 116.

10 Cyril Birch (trans.), *The Peony Pavilion* (Bloomington: Indiana University Press, 2002), p. 33 (Scene 8).

11 Xu, *Tang Xianzu pingzhuan*, p. 109.

12 Tang Xianzu, 'Ku Loujiang nüzi ershou youxu', in Xu Shuofang (ed.), *Tang Xianzu quanji*, p. 491.

13 Xu, *Tang Xianzu pingzhuan*, p. 164.

14 A translation of this essay is available in Faye Chunfang Fei (ed. and trans.), *Chinese Theories of Theatre and Performance from Confucius to the Present* (Ann Arbor: University of Michigan Press, 1999), pp. 55–7.

15 See Mei Dingzuo, 'Changming lüji xu', in idem, *Luqiu shishi ji, wenji, juan* 4, 32b–33b, *Xuxiu Siku quanshu* (Shanghai: Shanghai guji chubanshe, 1995), vol. 1379, p. 171.

16 Tang Xianzu, 'Xie Zou yugong', in Xu Shuofang (ed.), *Tang Xianzu quanji*, p. 491.

FIGURE 2 *Shakespeare's memorial bust on the north wall of the chancel of Holy Trinity Church, Stratford-upon-Avon. It is likely to have been installed before 1619 and is mentioned in the 1623 Folio. The inscription refers to Shakespeare's name decking a 'tomb', but there is no tomb nearby, only a gravestone with an epitaph but no name, believed to be Shakespeare's, and positioned next to the grave of his wife, Anne. Photo and copyright John Cheal.*

1.2 Stratford-upon-Avon: 1616

Paul Edmondson

Monday 25 April 1616 was a significant moment in the life and future of Stratford-upon-Avon. The playwright and poet, Master William Shakespeare, Gentleman, who had died two days earlier, aged 52, was buried in the chancel of Holy Trinity Church, a ceremony no doubt attended by his close family, friends and neighbours. Among those mourning were his wife, Anne, originally from nearby Shottery. They had been married for almost thirty-four years (ever since William was only 18 and Anne 26). Their eldest child, Susanna (1583–1649), her physician husband, John Hall (c. 1575–1635), and their daughter, Elizabeth (1608–70), were no doubt in attendance, as was Shakespeare's younger daughter, Judith (1585–1662) and her husband, Thomas Quiney (1589–?1662–3). Judith was two months pregnant with their first child whom they would proudly name Shakespeare Quiney. Funerals often call to mind earlier deaths. For his surviving family, Shakespeare's evoked memories of Hamnet Shakespeare, the twin brother of Judith who had died some twenty years earlier, aged 11. Shakespeare's sister, Joan Hart, would have been among the mourners, too. She was last surviving of his five siblings (three brothers and two sisters), the others having pre-deceased him by 1613. The vicar who presided over Shakespeare's funeral was John Rogers, who, from 1611, was Shakespeare's next-door neighbour, living in the old priest's house close to the Guild Chapel. Shakespeare's theatrical colleagues with whom he had worked for over thirty years in London were not able to be contacted in time to attend the funeral; Stratford-upon-Avon was a three- or four-day journey from London, and Shakespeare was buried two days after he died. But perhaps some of them were involved in the designing of the memorial bust for Shakespeare which was erected on the north wall of the church at some point in the succeeding years. Importantly, this bust tells us that he died on 23 April, aged 53 (if this is understood to be the beginning of his fifty-third year, rather than a mistake, then Shakespeare died on his birthday; to support this is his christening on 26 April 1564 when he was likely to have been three days old).

The bust was made by a Dutch sculptor, Geerhart Janssen, who two years earlier had made the tomb and effigy for Shakespeare's friend John Coombe (buried near the high altar in July 1614). Janssen's father's workshop was in Southwark near the Globe Theatre so the chances are that both father and son knew what Shakespeare looked like: high, rounded cheeks, small, sunken eyes, a high forehead and balding, auburn hair. We learn from the bust that Shakespeare was right-handed; he holds some paper in his left hand, while the other (usually furnished by the church with a local goose feather for his quill) is poised to compose. It looks as if he is wearing the scarlet livery tunic of the King's Men theatre company, harking back to the coronation of 1603. That had been among the greatest occasions in Shakespeare's life, certainly one of the most prestigious. He and some of his fellow actors and company shareholders were invited to help form part of the royal procession through London. We do not know precisely when the monument was installed but it seems to be a tribute to his memory by friends, colleagues and towns-people. Stratford-upon-Avon historian Mairi Macdonald points out that Thomas Wilson, a vicar with Puritan leanings, took over the running of the church in 1619 and that this colourful memorial is unlikely to have been to his taste.[1] The bust is likely therefore to have been installed by 1619 and was certainly in place by 1623 when it was referred to by Leonard Digges in his poem 'To the memory of the deceased author Master William Shakespeare' at the front of the 1623 Folio edition of his collected works, which begins:

Shakespeare, at length thy pious fellows give
The world thy works, thy works by which outlive

Thy tomb thy name must; when that stone is rent,
And time dissolves thy Stratford monument,
Here we alive shall view thee still.[2]

Shakespeare will live on in his works long after the bust in Holy
Trinity Church has vanished (the bust was restored in 2013
and is seen by the hundreds of thousands of people a year who
visit Shakespeare's grave). At the top of the memorial can be
seen Shakespeare's coat of arms, the official sign that he was a
'gentleman'. This was a significant achievement for the family
as a whole. Shakespeare's father, John Shakespeare (before
1530–1601) was born into a farming family from the nearby
village of Snitterfield. He was a tradesman all his life (a maker
of gloves and a trader of white leather) but achieved public
prominence and distinction through several civic offices he
held in Stratford-upon-Avon, including bailiff (the equivalent
of a mayor). During his year in office (1568–9), he authorized
two professional playing companies to perform in Stratford-
upon-Avon: the Queen's Men, and the Earl of Worcester's
Men. These occasions could have constituted his young son's
first theatrical experiences, and marked the first time the town
had formally welcomed visiting troupes. Shakespeare was
granted the title and social status of 'gentleman' for his father
by the College of Heralds in 1596 by being able to claim
ancestral service to King Henry VII (1485–1509), and the
motto 'Non sanz Droict', which means 'Not without Right'.
This sounds defensive, perhaps because twenty years earlier
an application by John Shakespeare himself for a coat of arms
had not come to fruition. As the eldest son, Shakespeare had
inherited and was able to use the title and the coat of arms for
himself. One likes to think that it was displayed in his family
home, New Place, in the centre of Stratford-upon-Avon.
Though Shakespeare was not alone among his fellow company
members in achieving the status of gentleman, it presents a
sharp contrast to his father's background and demonstrates
the Shakespeares' persistent social, personal and professional
ambition.

The first words on the memorial bust are in Latin:

Iudicio Pylium, genio Socratem, arte Maronem,
Terra tegit, populus maeret, Olympus habet.

These lines can be translated as:

Earth covers, the nation mourns, and heaven holds
A Nestor in counsel, a Socrates in mind, a Virgil in art.

In the first book of Homer's *Iliad,* Nestor is portrayed as
eloquent, wise, uttering 'winning words', a 'clear speaker',
whose language is 'sweeter than honey'[3] (*Iliad* 1: 247–53).
Clearly, the comparison with this classical counterpart
resonated for those seeking to honour Shakespeare's memory.
In 1598, for example, the scholar and clergyman Francis
Meres had referred to the 'mellifluous and honey-tongued
Shakespeare' and to his 'sugared sonnets'; in the same year,
a fellow poet, Richard Barnfield, wrote about Shakespeare's
'honey-flowing vein' in his *Poems in Divers Humours*; echoing
Meres, historian and poet John Weever referred to Shakespeare
as 'honey-tongued' the following year in his *Epigrams in the
Oldest Cut and Newest Fashion.* The mention of the Roman
poet Virgil pays tribute to the significant use that Shakespeare
made of Latin source material (especially for three of his four
Roman plays); and the way he uses Italy (in whole or in part)
as a location for seven of his other thirty-eight plays, and one
of his two narrative poems (*The Rape of Lucrece* takes place
in Collatium, twenty-four miles south of Rome). One hundred
and fifty-four of Shakespeare's sonnets, a poetic form which
originated in Italy and whose name derives from *sonnetto*
(little sound) were published in 1609. Virgil, of course, was
influential in shaping an Italian national identity, a role
that would be echoed by Shakespeare's place in a rapidly
expanding British imperial culture in the eighteenth century.
Interestingly, the mention of Virgil firmly contextualizes
Shakespeare as a European writer. Like his contemporaries,

Shakespeare was empowered by the continental, humanist ideals associated with what we now think of as Renaissance or Early Modern thought, a cast of mind and intellectual formation that was originally and firmly rooted, like Virgil, in Italy. Socrates would have evoked the dramatic tragedies in the minds of Shakespeare's contemporaries, as well as philosophical discourse and dialogue. So, Shakespeare's posthumous reputation begins with readers of Latin being invited to think of him as eloquent, wise, philosophical and, appropriately for a dramatist, someone who thought through dialogue, as well as using it as a vehicle by which to entertain.

The classical names on Shakespeare's monument call back to mind his earliest intellectual influences, namely his education at the King's Free School, re-established under King Edward VI in 1553. It was one of the king's many grammar schools that established Protestant thinking and religious reform in the state's developing educational system. The Tudor grammar schools were part of the government's machinery to ensure that (as one royal proclamation put it) 'good literature and discipline might be diffused and propagated throughout all parts of our Kingdom, as wherein the best government and administration of affairs consists'.[4] The school in Stratford-upon-Avon offered a free education to boys from the town from the ages of about 8 to 15. Its records for that period, like many others in England, do not survive, but we know about the educational curriculum and practice of the time. The boys were taught Latin rigorously six days a week through the whole year, going to school from 6.00 am in summer and from 7.00 am in winter. They stayed until dusk and had half days on Thursdays and Saturdays. The major Christian festivals provided the few annual holidays.

The emphasis of the whole educational enterprise, in light of the teachings of the early sixteenth-century Dutch scholar Desiderius Erasmus (1466–1536), was on the development of eloquence in speech and writing. Grammar schools were the perfect training grounds for politicians and playwrights. A key textbook was William Lyly's *Short Introduction of*

Grammar (1540) through which Shakespeare developed familiarity with a vast range of rhetorical devices. Classical moral
philosophy sat alongside the state's prescribed Christian ethos.
The boys were expected to speak Latin to each other in the
playground and even at home. The curriculum was highly
demanding. Authors studied in their original Latin included:
Cicero, Erasmus, Horace, Juvenal, Mantuanus, Palingenius,
Quintilian, Sallust, Susenbrotus, Terence, Virgil, and especially
Ovid, whose *Metamorphoses* with all its imaginative tales of
transformation was among Shakespeare's favourite books and
is alluded to many times in his work. His earliest published
works, the two narrative poems, *Venus and Adonis* (1593) and
The Rape of Lucrece (1594 – both printed by another Stratford
grammar-school boy, Shakespeare's friend, Richard Field), are
based in part on stories to be found in Ovid (the latter in the
Heroides). The only writing in Greek to feature on the school
syllabus was the New Testament. Shakespeare did not go to
university but he did not need to. His humanist schooling in
the crafts of language and classical literature is writ large across
the whole body of his work. A brief account by the diarist John
Aubrey (1626–97) tells us that Shakespeare was for some years
'a school master in the country', which could, since Aubrey
was writing in London, mean Stratford-upon-Avon itself. That
one of the brightest boys in the school should help out with the
teaching seems perfectly plausible. If so, then a picture emerges
of Shakespeare being an especially bright pupil and one who
stayed on to teach the same Latin and Greek literature by
which he too had been inspired and formed.

The memorial bust's Latin inscription is followed by one
in English:

Stay, passenger, why goest thou by so fast?
Read, if thou canst, whom envious Death hath placed
Within this monument: Shakespeare: with whom
Quick nature died; whose name doth deck this tomb
Far more than cost: sith all that he hath writ
Leaves living art but page to serve his wit.

These few lines are the first in English to establish Shakespeare's posthumous reputation as a writer. He was, they tell us, a poet and dramatist so attuned to verisimilitude, to 'living art', that 'quick' (again 'living') 'nature' has died with him. Shakespeare's published, printed pages are left behind and, like a pageboy, continue to 'serve his wit', his intelligence. The double-meaning of 'page' evokes the world of Shakespearian drama and glances to some of his characters: the boys playing the young women in his plays some of whom disguise themselves as boy-pages or young men. This was at a time when women were not allowed to perform with the professional companies; most of Shakespeare's plays can be performed by a cast of ten men and three boys, with doubling. The clever, witty or mischievous page was a stock character from the Italian tradition of drama, the commedia dell'arte, the influence of which can be traced through Shakespeare's work (Mote in *Love's Labour's Lost* is a good example). Two pages enter the stage to sing 'It was a lover and his lass' in the pastoral comedy *As You Like It*.

Of those watching Shakespeare's burial, his daughter Susanna inherited the most, and Shakespeare's wealth was significant. He left around £370 in cash as well as a substantial amount of extremely valuable real estate and land. Shakespeare had always been an entrepreneur and financial speculator, as well as a poet who wrote plays for popular entertainment. But his wealth had not accrued only by writing plays. A theatre company would pay a freelance writer a few pounds for a new play, but that was not enough to support and sustain a wife and family, as Shakespeare, from the age of 18, had needed to do. No other playwrights of the period were able to make financial investments to the extent that Shakespeare did. A writer who acted earned more money. Shakespeare, like Ben Jonson (early in his career) and a handful of others, managed to do both.

Shakespeare's substantial wealth came from his significant financial investments in the professional theatre. In 1594, he became a shareholder in the theatre company for which he was also the leading dramatist. Their patron was the

Lord Chamberlain and they performed at court before the monarch, for which they were paid handsomely. In fact all theatre companies had to have an aristocratic patron, and all public theatre performances were, during Elizabeth's reign, in theory, dress-rehearsals for the moment when the company would perform at Court. It is worth bearing in mind the number of times that Shakespeare, along with his fellow actors, performed in front of the monarch. During Shakespeare's lifetime, the Lord Chamberlain's (later the King's) Men performed a total of 170 times at Court before Queen Elizabeth I and, later, King James I.

By 1597 Shakespeare was rich enough to buy New Place, which it is estimated cost him around £120. This was a substantial family home which gave him space to write as well as social status (it had been built in the 1480s by Hugh Clopton who had gone on to become Lord Mayor of London). It was an impressive house by most people's standards and it is interesting that, in contrast to this permanent base in Stratford-upon-Avon, Shakespeare never owned property in London until just before he died. He saved money by lodging in London including, in order of residence: the parishes of St Giles Cripplegate, St Helen's Bishopgate (where he was fined for defaulting on his taxes in 1597, perhaps suggesting he was away, moving into New Place), St Saviour's near the Clink Prison, Southwark, and with the Mountjoy family on the corner of Monkswell and Silver Streets, again in the Cripplegate ward. The theatres were closed during Lent which would have given him plenty of time (six weeks) to spend at his Stratford-upon-Avon home with his family, to read and write in relative peace and quiet. Between 2010 and 2015 the Shakespeare Birthplace Trust commissioned an archaeological dig of the site (New Place was demolished in 1759) which confirmed it to be a grand manor house to be enjoyed by someone of considerable means. Traces of the family's inner dwelling on the far side of the courtyard were discovered along with many artefacts from Shakespeare's period, including evidence of feasting and cottage industries.

New Place was the home that his daughter, Susanna, inherited and in which, in 1642, during the English Civil War, she welcomed Queen Henrietta Maria, wife of King Charles I, a royal couple who loved the theatre and especially the works of Shakespeare. With a home like New Place, Shakespeare seems to have lived the life of a commuter, someone who lodged in London and thrived there professionally, but whose grandest, most prized address was in Stratford-upon-Avon. He divided his time between two quite different worlds and locales, the personal and the professional.

Shakespeare's means increased substantially in 1599 when he made another shrewd investment. Along with four other company men he spent £100 on shares in a new theatre, the biggest London had seen: the Globe. It was made from the recycled timbers of The Theatre which had stood on a site for which the ground lease was about to expire. The wood was carried south across a frozen Thames and the Globe opened for business later in 1599. You could stand in the yard and watch a play for a penny or you could pay a few more pence and have a cushion, or sit in one of the galleries. Sixpence bought you a place in the Lords' Room (where you could be seen by the audience, even though your view of the actors was poor). The audience capacity in the new theatre was around three thousand and, as the company's leading dramatist, the more successful Shakespeare's plays became the more money he would make. But income fluctuated year on year and takings were always contingent on outbreaks of the plague (when the theatres had to close and the companies often went on tour instead). In a lucrative year, it is estimated Shakespeare earned around £200 from his company shares and Globe receipts.[5] He continued to invest heavily in Stratford-upon-Avon. He bought a massive 107 acres of land for £320 in 1602. Only three years later in 1605 he spent £440 on a 50 per cent share in the annual tithes payable to the church, an investment that yielded about £60 a year.

Shakespeare's mother, Mary (from an old country family, the Ardens), died in 1608, the same year that the King's Men took over the running of the Blackfriars Theatre, an indoor playhouse which used to be part of a Dominican monastery. Shakespeare was among the founding group of investors, as he had been for the Globe, and another highly successful business was established. Although fewer people could attend each performance the cheapest admission price was six times higher (sixpence) and the theatre could operate more easily during the winter months. The plays were lit by candles and there was more scope for special effects than in the Globe. As a venue it had a strong reputation for music, having been used by a boys' company for the previous eight years. In 1613 Shakespeare bought a gatehouse at Blackfriars for £140. And all this at a time when the Stratford-upon-Avon schoolmaster's salary was £20 a year.

Clearly, Shakespeare was spending very large sums, so it may be worth bearing in mind a story from Poet Laureate William Davenant (1606–68), who liked to say he was Shakespeare's godson and illegitimate son. Where, for instance, did the money come from which enabled Shakespeare to co-found the theatre company in 1594 and to purchase shares in it? Davenant's view was published in Nicholas Rowe's attempt at the first ever biography of Shakespeare in 1709. According to Davenant, Henry Wriothesley, the third Earl of Southampton, gave Shakespeare £1,000 'to enable him to go through with a purchase which he heard he had a mind to'.[6] He was the dedicatee of Shakespeare's two narrative poems; even so, the level of patronage mentioned by Davenant is colossal. In 1806, a highly reliable antiquarian of Stratford-upon-Avon, Robert Wheler, corroborates Davenant's claim with local tradition: 'the unanimous tradition of this neighbourhood is, that by the uncommon bounty of the Earl of Southampton, he was enabled to purchase houses and land at Stratford'.[7] If Davenant's story is true, then the Earl of Southampton's injection of cash made an enormous difference to Shakespeare's livelihood. It would explain how he could afford to purchase the shares and, a few years later, New Place.

But what of the enormous sums he was able to invest in the real estate and the tithes from 1601, the year his father died? The traditional view of John Shakespeare's finances is that he experienced a downward trajectory from prosperity and the highest public office the town made available through to having to sell some of his real estate and becoming impoverished. His son, William, determined to rescue his family name and to ensure that he would never know the same fate, became keenly ambitious and hugely successful. An alternative view, first proposed by David Fallow of the University of Exeter, is that John Shakespeare continued to make significant sums of money through his wool dealing and that he sold some of his real estate not because he was encountering financial difficulty, but in order to re-invest the capital in wool. In 1576, as part of that earlier attempt to acquire a coat of arms for himself, John Shakespeare is said to be in possession of £500. Fallow suggests that Shakespeare himself first went to London in order to represent his father in the wool-dealing business (known as 'brogging'). This revisionist view of John Shakespeare's financial situation would explain how and why, after the death of his father in 1601, the size of Shakespeare's investments increased considerably. So, it may be that Shakespeare's money came from three major sources: a gift from the Earl of Southampton which positioned him socially and professionally, the investments he was able to make in the theatre company and theatres, and the estate he inherited from his father (including, of course, the family's business-home on Henley Street).

It seems that the earliest response to Shakespeare's death was a poem by William Basse.[8] Had Shakespeare died in London, he would almost certainly have been buried in Westminster Abbey. Basse's poem is important because in it he casts Shakespeare into a distinctly English rather than classical literary tradition. He imagines other poets having to move up in order for Shakespeare to be accommodated alongside them in the bed of the grave:

Renownèd Spenser, lie a thought more nigh
To learnèd Chaucer; and rare Beaumont, lie

A little nearer Spenser, to make room
For Shakespeare in your threefold, fourfold tomb.
To lodge all four in one bed make a shift
Until doomsday, for hardly will a fifth
Betwixt this day and that by fate be slain
For whom your curtains need be drawn again.
But if precedency in death doth bar
A fourth place in your sacred sepulchre,
Under this carvèd marble of thine own,
Sleep, rare tragedian Shakespeare, sleep alone.
Thy unmolested peace, unsharèd cave,
Possess as lord, not tenant, of thy grave,
That unto us or others it may be
Honour hereafter to be laid by thee.

'Tragedian', as Katherine Duncan-Jones notes, means 'actor', as well as a writer of tragedies. The poem survives in different manuscript versions. Initially, Basse seeks to establish a major, civic, London locale for Shakespeare (Westminster Abbey). A later version of his fine tribute is annotated 'was bury'd att Stratford upon Avon, his Town of Nativity'.[9]

Stratford and London are the dual locales in Shakespeare's life. The memorial bust in Holy Trinity Church may have been Stratford-upon-Avon's way of connecting with a London-centred project designed to construct and establish Shakespeare's posthumous reputation: the compiling and publication of the 1623 Folio, known as the First Folio (three reprints would follow from 1632 through to 1685). It was the work of many people, some of whom are acknowledged in the volume. The project seems to have been led by his friends and fellow actors, John Heminges and Henry Condell (who, along with the famous actor, Richard Burbage, received bequests from Shakespeare to buy mourning rings). Half of Shakespeare's plays were not published during his lifetime and first appear in the Folio. Some of the manuscripts from which the printed texts derive are based on Shakespeare's original papers, presumably acquired from his widow Anne or daughter Susanna. The works are divided up by genre: comedies, histories and tragedies, a literary critical act which set the tone for succeeding centuries of reception. But Shakespeare is a playwright who challenged genres, who pushed at the boundaries of comedy and tragedy and who, controversially for some of his contemporaries, liked to mix genres within a single play. All of Shakespeare's comedies contain either tragic or dark undertones; all of his tragedies lighter episodes. Some of the histories include elements of the comic form, for example *Henry IV Part One* and *Part Two*; others are identified as tragedies (*Richard II* and *Richard III*). At least four plays are missing from the Folio collection: the now lost *Love's Labour's Won*, *Pericles* (co-authored with brothel-keeper George Wilkins), *The Two Noble Kinsmen* and the lost *Cardenio* (both co-authored with John Fletcher, who succeeded Shakespeare as the leading playwright of the King's Men theatre company). It would have been far more useful for Heminges and Condell to arrange the plays chronologically, since scholars cannot agree on the order in which Shakespeare wrote them.

Canons of literary work vary and develop over time, as do an author's ways of writing, and our ways of understanding authorship. Two of the most significant developments in Shakespeare studies over the last thirty years are that Shakespeare regularly revised his work because of practical, theatrical considerations and that he seems to have collaborated on several more plays, most significantly at the beginning and end of his career. Collaboration was a standard practice among playwrights of Shakespeare's time. There is also a group of plays, which first appeared in the second issue of the 1664 Third Folio, in which there may be reasons to think that Shakespeare had some kind of helping hand.

Establishing an understanding of any author's locale, whether in England or China, has to start from somewhere. If Shakespeare's posthumous reputation began when those who attended his funeral walked away from it, then it continues with the memorials erected to his memory and in the places which have become and newly become associated with his memory through time. Descendants of Shakespeare's sister's family lived until 1806 on part of the site which by 1759 had become known as Shakespeare's Birthplace (it is marked as such on the earliest surviving map of the town). The earliest written mention by someone noticing Shakespeare's grave is in 1634 when a Lieutenant Hammond, during a tour of twenty-six counties, records 'a neat monument of that famous English Poet, Mr William Shakespeare; who was born here'.[10] Two centuries later, on 8 April 1828, the novelist Walter Scott would stand on the same spot and, looking upon Shakespeare's grave, call it 'the tomb of the mighty wizard'.[11] Now, people still want to do the same: to look at the monument, the grave, and to pay their respects. The epitaph on the gravestone itself, close to the high altar, comprises two rhyming couplets which address the passer-by as a Christian friend before going to arrest him or her with a blessing and a curse:

> Good friend, for Jesus' sake forbear
> To dig the dust enclosèd here.
> Blessed be the man that spares these stones,
> And cursed be he that moves my bones.

Some people have suggested that Shakespeare wrote these lines himself and left instructions for them to be carved in his memory. My guess is that they, like the words in the monument on the wall above them, may have started to form in the minds of his family as they walked out of the church on that Monday in April, 1616, as they made their way back through the liveliness of the town that was already becoming Shakespeare's Stratford-upon-Avon.

Notes

1   Mairi Macdonald, '"Not a Memorial to Shakespeare, but a Place for Divine Worship": The Vicars of Stratford-upon-Avon and the Shakespeare Phenomenon, 1616–1964', *Warwickshire History*, 11 (2001–2), pp. 207–26 (207).

2   William Shakespeare, *The Complete Works*, eds Stanley Wells, Gary Taylor, John Jowett and William Montgomery, 2nd edn (Oxford: Oxford University Press, 2005), p. lxxii. Unless otherwise stated all references to the Shakespeare memorial and commendatory verses are cited from this edition.

3   Homer, *Iliad*, trans. Robert Fagles (London: Penguin, 1991), Book 1.290–1.

4   Jonathan Bate, *Soul of the Age: The Life, Mind and World of William Shakespeare* (London: Viking, 2008), p. 81.

5   Andrew Gurr, *The Shakespeare Company 1594–1692* (Cambridge: Cambridge University Press, 2004), p. 115.

6   Nicholas Rowe, *Some Account of the Life of Mr William Shakespeare* (London: Jacob Tonson, 1709), p. x.

7   R. B. Wheler, *History and Antiquities of Stratford-upon-Avon* (London: J. Ward, 1806), p. 73.

8   A view supported by, among others, Katherine Duncan-Jones in *Shakespeare: Upstart Crow to Sweet Swan 1592–1623* (London: Bloomsbury, 2011), p. 255.

9   Duncan-Jones, *Shakespeare*, p. 256.

10 David Kathman, 'Shakespeare and Warwickshire', in *Shakespeare Beyond Doubt: Evidence, Argument, Controversy*, eds Paul Edmondson and Stanley Wells (Cambridge: Cambridge University Press, 2013), pp. 121–32 (131).

11 Walter Scott, *The Journal of Sir Walter Scott*, ed. W. E. K. Anderson (Edinburgh: Canongate Books, 1998), p. 509.

2

Classics, tastes and popularity

What kind of stories were being dramatized by 1616 and why? What determines popularity and what gives a play canonical status as a classic? These essays touch on developments of 'popularization' and changes in taste as seen on the early seventeenth-century English and Chinese stage, as well as the influence of major writers and masterpieces on playwriting in 1616 and beyond.

2.1 The 'popular turn' in the elite theatre of the Ming after Tang Xianzu: Love, dream and deaths in *The Tale of the West Loft*

Wei Hua

The popularity of *The Tale of the West Loft*

By the 1610s visits to the pleasure quarters in Chinese cities like Hangzhou, Nanjing and Suzhou in south of the Yangzi River became very popular. In a book published in 1616, a scholar-official wrote, 'Nowadays prostitutes are all over the country. In big cities there are hundreds and thousands of them. In other poor and isolated counties they are everywhere as well.'[1] The courtesans as a social group captivated the public's imagination to the extent that an anthology of some 500 poems by 180 courtesans in the late Ming was published. This book, titled *Enchanting Words from the Pleasure Quarters* (*Qinglou yunyu* 青樓韻語), was handsomely printed with twelve exquisite woodblock prints illustrating lines from the courtesans' poems. Juxtaposed with these poems are extracts regarding the patrons' and the courtesans' conduct from an earlier *Brothel Guidebook* (*Piaojing* 嫖經), as well as a new late Ming commentary. In so far as the subject matter revolves around male–female relationships at the pleasure quarters, *Enchanting Words from the Pleasure Quarters* is similar to quite a number of dramatic romance (*chuanqi* 傳奇) plays written and published during the late Ming.[2] Ten of these, all featuring love between scholars and courtesans, were put together and printed during the Chongzhen reign (1628–44) as the fourth set of ten plays (*Xiuke yanju shiben disitao* 繡刻演劇十本第四套) in what is now called *The Sixty Plays*

(*Liushizhong qu* 六十種曲), the most representative collection of Ming drama. Included in this set is *The Tale of the West Loft* (*Xilouji* 西樓記, hereafter *West Loft*). Believed to be based on the author's teenage experience with a rival for the love of a courtesan, *West Loft* has enjoyed wide popularity onstage to this day. Its author, Yuan Yuling 袁于令 (1592–1672), became one of the major dramatists after Tang Xianzu 湯顯祖 (1550–1616) in seventeenth-century China.

West Loft was most probably written between 1610 and 1611, before the author turned twenty. It tells the love story between Yu Shuye, a young scholar from a high official's family, and Mu Suhui, a famous courtesan in the city of Suzhou. Mu admires Yu for the lyrics he wrote for the song 'Love at the Chu River' (*Chujiangqing* 楚江情). When Yu pays her a visit at the West Loft, she, ill at the time, sings the song for him. Out of mutual admiration, they become a sworn couple instantly. But Yu's father expels Mu and her mother from the city lest his son's love for Mu should distract him from his studies. Mu's mother strikes a secret deal with the powerful and vulgar patron Chi Tong and takes her to his mansion in the city of Hangzhou. Mu vehemently refuses to marry Chi as his concubine and is locked up by him. Yu, not knowing Mu's whereabouts, falls seriously ill. When a rumour about his death reaches Mu, she tries to commit suicide. Although she is rescued, she still secretly plans her own death. She lies to Chi and tells him that she will marry him only after holding a mourning ritual for Yu. In the course of the ceremony, a knight-errant named Xu suddenly appears. He creates havoc, substitutes his concubine for Mu, and takes Mu to his mansion in Peking to wait for her beloved. Meanwhile, Yu is awarded the title of Top-ranking Scholar in the imperial examination in the capital. Realizing the many ordeals that his son and Mu have gone through, Yu's father eventually consents to their marriage. The play ends with a grand wedding scene.

After Tang Xianzu's *Peony Pavilion* in 1598, writing about *qing* (love, sentiment) became a leading creative force in Chinese drama. Quite a number of literati composed so-called scholar-and-beauty (*caizi-jiaren* 才子佳人) plays, in which true love between man and woman triumphs over the social norms of marriage. *West Loft* is representative of this subgenre. Following Tang's example, later author Yuan Yuling used dream and death to portray the profundity of love; nevertheless, in terms of dramaturgy, philosophy and gender perspective, this later play is substantially different and demonstrates the 'popular turn' in the elite theatre of the late Ming, in early-seventeenth-century China.

By 'popular turn' I mean a change in the literati's style of writing to accommodate the tastes of the general audience and reader, and a strong emphasis on a play's stage appeal over literary value.[3] For instance, the language Yuan Yuling used was easier to understand than that used in *Peony Pavilion*.[4] Quite a few scenes include vulgar jokes. A minor character, the gatekeeper, in Scene 10 speaks local Suzhou dialect to please the audience.[5] In addition, the dramatist adopted the then popular aria 'Love at the Chu River' as his theme song.[6] And unlike Tang Xianzu, he adhered closely to the rules of *Kunqu* 崑曲 (Kun Opera) music to conform to the fashion of the time. That the play's heroine is a courtesan also attracts much interest. According to the editor's preface in the fourth set, the scholar-and-courtesan play *The Embroidered Coat* (*Xiuru ji* 繡襦記) and others like it were performed every day and attracted a large audience of both men and women. 'All of them blew their noses in sorrow and then pressed their palms together in joy.'[7] Evidently, by the 1620s, the courtesans in those plays were already – or promoted as – familiar celebrities, for on the title page of the fourth set under the name of each play, the courtesan's first name is printed.

West Loft won immediate success. 'Soon after *West Loft* came out', wrote Chen Jiru 陳繼儒 (1558–1639), 'from the country's governing elite to men and women of the pleasure quarters ... people constantly copied and passed on the text to sing and perform.'[8] A good indication of the play's popularity among the general (non-courtly) audience is found in the following anecdote: one evening Yuan was in a sedan chair passing by the courtyard of a rich household holding a dinner party. From inside the walls an aria from the scene 'General Xiang Yu's Evening Banquet' was heard. One of his sedan carriers commented, 'In a moonlit night like this, they should sing "Tender words from the embroidered windows" instead of this.' Not knowing Yuan was the author of *West Loft*, from which the aria 'Tender words' came, the carriers moved on. Yuan, absolutely delighted, almost fell out of his sedan chair.[9] The fact that many drama anthologies published during the late Ming included scenes from *West Loft*, and that Feng Menglong 馮夢龍, a leading editor of popular fiction and drama, printed a revised edition of the entire play, are proof of its popularity both onstage and as a text.

The representation of *qing* through dreams: *West Loft* vs. *Peony Pavilion*

Tang Xianzu wrote in his preface to *Peony Pavilion*:

> Has the world ever seen a woman's love to rival that of Bridal Du? Dreaming of a lover she fell sick; once sick she became worse; and finally, after painting her own portrait as a legacy to the world, she died. Dead for three years, still she was able to live again when in the dark underworld her quest for the object of her dream was fulfilled. To be as Bridal Du is truly to have known love. Love is of source unknown, yet it grows ever deeper. The living may die of it, by its power the dead live again. Love is not love at its fullest if one who lives is unwilling to die for it, or if it cannot restore to life one who has so died. And must the love that comes in dream necessarily be unreal? For there is no lack of dream lovers in this world ... What cannot exist by virtue of reason or principle (*li* 理) *can* exist because of passion (*qing*).[10]

As Cyril Birch cogently observes, *Peony Pavilion* is the dramatist's 'most protracted and profound meditation on the nature of love'.[11] The above passage clearly manifests Tang's celebration of *qing* ('love' in Birch's translation) as a natural, irrepressible and life-generating force. And there is no doubt that the heroine Du Liniang ('Bridal Du' in Birch's translation) embodies *qing* in this play. The dramatist's central design is to use *dream* to reveal this innocent, cloistered maiden's erotic desire as completely natural and spontaneous despite the fact that it was morally and culturally forbidden. Bold and beautiful at the same time, 'The Interrupted Dream' (Scene 10 in a play with fifty-five scenes) is one of the most famous and critically acclaimed scenes in Ming dramatic literature.

Wai-yee Li has pointed out insightfully that the late Ming literati were fascinated by dreams and illusion.[12] After 'The Interrupted Dream', Yuan Yuling created his famous dream scene, 'The Confused Dream' (*Cuomeng* 錯夢). These two dreams have been lauded as the two best-written dream scenes in Ming *chuanqi* drama.[13] Yuan's scene presents the hero Yu Shuye dreaming of his beloved Suhui after their forced separation. When the scene opens, Yu has barely escaped dying of lovesickness, for a blank letter from Suhui has reached him by mistake and he therefore suspects that she wants to break up with him. It is a moonlit night. He feels weak and lonesome and hopes to dream of her. The stage direction then reads, 'He falls asleep. The *xiaosheng* 小生 (supporting young male actor) enters as his spirit.' We can imagine the latter is dressed in the same costume as the former. The 'double' arrangement apparently aims to arouse interest among the audience. With the introduction of a new actor, the dream is presented as 'a play within a play' with a music sequence of alternating northern and southern tunes. The author observes the generic convention of *chuanqi* drama, so all the northern arias are sung by the *xiaosheng* actor, while the southern arias are sung respectively by the other characters in his dream, first Mu's mother, then Mu's maid and, finally, Mu's patron in the company of Suhui and servants.

The dream begins with Yu searching Mu's residence late at night. He hears dogs barking when he arrives at her gate. Mu's mother enters but, to his surprise, refuses his request to meet with Mu, saying Mu does not know him and is entertaining a guest. She asks him to leave, closes the door and exits. When Yu knocks at the door again, Mu's maid enters. She repeats that Mu does not know him. He begins to feel angry and insists on seeing her. Ignoring the account Yu gives of suffering for Mu's sake, the maid asks him to leave or wait till her guest departs. She then shuts the door. Yu is left, anxious. He then notices that the music has stopped and the door is open. So he hides in the

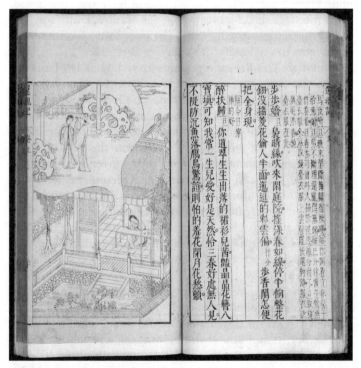

FIGURE 3 *The play text of Scene 10 of* Peony Pavilion *and the illustration of this dream scene. 1617 edition, No. 15097, National Central Library, Taiwan.*

shade of the tree and waits. When a lady enters looking intoxicated with sleeves covering her face, supported by her maid and followed by a patron and his servants, Yu rushes forward and grasps her by the arm, taking her to be his beloved. But she denies knowing him. Yu discovers that the woman – played by the *jing* 淨 (painted face) role-type – is strange-looking and ugly, not at all like the lady he has fallen in love with at the West Loft. But the woman insists that she *is* Mu Suhui. She exits with her patron, who orders his servants to beat Yu. Feeling outraged, Yu does not know if he has mistaken someone vulgar for Mu Suhui or if her appearance has changed. Suddenly, Yu finds himself surrounded by water and feels very frightened. Then the stage direction reads, 'Gongs are struck offstage. The *xiaosheng* actor hurriedly exits. The male lead wakes up, sobs and begins to cry loudly.' Yu's servant then enters.

Although Yu's dream represents as vividly as Du Liniang's dream the protagonist's innermost emotions (*qing*), it was created for different purposes. First of all, Yuan unlike Tang created his dramatic dream without any meditative or philosophical reason of the kind that Tang gives in his preface. As a result, it cannot be analysed from the philosophical perspective of authenticity (*zhen* 真) or heavenly endowment (*tianji* 天機) as can Tang's creation. Second, it lacks the culturally non-conformist, if not subversive, overtone when we consider the dreamer's sex and the dream's content against the social background of the chastity cult during the late Ming period. Third, structurally and thematically speaking, this man's dream does not occupy a pivotal place in the play as a whole.

'The Confused Dream' is, however, dramatically compelling and intriguing. For the audience, Tang's 'Interrupted Dream' has been performed with additional songs and dances of Flower Spirits not found in the original text since the late Ming, apparently to increase stage appeal.[14] From Yuan's commentary on Tang's *Purple Hairpin* (*Zichai ji* 紫釵記), we can detect Yuan's strong emphasis on an unexpected turn of events to enhance the audience's fun and pleasure.

The description of 'The Confused Dream' I have just given conveys a general sense of his idea of theatre and stagecraft. By keeping the audience enthralled with a series of unexpected happenings, Yuan ingeniously leads us to the hero's inner world of feelings of loss, longing and anxiety. He focuses attention on characters' arias, dialogues, gestures, movements and emotions, hence the reader as well as the audience of this scene is left with the strong impression that Yu is genuinely attached to Mu and very afraid of losing her. The psychological realism of this dream helps to deepen the audience's empathy with the protagonist and his love for the courtesan. The dramatist is therefore able to achieve his goal of celebrating the love between a top scholar and a courtesan regardless of their vast difference in social class.

According to Xue Cai 薛寀 (1598–1663), a contemporary and likely acquaintance of Yuan Yuling, the 'Confused Dream' demonstrates its author's fascination with *Peony Pavilion* because this scene derives entirely from 'The Interrupted Dream' and 'Spirit Roaming' (Scene 27).[15] Xue's statement is only partially true because, as we have discussed, Yuan's 'Confused Dream' is portrayed in a different way from Tang's representation of *qing* by way of a dream. Whereas Tang's aim was to show female interiority, Yuan wanted to convey a strange sensory experience. Yuan was more concerned with the audience's reception than with the gender issue or the philosophical concept of *qing* versus *li* (reason/principle). His dream involves the then commonplace social phenomenon of 'male rivalry over a courtesan'[16] and apparently appealed to a large audience. 'The Confused Dream' is the scene in *West Loft* that is most often selected in the drama anthologies published from the late Ming to the Qing. It also influenced the dream scene 'Dream on a Rainy Night' (*Yumeng* 雨夢) in Hong Sheng's (1645–1704) masterpiece, *Palace of Eternal Life* (*Changsheng dian* 長生殿) written in 1688, in the early Qing.[17]

Deaths in *West Loft*

Tang's *Peony Pavilion* preface states that 'Love is not love at its fullest if one who lives is unwilling to die for it.' What is unique about Tang's representation of love through death is that, unlike *Romeo and Juliet* and most love stories, when Bridal Du dies, she has never actually met her dream lover in real life. It is not so much for *whom* she dies as for *what* she dies that is significant. In *Peony Pavilion*, also named *The Soul's Return* (*Huanhun ji* 還魂記), death can be regarded as a willed protest and a necessary means by which the heroine is empowered to pursue love in a spiritual form without sociocultural constraints, hence the 'Spirit Roaming'. In *West Loft* the significance of death has little to do with insistence on individual subjectivity. It is mainly a plot device designed for theatrical effects and the audience's, as well as the author's, emotional satisfaction. The protagonists barely escape death whereas the antagonists are punished by death.

The famed Ming drama critic Pan Zhiheng openly expressed his fondness for the hero Yu Shuye. He said that Yu loves Mu Suhui so wholeheartedly that he can serve as 'an example of true feelings' (*zhongqing bangyang* 鍾情榜樣).[18] As the above discussion of Yu's dream has shown, the author portrayed Yu's character with great care. The image of Yu as a young man who values love far more than scholarly honour or official rank is presented in an unprecedented examination scene titled 'Crying During the Examination' (*Qishi* 泣試). Having just recovered from sickness, Yu takes the imperial examination against his will. He is shown crying involuntarily over the presumed death of Mu while writing his paper. When he sings, lamenting his loss: 'You became a ghost with great affection whereas I became a man with too little love', it is clear that the willingness to die for love is important for the characterization of the hero and the heroine as faithful spouses. Most scholars agree that Yu is the author's self-image. Some believe that as a young man Yuan Yuling was deprived of his student status and banned from imperial examinations because of his rivalry with Shen Tonghe over a courtesan named Zhou Wen.

In its forty scenes *West Loft* includes three violent deaths. Qinghong, the knight-errant Xu's concubine, slits her throat and jumps into the river and dies when she discovers her husband's intention to trade her for Lady Mu and leave her with Chi Tong. The play's villains, Chi and Zhao Bujiang, are killed onstage by the mysterious Xu. Feng Menglong and others have justly maintained that these deaths are unnecessary, so in Feng's revised edition all the deaths are revoked. Qinghong never appears in the play; Xu's new concubine, a courtesan named Hong Bao'er, is used to replace Mu and Hong willingly marries Chi because he is her old patron. Xu does not need to kill Chi because the latter never plots Yu's death, and Zhao becomes a matchmaker of some sort for Yu and Mu in the end.[19] However, Yuan Yuling's rationale appears to be different: love between the hero and the heroine is the most important thing in the world of *West Loft* and anyone – except Yu's father – who has impeded its fulfilment has to be punished. The knight-errant Xu can be seen as the idealized projection of the author himself because Xu's name 'Zhaoling' is the reverse of Yuan's name, 'Lingzhao'. Furthermore, Yuan is praised by his friend as having the character of a knight-errant.[20] Resembling the famous 'yellow-robed knight-errant' in Tang's *Purple Hairpin*, Xu represents individual agency at its best. He plays the role of a 'knight-errant for love' (*qingxia* 情俠),[21] a popular type of character in Feng Menglong's *Accounts of Love* (*Qingshi* 情史) as well as in late Ming drama. Yuan created him to crush the hero's powerful rival and deceitful friend, hence their fate in his hands. Perhaps Yuan was fond of a theatrical sensation and portrayed the killings despite the fact that the villains' crime does not justify death.

In *West Loft*, the death of Qinghong, the lovely concubine, is far more controversial than the deaths of Yu's rival Chi and the adversary Zhao. Though heroic and sensational, her death is unsettling to read and to watch. One cannot but disapprove of her knight-errant's deceit and selfishness. Although the author's objective is to sanction marriage between a scholar and a courtesan, his disposal of a concubine, another socially inferior member, reveals his inevitable patriarchal mindset. Contrary to Tang's yellow-robed knight-errant, who aids the helpless heroine to be reunited with her husband, the knight-errant Xu in Yuan's play focuses on fulfilling the hero's wish. The male-centred perspective can be further evidenced by Xu's rather unnecessary testing of Mu's love and fidelity. After Xu rescues her, he pretends to ask her to be his concubine in order to test whether her feelings for Yu are genuine. The implication is that Xu thinks Mu less trustworthy and sincere because of her inferior social class as a courtesan. A play that appears to be about true love regardless of class difference may in fact be ridden with subconscious contradictions.

Conclusion

We can see that *West Loft*'s dramatic plot twists, sensational scenes, theatrical effects and central theme contributed to its widespread popularity. Much can be gained by comparing the performance values of *West Loft* with those of *Peony Pavilion*. A classic is often the first of its kind and heavily influences later works in centuries to come. *Peony Pavilion*'s complex yet subtle philosophical inquiry and female interiority leave a special and long-lasting impact on its readers and audience. *West Loft* seems like a sensationalized imitation in comparison. It is the ability to touch the core of the human soul with its depiction of *qing* that makes Tang's *Peony Pavilion* an eternal classic.

Notes

1   See Xie Zhaozhe, *Wu zazu* (Beijing: Zhonghua shuju, 1959), *juan* 8, p. 225.

2　See Cyril Birch's discussion on his choice to translate the term *chuanqi* as 'dramatic romance' in his 'A Comparative View of Dramatic Romance: *The Winter's Tale* and *The Peony Pavilion*', in Roger T. Ames et al. (eds), *Interpreting Culture through Translation* (Hong Kong: The Chinese University Press, 1991), p. 60.

3　See, for example, Mao Yuanyi's (1594–1640) preface to an annotated edition of *Peony Pavilion* in Xu Shuofang (ed.), *Tang Xianzu quanji* (Beijing: Beijing guji chubanshe, 1999), vol. 4, p. 2574. Mao said the reason why Zang Maoxun revised Tang Xianzu's plays was because Zang thought they were 'books on the desk' (*antou zhi shu* 案頭之書) rather than 'plays for the stage' (*changzhong zhi ju* 場中之劇).

4　Li Yu (1611–80), one of the leading dramatists after Tang Xianzu, criticized the latter's use of language in 'The Interrupted Dream' (Scene 10) in *Peony Pavilion*. See Li, *Xianqing ouji*, in *Li Yu quanji* (Hangzhou: Zhejiang guji chubanshe, 1992), vol. 3, p. 18.

5　Yuan Yuling, *Xilouji pingzhu*, annot. Chen Duo, in *Liushizhong qu pingzhu* (Changchun: Jilin renmin chubanshe, 2001), vol. 15, pp. 546–8.

6　Wu Mei indicates that the song was originally written by Zhu Youdun (1379–1439) in the early Ming. Yuan changed some of the original lyrics to fit the situation of the female protagonist. See Wu, *Zhongguo xiqu gailun* (Shanghai: Shanghai shudian, 1989), vol. 3, p. 27.

7　Xianxian Daoren, 'Ti *Yanju sitao*', in Mao Jin (comp.), *Liushizhong qu* (Beijing: Zhonghua shuju, 1982), vol. 7, p. 2a.

8　Chen Jiru, 'Ti *Xilouji*', *Jianxiaoge ziding Xiloumeng chuanqi*, in *Guben xiqu congkan*, 2nd series (Shanghai: Shangwu yinshuguan, 1955), vol. 102.

9　See 'Yuan Yuling shengping ziliao huiji' (Collected information on Yuan Yuling's life) in Yuan Yuling, *Xilouji pingzhu*, p. 754.

10　Cyril Birch (trans.), *The Peony Pavilion* (Bloomington: Indiana University Press, 2002), 'Preface to the Second Edition', p. ix. The last sentence is my translation.

11　Ibid., p. x.

12   Wai-yee Li, 'The Late Ming Moment', in idem, *Enchantment and Disenchantment: Love and Illusion in Chinese Literature* (Princeton: Princeton University Press, 1993), pp. 47–88.

13   Chen Duo, '*Xilouji* jiqi zuozhe Yuan Yuling', *Xuzhou jiaoyu xueyuan xuebao,* 1998.4, p. 41.

14   For the performance history of this scene, see Lu Eting, '"Youyuan jingmeng" jishuo', in Hua Wei (ed.), *Tang Xianzu yu Mudanting* (Taipei: Zhongyang yanjiuyuan Zhongguo wenzhe yanjiusuo, 2005), vol. 2, pp. 699–736.

15   See Zheng Zhiliang, 'Yuan Yuling yu Liulangguan pingdian "Linchuan simeng"', *Wenxian*, 3 (July 2007), p. 52. I believe the dream scene in *Romance of the Western Wing* also influenced Yuan Yuling's composition of 'The Confused Dream'.

16   See Lu Eting, 'Tan Yuan Yuling', in idem, *Qingdai xiqujia congkao* (Shanghai: Xuelin chubanshe, 1995), p. 11.

17   The ending of this later dream with reference to water is similar to the dream scene Yuan composed.

18   See Wang Xiaoyi (comp. and annot.), *Pan Zhiheng quhua* (Beijing: Zhongguo xiju chubanshe, 1988), p. 56.

19   For details, see Feng Menglong, *Chujiangqing*, in *Feng Menglong quanji* (Nanjing: Jiangsu guji chubanshe, 1993), vol. 13, pp. 1020–4, 1038–40.

20   Lu Eting, 'Tan Yuan Yuling', pp. 12–13.

21   Feng Menglong, *Qingshi*, in *Feng Menglong quanji*, vol. 7, pp. 119–58.

2.2 Blockbusters and popular stories

Nick Walton

What do audiences want? This question must have focused the minds of dramatists writing in 1616, just as it continues to haunt playwrights in 2016. Playgoers then as now are a disparate body, and their tastes can be as subjective as they are fickle. Stanley Wells suggests that audiences flocked to see plays in the Elizabethan and Jacobean era for a wide variety of reasons:

> Some hoped for straightforward entertainment. Some looked for edification, for instruction in English and Roman history, in mythology and in stories of ancient and modern heroes. Some sought to enter a world of the fantasy and imagination, or romanticized reflections of their own lives. Some went to be provoked to think about contemporary social and political issues, even though legal restraints meant that these usually had to be indirectly treated.[1]

While playgoers would have entered the playhouse with different expectations, the power of a good story had the capacity to bring an audience together through the simple pleasure of watching it unfold. While many plays of the period speak to the particular interests of their original audiences, there are those that share a timeless resonance. Whilst blockbusters are customarily of an age, popular stories are for all time.

1616 – 'Seize the crown'

The tales dramatists chose to tell between the end of the sixteenth and the early years of the seventeenth century altered to reflect the playgoers' developing tastes and interests. Wells notices that 'until the late 1590s romantic and historical subject matter prevailed, with plays set in distant lands and in the more or less remote past', but from around 1597 onwards 'the emergence of what became the Jacobean generation of dramatists, including Jonson, Dekker and Middleton, saw a broadening of subject matter, with plays set (sometimes covertly) in contemporary London and satirical of the society that produced them'.[2] Tastes and acting styles began to alter as dramatists responded to what was fashionable. Dramatists adapted their subject matter to appeal to their spectators. But it could also be argued that some dramatists working in 1616 were more concerned with ensuring that their subject matter was topical rather than necessarily popular. Marion O'Connor asserts that topical dramas often have 'a short theatrical shelf life',[3] and are thus denied the opportunity to become celebrated stories of their own, or any subsequent historical period.

Ben Jonson's *The Devil is an Ass* is representative of the satirical style that had begun to appeal to some playwrights by 1616. Jonson chose to set the action of his drama in the year the play received its first performance by the King's Men at Blackfriars – 1616. It can reasonably be assumed that some spectators would have been surprised when the character Fabian Fitzdotterel announced his intention from the stage to 'see "The Devil is an Ass" today' (1.4.21). As Richard Dutton notes, Jonson's playful jest 'undermines any comfortable demarcations between the play and its audience'.[4] Ian Donaldson has noted that this play focuses 'as ever, on matters of immediate topical concern in England';[5] the devil sent from hell to earth is no match for London's venal society. As Donaldson goes on to explain, 'Jonson looks with equal scepticism at the inherited systems of belief which his society is struggling at this moment to discard, and at those it is now beginning eagerly to embrace'.[6] Whilst we can assume that Jonson's 1616 play reflects his own dramatic tastes, it is difficult to judge how far it represents the audience's. Margaret Jane Kidnie records that 'There is no clear evidence to confirm whether or not the earliest production of *The Devil is an Ass* by the King's Men at Blackfriars was a success, but the fact that there is no record of a revival during Jonson's lifetime perhaps suggests that the response was indifferent.'[7] Ultimately, Jonson always sought to develop his spectators' tastes in line with his own, rather than shape his dramas to satisfy popular demand.

As Anjna Chouhan and Will Tosh make clear in their essays included in this volume, dramatists writing in 1616 shaped their plays to cater to a diverse range of performance spaces. This fact poses certain difficulties when trying to determine the blockbusters and popular stories of 1616; a play that proved popular in one theatre would not necessarily receive the same response from a markedly different group of spectators in another venue. Although writing styles altered over time, holding the mirror up to reflect an ever-changing London and worlds elsewhere, certain narratives and plot devices evidently held a perennial appeal for dramatists – and presumably audiences – alike. While new plays were being written year upon year, some old plays also continued to hold the stage and evidently proved popular with spectators. Christopher Marlowe's tale of devilish necromancy *Doctor Faustus*, a veritable blockbuster of the 1590s, continued to entertain audiences at the Fortune Theatre during the period of our study, and beyond. Thomas Kyd's early revenge drama *The Spanish Tragedy*, and William Shakespeare's *Titus Andronicus* written in the early 1590s, also continued to hold the attention of playgoers by 1616. Stage devils, ghosts and scenes of physical mutilation continued to entertain some audiences, while others looked for more modish entertainment in the shape of 'domineering women, effeminate courtiers, smooth-talking gallants, grasping dishonest merchants, and gullible dupes'[8] who inhabited the world of Jacobean City Comedy.

Some stories become popular over time, and it is their growing familiarity with audiences that can ultimately lead to their becoming a 'classic'. A 'blockbuster' holds instant appeal for a large audience, encouraging people to part with their money. The blockbuster's sudden notoriety can prove a reason in itself for people to see it, though the sudden rush of interest does not mean that it will prove popular with audiences in years to come. Popular stories endure because of the individual elements they contain. The craftsmanship that goes into combining elements of popular stories is something that can be studied, emulated and refashioned. The success of a blockbuster on the other hand can owe more to chance than cultivation. Elements of popular stories pass readily from writer to writer, but the instant appeal of a blockbuster is impossible to recapture or reproduce.

In his essay included in this volume Peter Kirwan provides a list of playbooks published in 1616. Included in this list is the anonymous, early romantic comedy *Mucedorus* – 'Amplified with new Additions'. The play is thought to have been written around 1590, and its blockbuster status is suggested by the fact that it was frequently reprinted prior to the Restoration; seventeen quarto texts which were printed before the end of the seventeenth century still survive. The frequency with which this play was reprinted points to its status as a blockbuster and a popular story both on the stage and on the page. The drama charts the eventful romance of Mucedorus and Amadine and concludes with the prospect of their betrothal. Having approved his daughter's marriage to the man he was ready to sentence to death earlier in the drama, the King brings the proceedings to a close with the prospect of a celebratory feast. During the course of the drama the lover Mucedorus dons two disguises, kills a bear, evades an attempt upon his own life and reveals himself to be the Prince of Valeria, rather than a lowly shepherd as he had led people to believe. His rival for Amadine's love, Segasto, proves a jealous villain, determined to thwart their romance with wicked intent.

In its presentation of green-eyed jealousy and pastoral adventure *Mucedorus* shares similarities with Shakespeare's *Othello* and *The Winter's Tale*. Both of these plays are also known to have proved commercially popular with audiences in the period, and continued to be staged long after their first performances. Love, jealousy and rivalry proved popular ingredients for many playwrights writing across the Elizabethan and Jacobean period, and the fact that these three plays retained their popularity with playgoers and readers suggests that their core interests had an emotionally enduring rather than modish appeal.

It is interesting (although perhaps unsurprising) to note then that audiences in England and China in 1616 evidently enjoyed tales in which love was a prominent concern. In her accompanying essay in this section Wei Hua relates the story of *The Tale of the West Loft* in which Yu Shuye and Mu Suhui become a sworn couple, only to be separated and then reunited at the end. Like their English counterparts – Mucedorus and Amadine, Othello and Desdemona, Leontes and Hermione – Yu Shuye and Mu Suhui discover that the course of true love never did run smooth. As with *Mucedorus*, *The Tale of the West Loft* concludes with Yu's father giving his consent for the marriage, and the play ends with a grand wedding scene. It can be assumed that spectators would have felt moved by the sense of harmony that is engendered at the close of both plays. It would seem that both English and Chinese audiences in the period took pleasure in the triumph of love in spite of attempts to thwart it.

Had Shakespeare been able to visit any of the theatres in London in the year of his death, or cast an eye over his contemporaries' works in progress, he would certainly have recognized some of the conventions and dramatic techniques that playwrights in 1616 were using to entertain their audiences. Thomas Middleton's play *The Witch* is believed to have been written in the middle of 1616, and the memory of Shakespeare's own dramatic imagination seems to haunt the play. Middleton had collaborated with Shakespeare on the writing of *Timon of Athens*, so he would have had first-hand experience of working with a dramatist who had been entertaining what Gary Taylor phrases 'the shifting community of readers and spectators'[9] for many years. In his endeavour to write a blockbuster of Shakespearian proportions, Middleton recycles and reconfigures plots that had proved popular more than a decade earlier. This new play houses some old dramatic ingredients: a bed-trick, a love charm, a poisoned chalice and a character in disguise. These elements would have seemed instantly familiar to audiences who had enjoyed *Measure for Measure*, *All's Well that Ends Well*, *A Midsummer Night's Dream* and *Hamlet*. And it is conceivable that Middleton's witches would have reminded spectators of the Weird Sisters who had appeared in Shakespeare's *Macbeth* in 1606. Like love, witchcraft and supernatural soliciting held a perennial pleasure for audiences in the early seventeenth century; Middleton's own drama was followed by other tales of witchcraft including *The Witch of Edmonton* and *The Late Lancashire Witches*. Sadly it is difficult to conclude whether Middleton's choice of subject matter guaranteed his play stage success; Marion O'Connor surmises that:

> The stage history of *The Witch* begins in a cloud of ambiguity and promptly disappears into a void. No professional production is known to have occurred subsequent to its first performance(s), of which tantalizingly little is known. The manuscript subtitles *The Witch* as having been "long since acted by his Majesty's Servants at the Blackfriars". [...] Middleton's dedicatory epistle, however, clearly indicates that the play had in some sense failed: "I have ... recovered into my hands (although not without much difficulty) this (ignorantly ill-fated) labour of mine.[10]

In her accompanying essay to this section Wei Hua records the influence that Tang Xianzu had over other Chinese playwrights by 1616 and beyond. Martin Wiggins has provided a similarly comprehensive record of the ways in which Shakespeare's influence can be seen in the writing of some of his contemporaries and successors:

> In plays of the post-Shakespearian period you will find, among many others: a comic scene with a gravedigger, which

contemporaries recognised as a lift from *Hamlet* (in Thomas Randolph's *The Jealous Lovers*); a father who affects disapproval of his daughter's low born suitor, but, like Simonides in *Pericles*, communicates his true feelings to the audience in asides (John Ford's *Perkin Warbeck*); a husband who is tempted by a villainous schemer into believing his wife has been unfaithful (Ford's *Love's Sacrifice*), and another who became insanely jealous after his wife seems to have disposed of one of his love-gifts (Philip Massinger's *The Emperor of the East*); a plot centred on lovers from rival families (Thomas May's *The Heir*); a queen whose husband irrationally accuses her of adultery with a court favourite whom she has praised (Richard Brome's *The Queen and Concubine*); characters who pretend to be statues and are reanimated by supposedly magical means (Massinger's *The City Madam*); a murderer who cannot wash his hands clean of blood which only he can see (William Hemminges's *The Jew's Tragedy*); a clown who asks for guerdon and remuneration (Alexander Brome's *The Cunning Lovers*); and a group of artisans who are to perform before royalty, with a leading actor who wants to play all the parts (Thomas Rowlin's *The Rebellion*).[11]

This long list helps to identify those moments in Shakespeare's dramas that had proved particularly memorable for playwrights and audiences. The fact that these characters and moments are recycled must go some way to suggesting that they had achieved a certain level of local renown if not popularity with audiences at the time.

Shakespeare's contemporaries – Ben Jonson, Thomas Dekker, John Fletcher, Thomas Middleton and William Rowley – would all no doubt have watched Shakespeare's plays and have taken note of their effect on the spectators. As Shakespeare's junior by eight years, Ben Jonson would have been a teenager when Shakespeare's first plays came to the stage. Dekker, Fletcher, Middleton and Rowley would only have been schoolboys when Shakespeare's *Titus Andronicus* and his three plays about the contention between the Houses of York and Lancaster were the blockbusters of the 1590s. The fact that *Titus Andronicus* was still being presented on stage once these young men had become professional writers in their own right made it hard for them to ignore Shakespeare's popular appeal.

The year 1616 is ultimately as significant for the death of one of the period's most talented writers of popular stories as it is for the staging or publication of new works. While the new plays that reached the stage in 1616 would for the main part enjoy fleeting popularity at best, Shakespeare's legacy of blockbusters and popular stories would continue to hold the interest of playwrights and audiences alike resulting in the eventual publication of the First Folio of Shakespeare's works in 1623, some seven years after the dramatist's death.

Would any of the plays being written or staged in the year of Shakespeare's death have struck spectators as being 'Shakespearian' in their craftsmanship and stagecraft? In the remainder of this essay I will briefly rehearse Shakespeare's achievement by his death in 1616, and point towards some of the 'Shakespearian' qualities for which his plays would conceivably have been remembered in the year of our study.

1616 – 'Remember me'

When Shakespeare's great tragedian Richard Burbage died in 1619 a funeral elegy was composed in his memory:

> He's gone, and with him what a world are dead,
> Which he revived, to be revived so
> No more. Young Hamlet, old Hieronimo,
> Kind Lear, the grieved Moor, and more beside
> That lived in him have now for ever died.[12]

Understandably, Burbage's memory was immortalized in the characters for which he had provided a face, a voice and a physical presence. Burbage's talent and charisma as a performer cannot be overestimated in their contribution to the success of Shakespeare's tragedies on stage in his own time. The visceral power of performance allowed Shakespeare's tales to become fixed in his audience's memories. The elegy for Burbage could suggest that, at least in some playgoers' minds, there was a sense in which the characters of Hamlet, Lear and Othello (and more besides) belonged to Burbage, and with his death 'have now for ever died'. If the memory of dramatic characters was tied so closely to the actors who portrayed them, then where did this leave the characters' creator, the playwright himself, in people's memories? What sprung to theatregoers' minds in the April of 1616 when news arrived in London of William Shakespeare's death? Would Londoners have associated him immediately with the staging of a cannibalistic banquet, an exit pursued by a bear, the blinding of an old man and the baptism of the infant Princess Elizabeth? Or would their first thoughts have been of a dramatist whose star had waned, whose plays seemed outdated when compared to the freshly minted dramas of 1616?

As Ben Jonson's tribute to his friend and rival in the First Folio of 1623 attests, Shakespeare's name came to represent the 'applause, delight, the wonder of our stage!' But by 1616 some aspects of Shakespeare's dramatic technique and chosen subject matter would have differed markedly to the writing styles of some of his contemporaries. The presence of a Chorus in *Henry V* and *Romeo and Juliet* would certainly have seemed like an antiquated approach to storytelling for some spectators, including Ben Jonson himself who mocked the use of this device. By the same token, Shakespeare's tetralogy of plays about the reign of Henry VI, which had helped to make his reputation in the early 1590s, would by 1616 have seemed representative of earlier theatrical tastes. The title of Thomas Middleton's play *Hengist King of Kent* which was written between 1616 and 1620 sounds like it might be a historical blockbuster of Shakespearian proportions, but as Grace Ioppolo notes, 'the play drops its interest in history after the first act'.[13]

Retelling sad stories of the death of kings no longer appealed to playwrights or spectators in 1616 in the way it once had during the 1590s, a period saturated with popular stories about the lives of English monarchs some of whom, like *Richard III* and *Richard II*, Shakespeare cast into the tragic form.

The foundation underlying Shakespeare's popular stories remained the same across a period of nearly twenty years: imaginary force. Walking into Shakespeare's theatre spectators were encouraged to look beyond the familiar boards of the thrust stage and envision sea coasts, battlefields and grave-yards, and feel the sultry heat of Verona, Egypt and Rome. Shakespeare played to his spectators' desire for escapism and adventure, and characteristically chose to exploit the theatre's inherent artificiality. Pericles sails from shore to shore; Imogen roams around the British Isles in *Cymbeline*; and sixteen years pass in a single speech in *The Winter's Tale* (made up of sixteen rhyming couplets, one for each year). Shakespeare helped to shape an approach to storytelling that allowed large stories to be presented with great theatrical economy. The playgoers served as collaborators investing 'imaginary puissance' into the dramatist's creative efforts to transform the 'wooden O' of the theatre into worlds elsewhere. Whilst changing fashions dictated that playwrights tended to relocate the action of their plays to London, some of the dramas of 1616 continued to be set overseas. Thomas Middleton's *The Witch* and *The Widow*, both believed to have been staged in 1616, have Italian settings, always a popular location among Early Modern dramatists.

Tales of rivalry between family, friends and nations recur throughout Shakespeare's canon. Rivalry formed an important ingredient in shaping the writer's earliest dramas: Proteus competes with Valentine for Sylvia's love in *The Two Gentlemen of Verona*; Petruchio and Kate spar for dominance in *The Taming of the Shrew*; and Tamora and Titus Andronicus rival one another in acts of atrocious violence in the name of revenge. Later in Shakespeare's career feuding families would keep Romeo Montague and Juliet Capulet apart, and Iago would prove determined to dispose of all professional and sexual rivals who threatened his peace of mind. Sexual, social and political rivalry serve as the catalyst to a variety of jealous, rash and sometimes murderous acts across Shakespeare's canon. Tales of rivalry anticipate dramatic conclusions, whetting spectators' appetites for either savage confrontations or emotional reconciliations. Some rivals, like Orlando and Oliver in *As You Like It*, and Palamon and Arcite in *The Two Noble Kinsmen*, will finally become reconciled; but others like Coriolanus and Aufidius, and Tybalt and Mercutio in *Romeo and Juliet*, will fight until the end.

As Shakespeare garnered experience as a dramatist he would begin to stitch revenge narratives into the tapestry of his tales so that they became just one of a number of popular stories threaded through the drama. At the beginning of his career Shakespeare saturated *Titus Andronicus* with Seneca-inspired revenge plots, but would progress to create revenge dramas for the Jacobean stage that focused less upon sensational gore and more upon the inner thoughts of those confronted with the opportunity to wreak vengeance. Considered reasoning, and the expression of personal response to a situation, would come to characterize Shakespeare's use of soliloquy, bringing an increased sophistication to the dramatist's presentation of mental states and human behaviour. As Shakespeare developed modes of expression ever closer to the voices in his audiences' own minds, the bond between character and spectator would deepen. Audiences could begin to speak not only of what had happened in a drama, but also of how characters had felt about the dilemmas facing them.

As well as being the creator of popular stories of his own, Shakespeare must have shared his audiences' passion for hearing a good story well told. Throughout his career he reworked popular stories, adapting freely and inventing stage business that he sensed would work effectively. With time these new dramatizations of old source material would become popular stories in their own right. Stagings of *Romeo and Juliet* and *The Winter's Tale* could entertain thousands of people in the same moment, while their sources, Arthur Brooke's *The Tragical Historye of Romeus and Juliet* (1562) and Robert Greene's *Pandosto: The Triumph of Time* (1588) called for private study, and the ability to read. In choosing to write for the public playhouses Shakespeare chose a popular medium through which his stories could reach the widest audience quickly. By writing within and out of Shakespeare's popularity, his contemporaries helped to establish that the most popular stories, if not always blockbusters, tended to hold in themselves memories of or allusions to Shakespeare's own.

Notes

1   Stanley Wells, *Shakespeare & Co.: Christopher Marlowe, Thomas Dekker, Ben Jonson, Thomas Middleton, John Fletcher and the Other Players in His Story* (New York: Pantheon Books, 2006), p. 9.

2   Wells, *Shakespeare & Co.*, p. 9.

3   Marion O'Connor, 'The Witch', in *Thomas Middleton: The Collected Works*, eds Gary Taylor and John Lavagnino (Oxford: Oxford University Press, 2007), p. 1128.

4   Richard Dutton, 'Jonson's Satiric Styles', in *The Cambridge Guide to Ben Jonson*, eds Richard Harp and Stanley Stewart (Cambridge: Cambridge University Press, 2000), p. 67.

5   Ian Donaldson, *Ben Jonson: A Life* (Oxford: Oxford University Press, 2011), p. 348.

6   Donaldson, *Ben Jonson: A Life*, p. 348.

7   Margaret Jane Kidnie (ed.), 'Introduction', in *The Devil is an Ass: And Other Plays* (Oxford: Oxford University Press, 2001), p. xxx.

8   Kidnie, *The Devil is an Ass: And Other Plays*, p. xxi.

9   Gary Taylor, 'Lives and Afterlives', in *Thomas Middleton: The Collected Works*, eds Gary Taylor and John Lavagnino (Oxford: Oxford University Press, 2007), p. 41.

10 O'Connor, *Thomas Middleton: The Collected Works*, p. 1128.

11 Martin Wiggins, *Shakespeare and the Drama of His Time* (Oxford: Oxford University Press, 2000), p. 130.

12 Wells, *Shakespeare & Co.*, pp. 43–4.

13 Grace Ioppolo, 'Hengist, King of Kent; or, The Mayor of Queenborough', in *Thomas Middleton: The Collected Works*, eds Gary Taylor and John Lavagnino (Oxford: Oxford University Press, 2007), p. 1448.

3

Making history

How did England (or London) and China see and consume representations of the past in their theatres? To what extent was theatre used as a medium to comment on political affairs, historical or contemporary, on the stage?

3.1 *Shishiju* as public forum: *The Crying Phoenix* and the dramatization of contemporary political affairs in late Ming China

Ayling Wang

As a new subgenre of historical drama, *shishiju* (時事劇) or 'drama on current political affairs' first came into view in late Ming China and became prominent during the Ming–Qing transition period. The term *shishi* (current political affairs) was first used by the famous late Ming drama critic Qi Biaojia (1602–45) to categorize some plays in his classic work of drama review, *Classification of Plays from the Far Mountain Hall* (*Yuanshantang qupin* 遠山堂曲品).[1] Although there are only about ten plays of this kind extant, according to Qi Biaojia there must have been more than forty *shishiju* written during the late Ming period.[2] These plays are noteworthy for their wide-ranging themes focusing on all the major political issues of the period: the partisan activities at court under the high-handed Grand Secretary Yan Song 嚴嵩 (1480–1567) during the Emperor Jiajing's reign; the political strife against the dynasty's last powerful eunuch Wei Zhongxian 魏忠賢 (1568–1627); the security challenges of the coastal raiders in the Jiangnan area; the renewed Mongol invasion across the Great Wall near the capital; the conflicts between various ethnic groups; the civilian riots in the urban areas; and the peasant uprisings in the countryside. It is important to bear in mind that these political events did not occur separately in the political centre of the Ming Empire. They were widely publicized by the capital gazettes or literary sketches, and they effectively shaped the popular opinions of justice and morality. Following this new trend of dramatizing current affairs, the contemporary political events soon became popular topics frequently adopted by many subsequent authors of *shishiju*. In fact, as a medium for authors to convey their concerns and for spectators and readers to witness their concerns expressed, drama became a major literary genre more closely related to the social and political life of the time than it was during the previous periods of the Ming dynasty.

Being regarded as the first typical *shishiju* play dealing with contemporary political affairs in the history of Chinese drama, *The Crying Phoenix* (*Mingfeng ji* 鳴鳳記) was probably written between 1573 and 1582. It takes as its background the political struggle at the Ming court under the Grand Secretary Yan Song that happened just fifteen years before the play was written. Though conventionally attributed to Wang Shizhen 王世貞 (1526–90), the authorship of this politically sensitive work was actually disputed.[3] Its authorship was also attributed to a person in Wang's literary circle, to Liang Chenyu 梁辰魚 (1519?–91?), or to an anonymous author who intended to comment with righteous indignation on the contemporary, chaotic political situation.[4]

As a kind of public forum presented in the form of *chuanqi* drama, *The Crying Phoenix* would have played a primary role in the political debate of the time. By combining the northern and southern dramatic traditions at the beginning of the fifteenth century, *chuanqi* drama created its refined form in the southern drama *kunqu* style. The extended scope of the *chuanqi* drama form and vivacious dialogue as the principal mode of representation allow the playwright to present a variety of contradictory views among the characters, elucidating the relative value of their individual positions. *Chuanqi* drama thus became a significant means for the Ming literati to reflect on the contemporary political situation and their stance on it. As a lengthy *chuanqi* play with forty-one scenes, *The Crying Phoenix* was conventionally interpreted, on the one hand, as an admonition to the 'treacherous ministers' Yan Song and his faction and, on the other hand, as praise of the 'loyal officials and righteous men'. The most famous characters in the play are Xia Yan 夏言 (1482–1548) and Yang Jisheng 楊繼盛 (1516–55), who were executed for their resistance to Yan Song and his faction. While the play was written at the time when the remnants of Yan Song's faction had not completely lost power and Emperor Jiajing was still on the throne, the author was indeed audacious enough not only to overtly reprimand Yan Song's faction for its degrading surrender to the barbarians and brutal persecution of the loyalists, but also to laud the loyal subjects' and righteous men's persistent resistance to Yan Song's faction. In fact, the author of *The Crying Phoenix* did use the names of real people for the dramatic figures and depicted actual events of the recent past. The main plot and figures are mostly based on the contemporary political events which were familiar to contemporaries, and some of the people involved were still alive at the time of its writing. This explains why the play immediately caused a great sensation and remained popular until the end of the Ming dynasty.

Surrounding the two major contemporary events of the Jiajing period – the loss of the Ordos region in the north-western frontier and the Japanese pirates' invasion of the southeastern coastal provinces, *The Crying Phoenix* mainly depicts the conflict between the 'eight remonstrating ministers' or the 'ten righteous men'[5] and Yan Song's faction. Moreover, the author maintains that 'loyalty and treachery are conflicting in nature' and denounces the crimes that Yan Song and Yan Shifan 嚴世藩 (1513–65) have committed. The plot of forty-one scenes of the play, which covers a period of eighteen years, starts from Xia Yan's attempt to promote the Governor General Zeng Xian's 曾銑 (1509–48) plans to recover the Ordos region and ends with the execution of Yan Shifan. As a close ally of Zhao Wenhua 趙文華 (?–1557), Yan Song and his son Yan Shifan dominated court politics with the tacit consent of the fatuous sovereign who neglected his mission as emperor and devoted much of his time to sensual pleasures and Taoist practices. Under Yan Song's abuse of supreme power, the nation fell into an era of moral debauchery and corruption, in which morally upright officials were sidelined and the Ming national strength collapsed rapidly. Yan Song's wealth is said to have been so great as to have been equivalent to that of the emperor. He was also notorious for his corruption and had been known to openly sell government positions during the Jiajing reign. However, his corruption and treachery created many political opponents. Yan Song was finally disgraced in his later years and died in poverty not long after that, while his son, Yan Shifan, was executed for collaborating with Japanese pirates who invaded Chinese coastal provinces at the time.

Nevertheless, while the Jiajing court produced the most corrupt grand secretary, Yan Song, it also created the dynasty's moral icon of courage and integrity, Yang Jisheng. Forthright and vigorous, Yang repeatedly wrote memorials (*zouyi* 奏議, which were documents sent by an official to the emperor) protesting against government policies and criticizing the corruption of top officials, and consequently he was sent to jail, tortured and stripped of his position. Knowing that he had little hope of pulling down the powerful Yan Song, but believing it was his moral obligation to continue the fight, he delivered another memorial. As an epitome of the righteous Confucian martyr, Yang Jisheng was ordered to be beaten a hundred strokes, which was the most severe punishment, and was finally executed. In fact, for most historians, the Ming dynasty was a time that cultivated the great moral strength of the real Confucian, for many of these heroic ministers embodied the Confucian male virtue of political integrity. The Jiajing court exemplified their great moral strength.

By writing a historical drama about contemporary political events, the author of *The Crying Phoenix* released vivacious stories related to the anti-Yan Song factional rivalry which embodied the collective consciousness of the late Ming period. In most cases, Chinese drama has a preference for the dramatic structure with 'one main character and one key incident', or two parallel plots led by the male role of *sheng* and the female role of *dan*. In order to combine the complicated plots and many figures in the play as a whole, *The Crying Phoenix* developed a multiple structural pattern including more figures and more episodes than previous Chinese plays, which were conventionally presented by one main plot interspersed with several episodic subplots, or by interweaving the main plot with a second one. The theme of 'loyalty and uprightness' was thus brought to light by the main dramatic action of 'eliminating the treacherous officials and returning to correctness'.[6]

In general, the dramatic figures in *The Crying Phoenix* consisted of twelve types of theatrical roles which covered thirty-six named dramatic characters and nearly one hundred non-named cast members. As a matter of fact, the author utilizes the narrative techniques of 'group biographies' and 'separate biography' inspired by traditional historical writing to narrate the admirable political action of 'resisting the treacherous officials' performed by the 'two loyalists and eight upright men', alternated with their families' stories of grief and joy, separation and reunion. For presenting the characters' different personalities and dispositions effectively, the playwright employs various techniques of depiction to categorize the ten loyal subjects, which include the 'single depiction' of Yang Jisheng, the 'group depiction' of Zhang Xu, Dong Chuance and Wu Shilai, the 'direct depiction' of Xia Yan and the 'profiling depiction' of Zen Xian. Moreover, the playwright skilfully uses the technique of contrast to emphasize the dissimilarity between righteousness and evil, loyalty and treachery.

The plot of *The Crying Phoenix* involves complicated events and actually covers a period of eighteen years in which the correlated figures and events need to be compressed, and the irrelevant and chaotic historical materials must be reorganized into a complete unity. Since the playwright intends to represent the faction opposed to Yan Song, whose many members are from different social strata, he requires a multiple structure with several plots to present the incessant political strife which is the background of the late Ming period. To fulfil the thematic requirement, the play must take a multiple structural pattern. It contains ten loyalists' confrontations with three treacherous ministers in five major political struggles. Their victimized families are depicted as destitute and homeless, and we are shown the aggravation and invasion of the barbarian troops from the northern frontier and the southeastern coast. The author is interested in a single point of focus to lead the plot developing smoothly from beginning to end.

In his Preface to *The Commendation of Loyalty* (*Biaozhong ji* 表忠記), Guo Fen 郭棻 (1622–90) points out, 'The reason why the play could be used to educate loyalty and admonish treachery is because the play not only focuses on Zou Yinglong and Lin Run, but also elaborates the stories of Yang Jisheng and Xia Yan.'[7] In fact, the author breaks the theatrical convention of *chuanqi* by using the roles of *sheng* 生 (male lead) and *jing* 淨 (the painted-face male role), instead of *sheng* and *dan* 旦 (female lead), as protagonists who connect the whole play. In a play as lengthy as *The Crying Phoenix*, the roles of *sheng* and *dan* have uncommonly finished their actions before Scene 15, leaving the remaining twenty-six scenes to other characters. Such an experiment in *The Crying Phoenix* anticipates a consequential later development of Ming–Qing drama, an innovative device that allows for a more flexible arrangement of characters and role types in relation to the plot structure.

This device is beneficial to the presentation of the theme of a lengthy play with forty-one scenes such as *The Crying Phoenix* and the development of the main plot, for which the traditional convention of focusing on the roles of *sheng* and *dan* is apparently inadequate. *The Crying Phoenix* takes the life course of Zou Yinglong (*sheng*) and Lin Run (*xiaosheng*, supporting male role) as the main plot, which is interspersed with several subplots. The first subplot of anti-Yan Song activities is connected by several short plots which mainly present episodes related to Xia Yan and Yang Jisheng. The second subplot is Zou Yinglong and Lin Run's emotional experience and growth. The third subplot is the story of Xia Yan's orphan. The continuous political strivings between the loyalist and the treacherous groups motivate Zou and Lin to grow stronger emotionally and to reverse the situation by the end of the play.

This theatrical device which takes *sheng* and *jing* as leading figures also means that Yan Song (played by the *jing* role) and his corollary figures (Yan Shifan, Zhao Wenhua and Yan Maoqing) are depicted as caricatures. Though Yan Song is able to counteract Zeng Xian's impractical plan to recover the Ordos region, he is on the whole depicted merely as an incompetent, irresponsible and insatiable conspirator. He abuses his access to the emperor and makes sure that his opponents are tortured, imprisoned and executed as soon as possible. As for Zhao Wenhua, portrayed through the *chou* 丑 (clown) role, he is depicted as a coward, a sycophant and a cynical opportunist who always tries to fawn upon the rich and powerful while striving for the position of favourite. The depiction of Yan Shifan, though, seems quite faithful to historical reality: he was arrogant, self-indulgent, debauched and engaged in the corrupt practice of selling official positions. He manipulated Yan Song during his father's later years in court. The playwright never portrays Yan Song and his faction as evil; instead he simply lets his figures self-mock and label themselves as deceitful, avaricious and opportunistic. By portraying Yan Song and Zhao Wenhua through the theatrical roles of *jing* and *chou* respectively, the playwright encouraged the contemporary audiences and his readership to relate the dramatic irony on to contemporary affairs.

There are at least six scenes which unveil Yan Song and his allies' sinful attitudes and corrupt deeds. Scene 21 'Zhao Wenhua Offers Sacrifices to the Sea' (*Wenhua jihai* 文華祭海)[8] is the most outrageous. When the news arrives of the Japanese pirates' assaults on the southeastern coast, Emperor Jiajing commands Yan Song to despatch a troop to destroy them. Fearing that the general who won military exploits would acquire the emperor's trust and threaten his own authoritarian position, Yan Song shrewdly assigns Zhao Wenhua as the minister of war to lead the troops to the southern coast.

However, since Zhao Wenhua is utterly ignorant of military affairs, all he does is simply offer a box of golden and silver drinking vessels as a sacrifice to the Dragon King of the Eastern Sea, then kill some innocent and ordinary people, whilst at the same time rewarding the chieftain at court. When Yan Song sends Zhao Wenhua off to defend against the Japanese pirates' attack to the south in the preceding scene, his son actually anticipates the outcome: 'The Jiangnan area is rich and prosperous. Perhaps this time Minister Zhao will hopefully come back with a full load of treasures in gold and silver, at least half of which will go to our family!'[9] Because he has someone powerful to rely on at court, Zhao Wenhua ignores the rampant Japanese pirates and tormented ordinary people, and disregards the nation's hazardous situation.

In addition, the playwright utilizes some short episodes to disclose the tyranny of Yan Song's faction. For example, in Scene 23 'Paying Homage to the Loyalists' Souls' (*Baiye zhongling* 拜謁忠靈),[10] Guo Xiyan, a member of the Imperial Academy, takes a stroll with his students Zou Yinglong and Lin Run, and they bump into an emaciated, blind female beggar singing in the street. It turns out that this pitiable woman, who originally came from a good family in Yangzhou, was wrested from her home against her will by Yan Shifan. Her father was killed and her family was stripped of its property. Moreover, when she lost the master's favour because of the fading away of her beauty, she was blinded by Yan Shifan's wife and was pitilessly expelled from Yan's house. As a result the blind woman could only sing and beg for a living in the street. In the same scene, Guo, Zou and Lin also meet a male beggar called Hu Yi who is a fellow townsman of Yan Song. While Yan Song was frequently given financial help by Hu's family before he gained fame and fortune, after he rose to power and position, he allowed his housekeeper to take Hu's property illegally. Though Hu Yi went to the capital and took half a year to file a lawsuit against Yan Song, he had no success and tragically ended up as a beggar. By depicting contemporary incidents at intervals throughout the play, the overall effect is almost one of reporting and updating the news, and demonstrates one of the major characteristics of *shishiju*: recording reality.

One of the central themes of the play is the conflict between filial piety and loyalty. The main character who embodies this theme is Yang Jisheng, a representative figure of loyalty. The choice of whether or not to behave ethically or to expect that such behaviour should occur unconditionally is a recurrent theme in many of the historical plays during the late Ming period. In Scene 14, entitled 'Drafting a Remonstrance by Lamp Light' (*Dengqian xiuben* 燈前修本),[11] Yang Jisheng stays up late at night in his study drafting a memorial against Yan Song. By means of this memorial, he aims 'to eliminate the court and the provinces of all evil-doers'. Yang Jisheng knows that, not being a censorial official, he will put himself in danger by trying to impeach Yan Song. In submitting his memorials against Yan Song, he will contravene the established censorial procedure and be punished. He is, however, acting out the relationship of ruler and minister by a public gesture of loyalty to the emperor in order to maintain the legitimacy of his position within the imperial system. Yang feels strongly that it is his moral obligation to protest, and his strong commitment to the emperor leads him to disregard his own interests in order to save the country. It is improbable that Yang anticipates that his actions will result in the fall of Yan Song; rather, it is a matter of demonstrating his own integrity in the face of the political circumstances. The unexpected cry of a ghost reminds Yang that he is morally responsible not only to the emperor but crucially also to his family and his ancestors. As the personification of Yang's own sense of morality and integrity, the ghost disapproves of him sacrificing himself for the state and urges him to reassess his duties towards his parents and ancestors. Confronted by the contradictory demands of loyalty and filial piety, Yang cannot find a way of reconciling the two and finally chooses the demands of loyalty rather than those of filial piety. However, to heighten the drama of Yang's moral dilemma between filial piety and loyalty, the playwright brings Yang's wife Madame Zhang into the scene who engages in a lively debate with Yang. While Madame Zhang is sympathetic to her husband's resentment of the current political chaos, she tries to dissuade him from indicting Yan Song. Regarding filial piety as a higher value than loyalty to one's ruler, Madame Zhang advises her husband that one is obliged to preserve one's life for the sake of one's family. Yang Jisheng, on the contrary, maintains determinedly that filial piety has to be given up in favour of loyalty to the emperor. Thus the moral dilemma in which Yang Jisheng finds himself is laid bare. In this way, *The Crying Phoenix* reflects the uncertainty and the related tension in its assessment of different patterns of moral behaviour typical of an age in which contemporaries perceived themselves as being caught up in a moral and political crisis.

It is worth mentioning that in facing political problems squarely rather than skirting round them the playwright does not avoid directing his attack against the Jiajing Emperor in the play. In fact, *The Crying Phoenix* is not a laudatory account, but, on the contrary, a daring and harsh criticism of the Jiajing emperor. This criticism actually permeates the whole text and relates to the Jiajing emperor's obsession with Daoist practices and his failure to fulfil the people's expectations of an emperor. The criticism of the Jiajing emperor is best demonstrated by the eulogy of the emperor in the final scene of the play, in which an imperial edict is presented as a rehabilitation and promotion of all the ministers involved in Yan Song's downfall, but is in fact a criticism of the Jiajing emperor.[12]

As the first *shishiju* play directly presenting the significant contemporary politics on stage during the late Ming period, *The Crying Phoenix* became the pioneering artistic model which inspired many subsequent historical plays such as Li Yu's 李玉 (c.1591–c.1671) *Register of the Pure and Loyal* (*Qingzhong pu* 清忠譜) and Kong Shangren's 孔尚任 (1648–1718) *Peach Blossom Fan* (*Taohua shan* 桃花

扇). It is notable that *The Crying Phoenix* is not only the first *shishiju* play about contemporary politics, but also a well-liked, theatrically innovative play. In fact, the performance of *The Crying Phoenix* remained popular on stage from 1616 until the end of the Ming dynasty. The Ming anthologies of dramatic songs such as *Categorized Selection of Various Tunes* (*Qunyin leixuan* 群音類選), *The Essence of the Ballad* (*Yuefu jinghua* 樂府菁華) and *A Collection of Intoxicating Delight* (*Zuiyiqing* 醉怡情) all included several scenes from *The Crying Phoenix*. It is obvious that because of the frequent emergence of authoritarian, treacherous officials and sycophantic courtiers at court during the latter part of the Ming dynasty, *The Crying Phoenix* was in great demand and was continually performed. The fact that *A Cloak of Patchworked White Fur* (*Zhuibaiqiu* 綴白裘), one of the most famous Qing collections of dramatic songs, included nine scenes or dramatic excerpts (*zhezixi* 折子戲) from *The Crying Phoenix* might be strong evidence of the play's appeal to and influence on the theatre of later generations.

Notes

1   Qi Biaojia, *Yuanshantang qupin*, in *Zhongguo gudian xiqu lunzhu jicheng* series (Beijing: Zhongguo xiju chubanshe, 1959), vol. 6, pp. 29, 38, 111.

2   See Dietrich Tschanz, 'History and Meaning in the Late Ming Drama *Ming feng ji*', *Ming Studies* 35 (1995), p. 1.

3   For an overview of the editions of *Mingfeng ji*, see Ye Yongfang, 'Mingfeng ji yanjiu' (MA Thesis, Dongwu University, 1982), pp. 18–20.

4   About the authorship of *Mingfeng ji*, see Wang Yongjian, 'Guanyu *Mingfeng ji* de zuozhe wenti', in idem, *Tang Xianzu yu Ming Qing chuanqi yanjiu* (Taipei: Zhiyi chubanshe, 1995), pp. 119–33, and Yan Baoquan, '*Mingfeng ji* de zuozhe ji juzuo sixiang neirong he yishu chengjiu', in Huang Zhushan

and Feng Junjie (eds), *Mingfeng ji pingzhu* (Changchun: Jilin renmin chubanshe, 2001), pp. 759–78.

5 The so-called 'eight remonstrating ministers' refer to Yang Jisheng, Dong Chuance, Wu Shilai, Zhang Xu, Guo Xiyan, Zou Yinglong, Sun Piyang and Lin Run, who were also called 'ten righteous men' with another 'two loyalists', Xia Yan and Zeng Xian, included.

6 Huang Zhushan and Feng Junjie (eds), *Mingfeng ji pingzhu*, p. 253.

7 Guo Fen, '*Biaozhong ji* bianyan', in Li Zengpo (ed.), *Ding Yaokang quanji* (Zhengzhou: Zhongzhou guji chubanshe, 1999), vol. 1, p. 914.

8 Huang Zhushan and Feng Junjie (eds), *Mingfeng ji pingzhu*, pp. 473–8.

9 Ibid., p. 467.

10 Ibid., pp. 486–500.

11 Ibid., pp. 411–22.

12 Ibid., pp. 650–1.

3.2 Dramatizing the Tudors

Helen Cooper

1616 is not the most obvious year one would choose for thinking about the dramatization of English history. The great period for the history play had been the last decade of Elizabeth I's reign, the 1590s, which saw the composition of all but one of Shakespeare's histories, Marlowe's *Edward II* and a good many others too. But the dramatizing of English history continued after Elizabeth's death in 1603, though with a very different focus: at last, it became safe to dramatize the history of the Tudors themselves, an area that had been too hot to handle while they were on the throne. Shakespeare's *Henry VIII* of 1613, co-written with John Fletcher, brings us close to 1616; it was also almost the last of these plays of Tudor history to be written, only two such plays being written later, and the final one, John Ford's *Perkin Warbeck*, acknowledges how out of fashion the form had become. What follows is an overview of these Stuart plays of Tudor history, to note how and why their material might have been contentious earlier, and their connections with their own moments of composition.[1] Unlike in China, and in contrast to the making of history described in Ayling Wang's essay in this section, direct comment on contemporary affairs was impossible on the stage, but many of these plays none the less echo current events in disguised form. The appendices at the end of this essay summarize these plays and their selection of material.

The Elizabethans loved history and wrote it in a whole variety of genres, drama included. The closer history drew to the contemporary, however, the more dangerous it became. Drama of English history written under Elizabeth mostly stopped with events of a century earlier, with the advent of the Tudors, as found in Shakespeare's *Richard III* with its presentation of the future Henry VII as the providential saviour of England. The play was both politically safe and very popular: it was published eight times in quarto, and had its last known royal performance in 1633. *Henry IV Part I* was almost equally popular; and so was *Richard II*, though its history was a good deal more troubled, and it was not until after Elizabeth's death that the scene showing the king's deposition was printed. Notoriously, a performance commissioned by the Earl of Essex on the eve of his rebellion in 1601 landed the acting company in serious trouble. History was recommended as showing a mirror to the present, from which it could learn; but that had as its corollary that the precedents it offered could be dangerous. Distance in time was not necessarily adequate protection against a suspicion of causing civil dissension, and therefore even of treason. There was an attempt in the mid-1590s by a number of authors, led by Anthony Munday and apparently including Shakespeare, to compose a play on Sir Thomas More; but even though it never mentions either the break with Rome or Henry VIII's divorce from Catherine of Aragon, the Master of the Revels, who was responsible for approving plays, wanted to censor it out of existence – the manuscript still exists, with his damning annotations – and it was killed before it was born.[2]

Other Elizabethan plays of Tudor history of which we have records, all written in the Queen's very last years – one by Henry Chettle on Wolsey, and his two-parter on Lady Jane Grey – have been lost, perhaps indicating some problems with performing or preserving them. If the suggestion is correct that a sympathetic treatment of Wyatt's rebellion in the *Lady Jane* plays was designed as a comment on the rebellion of the Earl of Essex, they would certainly have fallen into that category. The other surviving text from this period, the anonymous *Life and Death of Lord Cromwell*, plays almost ludicrously safe with the life of the man who had masterminded the execution of Elizabeth's mother, Anne Boleyn, and overseen the break with Rome and the dissolution of the monasteries.[3] The play mentions none of this, focusing instead on the difficulties of Cromwell's early life and the kindness of those who helped

him, which he repays in adulthood with comparable benef-
icent acts. The play turns into something more like a citizen
play about the London boy who makes good; and his final
downfall is ascribed to the envy and false testimony against
him of various jealous lords, in league with Stephen Gardiner,
bishop of Winchester, who is the play's chief villain. It comes
close, in fact, to being history with the politics and the religion
taken out: the kind of thing that would not have troubled even
Elizabeth's touchy council.

Given the attitude of governmental suspicion, or of outright
suppression, it is not surprising that so little Tudor history was
dramatized under Elizabeth, especially as the most dramatically interesting material was the most risky. Principal among
such topics was the descent of the crown. Too much of what
had happened since the Tudor appropriation of the throne –
including that appropriation itself, since Henry VII's accession
marked the biggest rupture in the lineal descent of the crown
since the Norman Conquest of 1066 – was still dangerous.
No one bothered to dramatize the uncontested descent of the
crown from Tudor father to son; but the contested inheritances,
of Mary and of Elizabeth, were much more interesting, and so
too – though it was left until the very last – were the challenges
to Henry VII himself. The messy end of Henry VIII's first two
marriages had the potential to call into question Elizabeth's
own legitimacy. Her own refusal to name an heir had further
ruled out the descent of the crown as a topic throughout her
lifetime, as any discussion of it was fiercely suppressed. Those
problematic Tudor successions were rendered safe for dramatization at last only by the accession of the Stuart, James VI of
Scotland, as James I of England, in 1603.

Almost equally dangerous, though of crucial importance
to sixteenth-century history, was material directly relating
to the Reformation. All discussion of doctrine on stage had
been forbidden since the time of Henry VIII, and the plays
that cannot altogether avoid sectarian controversy replace
theological difference with the officially approved categories
of vice and virtue. The Reformation is a strong presence in the

plays in the sense that approval of Protestantism is a given; but it is almost always replayed in moral terms, wicked Roman Catholics opposed to virtuous Protestants, without touching on actual doctrinal questions. By the time the transition to the Protestant James I had been smoothly accomplished, however, political conditions were changing sufficiently to allow for some mention of religious difference too, and the playwrights began, cautiously at first, to move into Tudor territory. Eight such plays written after James's accession survive.

The first of these plays, Samuel Rowley's *When You See Me, You Know Me* of 1604, manages to replace theological controversy with high politics partly by playing fast and loose with historical chronology.[4] Its plot is driven by the machinations of Cardinal Wolsey, one of the chief all-purpose villains in Protestant eyes, to get himself elected to the papacy by means of manipulating Henry's foreign policy; and it ends with his downfall, which took place in 1529. The final event of the play, however, is the visit of the Catholic Holy Roman Emperor, Charles V, to England: he actually made the visit in 1520, to see his aunt Catherine of Aragon, but the play relocates it to the time of Henry's wife of the 1540s, the Protestant Katherine Parr, and the whole historical sequence is recast to show Catholic wickedness, in the form of Wolsey, opposed to Katherine Parr's virtuous Protestantism. The play is given a contemporary spin by the positive presentation of Charles, whose territories included Spain. The warmth might seem surprising; but 1604 was also the year of the Treaty of London that at last, after many decades of hostility, established peace with Spain. Tudor foreign policy, in fact, is inflected to mirror that of the Stuarts.

The other play to concern itself with Henrician politics, Shakespeare and Fletcher's *Henry VIII*, originally played under the title *All is True*, was written some nine years later.[5] This covers some of the same historical ground, not least the fall of Wolsey, but it includes the woman who displaced Catherine of Aragon as queen, Anne Boleyn. This is the only play in which she figures, and Shakespeare and Fletcher manage to bring off the remarkable feat of treating both her and Catherine with sympathy. Catherine is indeed the central woman character, her determined Catholicism overlooked in favour of her treatment as another in the line of falsely accused women that Shakespeare had made the focus of half a dozen of his earlier plays, from *Much Ado about Nothing* to *The Winter's Tale* and *Cymbeline*. Catherine joins the Thomas More of the suppressed play as the only ardent Catholics to be treated with full sympathy on stage, though both plays manage to avoid mentioning their theology. Instead, Shakespeare and Fletcher stress Anne Boleyn's Protestant sympathies, as Rowley had done Katherine Parr's. The play also pays homage to the future, in Archbishop Cranmer's prophecy of the peace and well-being of the country that will follow under Elizabeth; and he looks forward too to her own successor, James himself, so carrying forward the closing prophecy of peace under the Tudors at the end of *Richard III* to the next royal house, in a comparable act of royal propaganda.

The next play in terms of the events it dramatizes was probably also the first to be written after James's accession in 1603: Dekker and Webster's *Sir Thomas Wyatt*.[6] This is the first play to concern itself centrally with the transmission of the crown. It covers the death of Edward VI, Wyatt's support of the lineal heir Mary against the attempt to put Jane Grey on the throne and then his rebellion against her over her marriage to Philip of Spain. It thus manages both to support the principle of linear succession – Mary as rightful queen – while opposing her Catholicism: a joint emphasis that made it eminently suitable for playing after the transfer of the crown to the Protestant James.

Wyatt was closely followed by the first part of Thomas Heywood's *If You Know Not Me, You Know Nobody*, subtitled 'The Troubles of Queen Elizabeth'.[7] The troubles in question are those she endured under the reign of her sister Mary on account of her refusal to give up her Protestantism: this is very overtly about Reformation politics as well as personal suffering. One of Heywood's major sources was John

Foxe's *Acts and Monuments*, popularly known as *The Book of Martyrs*, which includes the Princess Elizabeth as one of those who were persecuted for their faith. This play too, however, contains a surprising element, in that Philip of Spain, like Rowley's Charles V, is presented favourably: it is he who, in opposition to the ecclesiastics Stephen Gardiner and Cardinal Pole, insists that Mary be reconciled to her sister, and who speaks warmly in her praise. Again, James's new treaty with Spain seems likely to have influenced his portrayal. 1604 was also, however, the year that saw the start of work on the new Authorized Version of the Bible, an event that is foreshadowed at the very end of the play when Elizabeth, acceding to the throne after Mary's death, declares that she will make the English Bible 'the Iewell that we still loue best' (line 1582), universally available to all her subjects, 'that happy yssue that shall vs succeed' (line 1595): a phrase that seems to enfold both the Bible and James himself. The play went through eight editions down to 1639, putting it on a par with the other most-reprinted history play, Shakespeare's *Richard III*.

Its popularity encouraged a sequel, though Part II of *If You Know Not Me* is much more of a citizen comedy than a political drama. The figure at the centre is Sir Thomas Gresham, who built the Royal Exchange, and it is enlivened by the antics of his shameless con-man son. The Queen appears at the end in what is very much an appendage to the main action, to hear of the defeat of the Spanish Armada. It is a celebration both of England and of London's mercantile pre-eminence, with an obvious audience appeal on both counts.

The Armada also forms the end point of the most overtly anti-Catholic play of them all: Dekker's allegorical *The Whore of Babylon*.[8] This is an account of the struggle between the Catholic powers of continental Europe, led by the Empress of Babylon (i.e. the Roman Church), and an Elizabeth transformed along the lines of Spenser's *Faerie Queene* into Titania, who rules over a fairy court of thinly disguised English aristocrats. Following the Spenserian model, the rival sets of characters are presented as unremittingly evil or good, and indeed the mode of personification prevents anything resembling normal characterization. It was written in or before 1607, and its central theme of the dangers of Roman Catholicism is not surprising given that it was written in the wake of the Gunpowder Plot, a plan to blow up the Houses of Parliament with the king inside, and the major attempt at a Catholic coup against James.

With the exception of the Shakespeare–Fletcher *Henry VIII* discussed above and a lost play of the same year on Perkin Warbeck, there was a long gap before the next play of Tudor history was written, Thomas Drue's *The Life of the Duchess of Suffolk* of c. 1623–4.[9] As it was originally composed, this may have been the most politically engaged of them all, to the point that it was heavily censored by the current Master of the Revels. He noted that, 'being full of dangerous matter [it] was much reformed by me',[10] so the rather messy state of the text as it was printed in 1631 may be in part the result of his interference. It tells the story, taken from Foxe's *Acts and Monuments*, of the widowed Protestant Duchess of Suffolk, Katherine Willoughby, her love for and marriage to her gentleman usher, their flight with their children across Europe from the persecutions of Mary's reign and their eventual return to London after Elizabeth's accession. Its confessional allegiance is unusually explicit, being surpassed only by Dekker's *Whore*, as it briefly includes the deaths of the Reformation martyrs Latimer, Ridley and Cranmer. At first glance, however, and with the exception of that scene, the play as we have it appears as if it would appeal most directly to the Jacobean taste for romance, as if it were a happily ending *Duchess of Malfi*. It was performed by the Palsgrave's Men, a troupe sponsored by the Protestant Palsgrave, the Elector Palatine Frederick V, husband to James's daughter Elizabeth; and by the early 1620s, he and his family were themselves refugees, seeking sanctuary from international Catholic opposition with various European Protestant rulers, some of whose forebears appear in the play giving succour to Katherine. The parallels with the Duchess's flight of the 1550s offer an opportunity for some strenuous criticism of court policies, presumably explicit in the text as Drue wrote it, on account of James's lack of support for the Palsgrave – an anti-Protestant stance emphasized by the possibility of a Spanish, and therefore Catholic, marriage for his son. The censorship of the text is an indicator of the continuing, and justified, anxiety over the capacity for historical drama to carry covert resonance for the present.

The final play to be written, John Ford's *Perkin Warbeck*, dramatizes the subject furthest distant historically, but it was also potentially the most dangerous in that it offered to undermine the very basis of the Tudor monarchy. Ford himself notes, 'In it I have endeavoured to personate a great attempt, and in it a greater danger.'[11] It concerns the challenge to Henry VII's right to the throne (itself very tenuous) offered by Perkin Warbeck, who gave himself out to be Richard Duke of York, son of Edward IV, one of the 'princes in the Tower' supposedly killed by Richard III. Henry had married the princes' eldest sister, Elizabeth of York, who was the heir of the Yorkist line – but not if either of her brothers were still living. Warbeck's assertion, if true, would have denied any element of right by marriage in Henry's claim to the throne, and denied his children's claim to be descendants of the rightful Yorkist heir. Warbeck was recognized as Prince Richard by various European sovereigns including James IV of Scotland, who gave him a close kinswoman as his bride. Henry insisted that he was in actual fact a Flemish impostor; but it is still impossible to be quite sure whether the king or the pretender was speaking the truth. History is, after all, written by the victors.

The degree of danger attaching to a dramatization of the Warbeck story would depend on how its protagonist is presented. The safe way would be to show him simply as a fraud, and that may well have been how the lost play of 1613 presented him. Between that play and Ford's own, however, a historical account of him had appeared by Francis Bacon, in his *Life of King Henry VII*, and Bacon calls attention to the oddities within the story. He introduces his account by noting that it was 'one of the strangest examples of a personation, that ever was in elder or later times', and that part of that strangeness was due to the King's own puzzling reactions: his 'manner of shewing things by pieces, and by dark lights, hath so muffled it, that it hath left it almost as a mystery to this day'.[12] That seems to have given Ford his cue, and perhaps also his subtitle of 'A Strange Truth'. His Warbeck is more kingly than the King, and always insists on his royal identity. The very first scene shows Henry stressing his own lineal right to the crown, but it is striking that he is the only person who does so. He is not presented as a villain, but his less attractive qualities, including his keenness to extract money from his subjects, open the way for Warbeck to capture the audience's sympathies. He by contrast is always shown in honourable mode, not least in his role as husband. His wife is presented as loyal and loving, and her belief in her husband never wavers. His downfall is ascribed to fate or destiny, not to Providence or God; the play indeed rigorously avoids declaring for or against Warbeck's claims. It is the play that potentially most strongly threatens the house of Tudor, but the Tudors were by this time very safely in the past.

Ford was none the less well aware that the day of the history play had passed. *Perkin Warbeck* abounds with echoes of Shakespeare's histories, especially those favourites *Richard II* and *Henry IV 1*; but he acknowledges at the start of his play's Prologue that such plays are 'out of fashion' (line 2). He justifies it on the grounds that its sources are pure English, and that its twin bases are 'Truth and State' (line 26). He follows his sources more closely than most of the other dramatists of Tudor history, with none of the chronological upsets of the earlier plays; but he avoids making any decision as to where 'truth' might lie. For most of the thirty years after Elizabeth's death, the Tudor myth itself is no longer quite sacred.

Notes

1 The only single study devoted to these plays as a group (Ford excepted) is by Marsha S. Robinson, *Writing the Reformation: Actes and Monuments and the Jacobean History Play* (Aldershot: Ashgate, 2002). See also Janette Dillon, 'Theatre and Controversy, 1603–1642', in Jane Milling and Peter Thomson (eds), *The Cambridge History of British Theatre, Vol. 1: Origins to 1660* (Cambridge: Cambridge University Press, 2004), pp. 364–76.

2 Anthony Munday et al., *Sir Thomas More*, ed. J. Jowett (London: Bloomsbury Arden Shakespeare, 2011).

3 In C. F. Tucker Brooke (ed.), *The Shakespeare Apocrypha* (Oxford: Clarendon Press, 1908).

4 F. P. Wilson (ed.) (Oxford: Malone Society, 1952).

5 In all complete editions of Shakespeare; also e.g. *Henry VIII* ed. Gordon McMullan (London: BloomsburyArden Shakespeare, 2000).

6 In *The Dramatic Works of Thomas Dekker*, ed. Fredson Bowers (Cambridge: Cambridge University Press, 1953), vol. 1. See also Cyrus Hoy, *Introductions, Notes and Commentaries to Texts in 'The Dramatic Works of Thomas Dekker'* ed. Fredson Bowers (Cambridge: Cambridge University Press, 1980), vols 1–2.

7 There are separate editions of both this and Part II by Madeleine Doran (both Oxford: Malone Society, 1934). See further Curtis Perry, *The Making of Jacobean Literary Culture* (Cambridge: Cambridge University Press, 1997), pp. 153–87, on Heywood's and Dekker's Elizabeth plays.

8 In *Dramatic Works of Thomas Dekker*, ed. Bowers, vol. 2 (1955).

9 Printed in 1631, and available on *Early English Books Online*; the only modern edition is an unpublished PhD thesis by Robert Anthony Raines, 'Thomas Drue's *The Duchess of Suffolk*: A Critical Old-spelling Edition' (University of Delaware, 1968).

10 A full account of its political engagement is given in Jerzy

Limon, *Dangerous Matter: English Drama and Politics in 1623/24* (Cambridge: Cambridge University Press, 1986), pp. 40–61 (80).

11 John Ford, *The Chronicle History of Perkin Warbeck*, ed. Peter Ure (London: Methuen, 1968), p. 5. On the date and possible censorship, see pp. xvii, xxviii–xxx.

12 Francis Bacon, *The Historie of the Raigne of King Henry the Seventh*, ed. Michael Kiernan, The Oxford Francis Bacon series, vol. 8 (Oxford: Clarendon Press, 2012), p. 80 (spelling modernized). Ford also used a more hostile account by Thomas Gainesford.

Appendix 1: Plays in order of composition

(Surviving plays are printed in bold.)

Probable date of composition	Author/Title	Printing history
1590s	Anthony Munday and others (including Shakespeare), **Sir Thomas More** (?never acted)	MS only
>1602	Anon, **The Life and Death of the Lord Cromwell**	1602
1601	Henry Chettle, *Life of Cardinal Wolsey*; *Rising of Cardinal Wolsey*	lost
1602	Henry Chettle and others, *Lady Jane I and II*	lost
1603	Thomas Dekker and John Webster, **The Famous History of Sir Thomas Wyatt**	1607, 1612
1604	Samuel Rowley, **When You See Me, You Know Me: The enterlude of K. Henry 8**	1605, 1613, 1621, 1632
1604	Thomas Heywood, **If You Know Not Me, You Know Nobody I: or, the Troubles of Queene Elizabeth**	1605, 1606, 1608, 1610, 1613, 1623, 1632, 1639
1604	Thomas Heywood, **If You Know Not Me, You Know Nobody II**	1606, 1609, 1623, 1633
1606	Thomas Dekker, **The Whore of Babylon**	1607
1613	William Shakespeare and John Fletcher, **Henry VIII (All is True)**	1623
1613	Anon, *Perkin Warbeck*	lost
1623–4	Thomas Drue, **The Life of the Dutches of Suffolke**	1631
>1634	John Ford, **The Chronicle History of Perkin Warbeck: A Strange Truth**	1634

Appendix 2: Plays in chronological order of events dramatized

Historical events	Author	Title	Likely date of composition
1490–9	Anon	*Perkin Warbeck*	1613
1490–9	**Ford**	***The Chronicle History of Perkin Warbeck*** (A Strange Truth)	1629–34
		Warbeck's claim to Henry VII's throne, marriage, execution	
[1507–30]	Chettle	2 plays on the rise and fall of Cardinal Wolsey	1601
1517–35	Munday and others	***Sir Thomas More***	?1594–5 ?never performed
		'Ill May Day' riots; More's Chancellorship and execution	
1527–36	**Shakespeare and Fletcher**	***Henry VIII*** (All is True) *Divorce and death of Catherine of Aragon; fall of Wolsey; marriage to Anne Boleyn; birth of Elizabeth*	1613
[1520]–40	**Anon ('W.S.')**	***The Life and Death of the Lord Cromwell***	1590s>1602
		Citizen-type play: Cromwell's early life, rise to power and fall	

Historical events	Author	Title	Likely date of composition
1537–46	Rowley	*When you see me you know me* (The enterlude of K. Henry the 8th)	1604
		The birth of Prince Edward to near Henry's death, overarched by Wolsey's attempts at the papacy and the visit of Charles V	
1553	Chettle and others	*Lady Jane I and II*	1602
		The attempt to place Lady Jane Grey on the throne; probably incorporated into Dekker and Webster's 'Wyatt', below	
1553–4	Dekker and Webster	*The Famous History of Sir Thomas Wyatt*	after 1603
		Death of Edward VI, succession of Jane Gray and Mary; Wyatt's rebellion over her marriage to Philip of Spain; executions of Jane, her husband and Wyatt	
1553–8	Drue	*The Life of the Dutches of Suffolke*	1629
		Flight of Katherine Willoughby, Duchess of Suffolk, from Marian persecution; the deaths of the Protestant bishops Latimer, Ridley and Cranmer	
1554–8	Heywood	*If You Know Not Me, You Know Nobody I* or, The Troubles of Queene Elizabeth	1604
		Elizabeth's imprisonment under Mary; her accession	

Historical events	Author	Title	Likely date of composition
1558–88	Dekker	*The Whore of Babylon*	1606
		Allegory of the Catholic opposition to Elizabeth; the Armada	
1570s–88	Heywood	*If You Know Not Me, You Know Nobody II*	1605
		Citizen play inc. building of Royal Exchange; Parry's plot; Armada	

Appendix 3: Events dramatized

Henry VII (reigned 1485–1509)

1485   defeat of the Yorkist Richard III at the Battle of
            Bosworth (Shakespeare, *Richard III*)
            accession of the Lancastrian Henry Tudor (Henry
            VII)
1491–9   claim of Perkin Warbeck to be the rightful Yorkist
            heir to the throne

Henry VIII (1509–47)

1509   accession of Henry VIII; marriage to Catherine of
            Aragon, his brother's widow
1514   the 'Ill May day' riots in London
1520   visit of Emperor Charles V (uncle of Catherine of
            Aragon) to England
1520   Field of the Cloth of Gold (English-French
            summit)
1527–33   negotiations for divorce from Catherine of
            Aragon (mother of Princess Mary)
1530   death of Cardinal Wolsey
            rise of Thomas Cromwell, strong proponent of
            the Reformation
1533   divorce of Catherine of Aragon, marriage to Anne
            Boleyn; birth of Princess Elizabeth
1535   execution of Sir Thomas More, former Chancellor
1537   birth of Prince Edward to third wife Jane
            Seymour, her death
1540   execution of Thomas Cromwell
1543   marriage to Katherine Parr
1547   death of Henry VIII

Edward VI (1547–53)

Mary I (1553–8)

1553	attempted elevation of Lady Jane Grey to the throne, as the Protestant claimant; accession of Mary Tudor; return to Roman Catholicism
1554	marriage of Mary to Philip II of Spain
	Wyatt's rebellion
	imprisonment of the Protestant Princess Elizabeth
1555	flight to the continent of Katherine Willoughby, Duchess of Suffolk
1555–6	burnings of Latimer, Ridley and Cranmer
1558	death of Mary

Elizabeth I (1558–1603)

1558	accession of Elizabeth
1571	opening of Royal Exchange (founded by Sir Thomas Gresham)
1585	Parry's plot to assassinate Elizabeth
1588	defeat of the Spanish Armada

Appendix 4: Tudor family tree (with regnal dates)

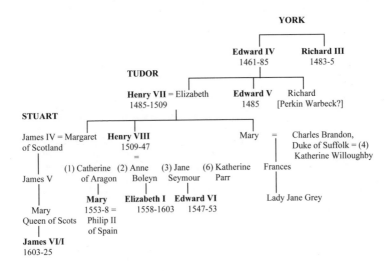

4

The state and the theatre

How were performances controlled and censored, and what was the function of theatrical performances at court? How did the power of the state manifest itself around the production of theatre?

4.1 Sixty plays from the Ming Palace, 1615–18

Tian Yuan Tan

In the year 1616, the Chinese emperor on the throne was the notorious Wanli (r.1573–1620), infamous for his apathetic attitude towards politics and often associated with the decline of the Ming dynasty. He was, however, a sovereign known to be fond of watching and reading drama.[1]

Theatrical performances had long been part of Chinese court culture. The Office of Music Instruction (*Jiaofang si* 教坊司), which was in charge of songs and drama for court performances, was set up as early as during the Tang dynasty (618–906).[2] Court theatre continued to flourish in late imperial China owing to the great interest shown by the emperors and their families. The Ming dynasty witnessed an expansion in the scale of theatrical organizations with the addition of three agencies.[3] The Bells and Drums Office (*Zhonggu si* 鐘鼓司), a department for palace eunuchs in charge of providing intimate palace theatrical entertainments for the emperor, was established in 1390 followed by two additional ones during the reign of the Emperor Wanli to meet the growing need for theatrical entertainments and new styles of performances in the imperial palace.[4] In terms of the scale of performance, contemporaneous records show, for example, that the two later agencies housed court drama troupes of over two hundred and three hundred members respectively.[5] Theatrical activity at the Ming court must therefore have been vibrant.

Unfortunately there are very limited extant sources and direct accounts of which plays were performed and when in the Ming court. The level of detail and chronological evidence found in Chambers's 'A Court Calendar', to which Janet Clare refers in the companion piece to this essay in this section, is unavailable in the documents for the history of Ming court theatre. Accounts of court payments to acting companies, which serve as key chronological evidence for the English courtly performances, were non-existent in the case of Ming court theatre, where theatrical performances were largely undertaken by the imperial troupes.

It is in this context that I approach the relationship between the Ming state and the theatre, particularly on its circulation, authorship and state control, through a group of sixty dramatic texts copied from palace editions around the year 1616. By focusing on these dramatic texts from the palace, we can see that the Ming court in 1616 was not only a unique milieu of theatre and performance space, but it also functioned as an archive of dramatic texts that extended its influence beyond the palace compounds.

In the 1610s, Zhao Qimei 趙琦美 (1563–1624), who was then serving a minor post in the capital as the Assistant Minister at the Court of the Imperial Stud, copied and collated over ninety plays in his leisure time using editions from the imperial palace as his base texts. Zhao referred to his source texts as 'palace editions' (neifuben 内府本 or neiben 内本), to be distinguished from other commonly transmitted sources (shiben 世本).[6] These plays now survive as part of a larger collection of drama texts named after Zhao's studio.[7] Among these plays, Zhao's colophons indicate clearly that sixty of them were copied and collated between 4 February 1615 and 15 January 1618.[8]

This must not be taken as an exhaustive list of the plays available in the Ming court during this period. We know that a wide variety of theatrical styles were performed in the imperial palace, and the sixty plays we are discussing here concern only one particular form, the northern style of Chinese drama known as zaju (literally, variety drama), a form of music theatre with sung arias and spoken dialogues in four acts that flourished during the preceding Yuan dynasty (1260–1368). For a long time, zaju remained the mainstream performance in the Ming court and enjoyed a higher prestige, though it faced increasing competition from the newly popular southern styles around the turn of the seventeenth century.

According to an early seventeenth-century account, there was a great demand for new plays in the Ming court:

> Short farces (*yuanben* 院本) always took the form of marionette dances. As for drama (*zaju*), it was in the northern style of the nine modes as used by the Jin and Yuan dynasty writers. On occasions when flowers and other seasonal items were to be presented to the court, the Office of Music Instruction would compose drama in four acts and submit them to the historian-officials for examination and finalisation, before presenting the arias and performing their theatrical skills in the presence of His Majesty. A few days later, they would again submit other presentations. The old texts were no longer presented.[9]

For plays to be checked by the historian-officials (*shiguan* 史官) in the Hanlin Academy, they had to be written out as full scripts, resulting in the production of the so-called 'palace editions' of drama in the Ming court. The actual production of these court manuscripts and their performances might have first taken place a few decades before 1616. Komatsu Ken argues that these palace editions can be dated to the Jiajing period (1522–67) and some plays might have also been re-adapted for performance later during the Wanli era.[10] As transcriptions of Ming court performance texts, the sixty plays copied from the palace editions in the period from 1615 to 1618 are therefore the most direct extant sources of what were perceived and still accessible as Chinese 'court plays' around the year 1616.

In terms of authorship, the Ming court was largely a world of anonymous drama. Among these sixty plays from the Ming court, only nine are of known authorship and all of them are attributed to earlier Yuan dynasty playwrights of the fourteenth century. The rest are either anonymous or said to be compiled by the Office of Music Instruction under a form of collective authorship with no names identified.

Two observations can be made from the composition of these sixty plays. First, during this period, there were no identifiable contemporary Chinese 'court dramatists' who wrote plays for palace performance in the same manner that Shakespeare could be regarded as being the 'King's Playwright'.[11] This suggests that either the idea of a court playwright composing drama under court patronage is not applicable to the Chinese court in the early seventeenth century, or that such playwrights are simply not visible in our sources. Second, most of the plays performed in the Ming court are not newly composed plays, but are instead revised or adapted versions from earlier dramas of the Yuan dynasty. Though the plays might have been originally composed by Yuan dramatists, it is clear that the versions that we see in the group of sixty plays had undergone changes in the Ming court.

Censorship was no doubt present during this period, but the extent and actual impact of the state's control over theatre is far from clear due to limited sources. On the one hand, we know from the Ming legal code that statutes were issued giving clear instructions on what kinds of plays were acceptable, and what were not. For example, as recorded in the *Great Ming Code* first issued in 1397 and repeated throughout the later reigns of the Ming dynasty:[12]

In all cases of theatrical performances, actors shall not be permitted to dress up as former emperors, empresses, or other imperial consorts, loyal ministers, martyrs, sages, or worthies. Any violations shall be punished by 100 strokes of beating with the heavy stick. If the households of officials or commoners allow them to dress up this way for performances, the penalty shall be the same. As for acting as immortals, righteous husbands, chaste wives, filial sons, or

> obedient grandsons with the aim of motivating others to be good, it shall not be prohibited.[13]

On the other hand, it is unclear whether or how these prohibitions were indeed implemented. Part of the problem lies in the scarcity of specific references to who or to which agency was in charge of such control and censorship. We recall from one of the passages cited earlier that drama texts compiled by the Office of Music Instruction needed to be examined and finalized. However, the passage only tells us that these texts were given to the 'historian-officials', which is no more than a generic reference to officials engaged in the compilation of various kinds of historical records and documents.[14] To my knowledge, nor are there any Chinese drama texts from this period that preserve markings of omissions or censorship in the early seventeenth century similar to the kind of marginal notes or markings made by the Master of the Revels, Edmund Tilney, as discussed by Janet Clare in her essay. For that level of well-preserved detail in drama censorship, we need to wait another two centuries until the late eighteenth and especially the nineteenth century, with the later Qing dynasty court drama manuscripts.

In this context, palace editions of drama functioning as inspection copies at the Ming court serve as an invaluable source. A comparison between palace and non-palace texts of the same title can help to suggest that some form of drama censorship and state control was in place.[15] To illustrate these points, let us look more closely at one example, the play titled *Duke Zhao of Chu: The Most Distant Relative Goes Overboard* (*Chu Zhaogong shuzhe xiachuan* 楚昭公疎者下船). According to the colophon, this play was copied and collated from a palace edition on the 28th day of the second month in the *bingchen* year, the 44th year of the Wanli reign 萬曆四十四年丙辰二月廿八日 (14 April 1616).[16] Chronologically, according to the order in which the plays were copied, this is No. 58 in the group of sixty plays. On the first page of the manuscript, one could see that this play was attributed to the early Yuan dynasty playwright Zheng Tingyu who probably lived in the late thirteenth or early fourteenth century. But to what extent can we see Play No. 58 as a work of Zheng Tingyu?

Several editions of Zheng Tingyu's play survive to the present day.[17] If we compare the version in No. 58 with its fourteenth-century 'Yuan dynasty edition', we will find that there are parts of No. 58 that are completely unrecognizable from the earlier commercial print edition of the same play. The two versions are so different from each other that the palace edition in the sixty plays is best regarded not as a censored or amended version, but as a new anonymous play rewritten in the Ming dynasty using parts of the old material from the Yuan drama.[18]

As its short title *The Most Distant Relative Goes Overboard* suggests, this play centres on a climactic moment in Act Three when Duke Zhao of Chu, during his flight from the capital after defeat by Wu Zixu's army, has to make the difficult decision about whom to sacrifice because his boat can no longer carry all the people on board. In the end, Duke Zhao's wife and son throw themselves into the river as we are told Duke Zhao considered them as more 'distant relatives' than his brother whom he chooses to save.

There are several major differences between the Yuan dynasty commercial print version and the Ming palace edition. First, the Ming palace edition clearly tones down the element of Wu Zixu's revenge against his former lord found in the Yuan version, which understandably might not sit well with the imperial audience at court. In Act One of the Ming palace edition, the dispute between the states of Wu and Chu is instead accounted for by Duke Zhao's refusal to return a precious sword to the prince of the Wu state.[19] Second, the Ming palace version also adds an element of divine intervention which changes the nature and tone of the play. The Duke's wife and son who are sacrificed in the play are later saved by the Dragon God guarding the river, hence leading to a happy reunion meeting at the end of the play. Third, whereas the title of the play appears as 'King Zhao of Chu' in the Yuan dynasty edition, it was changed to 'Duke Zhao of Chu' in the Ming edition, stressing that Chu was only a tributary state of Zhou, as the play underlines the power and authority of the King of Zhou. Moreover, the play concludes with a fourteen-line verse serving as an encomium to the King of Zhou and most probably directed towards the Ming emperor watching the play, which is a common feature in Ming court plays.[20] In terms of the content, one can also see this as a kind of morality play ('motivating others to be good') approved and promoted by the Ming court as another aspect of its control over theatre.

More interestingly, there is yet another version of this play printed around the same time as Zhao was copying and collating Play No. 58. This is the version in the influential anthology *A Selection of Yuan Plays* (*Yuanqu xuan* 元曲選) published in 1615 to 1616 by Zang Maoxun, an important figure in the history of Chinese drama who will be discussed in fuller detail in the essays by Stephen H. West and Patricia Sieber. Here, I shall only note that Zang also obtained many of his texts from the Office of Bells and Drums, the same source from which our sixty plays derived.

Comparing three editions, we will find that the third version in the *Selection of Yuan Plays* is textually very close to, and likely to have derived from, the palace edition No. 58, but appears to be unrelated to and unaware of the earliest Yuan edition.[21] As the *Selection of Yuan Plays* became the main anthology and reading text of Yuan drama from the late Ming to this day, the presence and influence of the palace edition can therefore be continuously felt.

This is where we need to re-examine the relationship between theatre and state, not just in terms of censorship but in the broader roles that the Ming court played in the development of Chinese theatre. The world of Ming court theatre was more than just an isolated *milieu* or *type* of theatre created and consumed within the compounds of the imperial palace. We know that the Office of Music Instruction performed not only for the imperial family, but also for the officials. Furthermore, it is arguably through these dramatic texts that we see the fuller impact of the Ming court on the history of Chinese theatre. As inspection copies, palace editions of drama might be regarded as products of state censorship. Yet it was precisely because of this need for court inspection that the textual recording of dramas was initiated. They would otherwise have been lost. In fact, many of the texts preserved in the sixty plays from the Ming palace are the earliest editions we have of these dramas. Only four of them, including Play No. 58 discussed here, have earlier so-called 'Yuan dynasty editions' from the fourteenth century.[22] Since the majority of the extant Yuan plays in one way or another was derived from the Ming court,[23] it is clear that the palace editions helped shape modern researchers' knowledge and understanding of early modern Chinese drama. But perhaps the same applies to Ming writers as well? What drama texts were available to a typical Chinese elite writer in the year 1616? How important was the Ming court in terms of the preservation and circulation of drama texts?

Returning to the case of Zhao Qimei's copying and collation of the sixty plays from the Ming palace, we need to ask: why did Zhao bother to copy these texts? We can certainly attribute this to his relish for drama, but it would also appear that these palace editions are no ordinary texts easily accessible to any writer. Otherwise, Zhao would not have invested the time and effort in copying and collating them. Several other Ming playwrights and literati were known to have read a sizable number of drama texts in the imperial court. An earlier example is Kang Hai 康海 (1475–1541), who claimed he came across hundreds and thousands of Yuan plays in the Hanlin Academy during his time serving as a senior compiler after his success as the Top Graduate in the 1502 examination. Closer to the period we are discussing, the famous calligrapher and painter Dong Qichang 董其昌 (1555–1636) had a hand in several colophons found in Zhao's Maiwangguan collection and in one case specifically mentioned that he had previously read the play in the *neifu* (palace storehouses).[24]

The sixty plays discussed in this essay derived from palace editions which were transcriptions of court performances, and in this regard they also serve as a valuable source of the theatrical styles and practices in the imperial court. For instance, costume lists of every character coming on stage in each play are appended to these palace editions. But one can safely speculate that, apart from these palace editions of performance texts, there were also other drama texts kept and produced in the Ming court primarily for reading purposes. For instance, *The Grand Canon of the Yongle Era* (*Yongle dadian* 永樂大典) commissioned by the Yongle Emperor (r. 1403–24) included plays and would have been another important source of drama texts in the palace before it was lost in the final years of the Ming dynasty.[25]

During the Ming dynasty, the imperial court is likely to have been the most central archive for access to a sizable body of drama texts. Much has been said about Chinese drama as a form of popular art and literature more usually associated with the common folk than with the imperial house, but it is time to reassess the roles played by the Ming court in the development and circulation of Chinese drama.

Notes

1   A seventeenth-century record describes Emperor Wanli as an avid reader who often instructed his officials to collect and present to him new books, including dramatic texts, from the markets and bookshops. See Liu Ruoyu, *Zhuozhong zhi* (Beijing: Beijing guji chubanshe, 1994), *juan* 1, p. 1.

2   On *jiaofang* from the Tang to Ming dynasties, see Wilt L. Idema and Stephen H. West, *Chinese Theater, 1100–1450: A Source Book* (Wiesbaden: Franz Steiner, 1982), pp. 95–118, and Zhang Ying, *Lidai jiaofang yu yanju* (Jinan: Qi Lu shushe, 2007).

3   See Iwaki Hideo, 'Min no kyūtei to engeki', in idem, *Chūgoku gikyokyu engeki kenkyū* (Tokyo: Sōbunsha, 1972), pp. 602–24; Tseng Yong-yih, 'Mingdai diwang yu xiqu', *Wenshizhe xuebao*,

40 (1993), pp. 1–23; Wilt L. Idema, 'Stage and Court in China: The Case of Hung-wu's Imperial Theatre', *Oriens Extremus* 23 (2) (1976), pp. 175–89. For a recent book-length study on Ming court theatre, see Li Zhenyu, *Mingdai gongting xiju shi* (Beijing: Zijincheng chubanshe, 2010).

4   Li, *Mingdai gongting xiju shi*, pp. 139–45.

5   Liu Ruoyu, *Zhuozhong zhi*, *juan* 16, p. 109.

6   For studies on *neifuben*, see especially Komatsu Ken, 'Naifuhon-kei shohon kō', in *Tanaka Kenji hakushi shōju kinen Chūgoku koten gikyoku ronshū* (Tokyo: Kyūko Shoin, 1991), pp. 125–59, and Nagamatsu Junko, 'Mingdai neifuben zaju yanjiu' (PhD dissertation, Sun Yat-sen University, 2009).

7   Full title: *Zaju, Old and New, Copied and Collated, from the Studio of the Transformed Bookworm* (*Maiwangguan chaojiaoben gujin zaju* 脈望館鈔校本古今雜劇). For a critical review of the existing scholarship on this collection, see Li Zhanpeng, '*Maiwangguan chaojiaoben gujin zaju* zhengli yanjiu shuping', *Mianyang shifan xueyuan xuebao*, Vol. 31, No. 3 (2012), pp. 72–6.

8   See a list in Sun Kaidi, *Yeshiyuan gujin zaju kao* (Shanghai: Shangza chubanshe, 1953), pp. 78–85. The sixty plays are found in *Maiwanguang chaojiaoben gujin zaju*, Vols 2, 4, 8, 10–12, 15, 16, 18, 20, 23–6, 28–30, 41–8, 50, 52, 57, 59–65, 68–71, 73–80, 82–4, *Guben xiqu congkan*, 4th series (Shanghai: Shangwu yinshu guan, 1958). There are some discrepancies between Sun's transcriptions and the dates of the colophons in the source text.

9   Song Maocheng, *Jiuyueji* (Beijing: Zhongguo shehui kexue chubanshe, 1984), p. 218.

10 Komatsu Ken, *Chūgoku koten engeki kenkyū* (Tokyo: Kyūko Shoin, 2001), pp. 131–4.

11 Alvin Kernan, *Shakespeare, the King's Playwright: Theatre in the Stuart Court, 1603–1613* (New Haven: Yale University Press, 1995).

12 See, for example, *Da Ming lü jijie fuli* (Wanli edn, reprint, Taipei: Xuesheng shuju, 1970), 26.14a.

13   Quoted in Wang Liqi (comp.), *Yuan Ming Qing sandai jinhui xiaoshuo xiqu shiliao*, rev. edn (Shanghai: Shanghai guji chubanshe, 1981), p. 13. English translation cited from Yonglin Jiang (trans.), *The Great Ming Code* (Seattle: University of Washington Press, 2004), pp. 220–1, with minor amendments.

14   Charles O. Hucker, *A Dictionary of Official Titles in Imperial China* (Stanford: Stanford University Press, 1985), p. 345.

15   See Wilt L. Idema, 'Why You Never Have Read a Yuan Drama: The Transformation of *Zaju* at the Ming Court', in S. M. Carletti, M. Sacchetti and P. Santangelo (eds), *Studi in onore di Lanciello Lanciotti* (Naples: Istituto Universitario Orientale, 1996), pp. 765–91; Stephen H. West, 'Text and Ideology: Ming Editors and Northern Drama', in P. J. Smith and R. Von Glahn (eds), *The Song-Yuan-Ming Transition in Chinese History* (Cambridge, MA: Harvard University Asia Center, 2003), pp. 329–73; Tian Yuan Tan, 'The Sovereign and the Theater: Reconsidering the Impact of Ming Taizu's Prohibitions', in Sarah Schneewind (ed.), *Long Live the Emperor: Uses of the Ming Founder across Six Centuries of East Asian History* (Minneapolis: Society for Ming Studies, 2008), pp. 149–69.

16   *Chu Zhaogong shuzhe xiachuan*, in *Maiwanguang chaojiaoben gujin zaju* collection, vol. 18, *Guben xiqu congkan*, 4th series, p. 37b.

17   On editions, see Ma Xiaoni, 'Yuan zaju *Shuzhe xiachuan* de banben wenti', *Dongnan daxue xuebao (zhexue shehui kexue ban)*, 10(3) (2008), pp. 81–5.

18   See Yan Dunyi, *Yuanju zhenyi* (Beijing: Zhonghua shuju, 1960), pp. 395–6; Zheng Qian, 'Yuan *zaju* yiben bijiao (di'er zu)', in *Guoli Bianyiguan guankan*, II(3) (1973), p. 100.

19   Zheng Qian, 'Yuan *zaju* yiben bijiao (di'er zu)', p. 101.

20   See Komatsu, *Chūgoku koten engeki kenkyū*, pp. 127–31; Nagamatsu, 'Mingdai neifuben zaju yanjiu', pp. 89–94.

21   Zheng Qian, 'Yuan *zaju* yiben bijiao (di'er zu)', p. 101.

22   'Yuan dynasty editions' of Yuan plays are rare and only thirty such editions survive to the present day. See Stephen H. West and Wilt L. Idema (eds and trans.), *The Orphan of Zhao and Other Yuan Plays: The Earliest Known Versions* (New York:

Columbia University Press, 2014) and Wang Shih-pe, 'Cong Yuankanben chongtan Yuan zaju: yi banben, tizhi, juchang san'ge mianxiang wei fanchou' (PhD dissertation, National Tsing Hua University, 2006).

23 Sun, *Yeshiyuan gujin zaju kao*, p. 152; Komatsu, *Chūgoku koten engeki kenkyū*, p. 38.

24 See Dong's colophon to *Cheng Yaojin fupi laojuntang* 程咬金斧劈老君堂, in *Maiwanguang chaojiaoben gujin zaju* collection, vol. 56, p. 38a.

25 A catalogue of the plays included was cited in Wang Liqi (comp.), *Yuan Ming Qing sandai jinhui xiaoshuo xiqu shiliao*, pp. 5–9. By the end of the Ming dynasty, Liu Ruoyu lamented that the whereabouts of this significant collection was no longer known after several fires in the palace. See Liu, *Zhuozhong zhi, juan* 18, p. 162.

4.2 Licensing the King's Men: From court revels to public performance

Janet Clare

The Prince being disposed to pastime would at one time appoint one person, at some time another, such as for credit, pleasant wit and ability in learning he thought meet to be the Master of the Revels for that time.

FROM A REPORT PREPARED FOR LORD BURGHLEY ON THE ORIGINS OF THE REVELS OFFICE, c.1573

These things are but toys to come amongst such serious observations; but yet since princes will have such things, it is better they should be graced with elegancy, than daubed with cost.

FRANCIS BACON, 'OF MASQUES AND TRIUMPHS', *IN ESSAYS AND COUNSELS, CIVIL AND MORAL*, 1625

It is a well-known fact that princes are disposed to pastimes and have a need to be entertained, a sentiment acknowledged by both Francis Bacon and the unknown author of a document concerning the Office of the Revels prepared for Lord Burghley, Elizabeth I's Lord Treasurer. In the companion piece to this essay Tian Yuan Tan demonstrates that Ming court theatre production was crucial to the historical development of Chinese theatre. By 1616 in England, theatre was established as a regular component of court entertainment, but plays were not written primarily or exclusively for court performance, nor – unlike in Ming China – can we identify a corpus of 'court plays'. At religious and secular feasts

– Christmas, Shrovetide, All Hallows on 1 November – and at dynastic and state occasions the Tudor and Jacobean court was entertained by revels, including not only plays but also moral interludes, maskings, tilts and, increasingly during Shakespeare's career, plays. Bacon's observation might seem disingenuous or drily ironic. Spectacles and drama of different kinds were more than mere 'toys'. Interludes, plays and masques could be both political and personal, often obliquely counselling the monarch or serving as propaganda for factional or dynastic interests. Tian Yuan Tan argues that, in the same period in China, the court approved and promoted plays which were, broadly speaking, morality plays, and that the differences between the palace version of a play and its commercial print version indicate censorship of the text to make the play more congenial for imperial entertainment. Similarly, plays performed at court during Shakespeare's working life were subject to some censorship, aesthetic as well as ideological. For playwrights, close to the court and mindful of producing plays to be performed before the king, we can assume a degree of circumspection or inner censorship. In this essay I will explore the dynamics between theatre practice, court performance and state censorship, focusing on specific cases, as, unlike Ming court theatre, the influence of the court's Office of the Revels extended beyond court drama to popular theatre.

Elizabeth I depended largely on a troupe of boy actors, the Children of the Chapel, and the companies under the patronage of her nobles to provide dramatic entertainment at court. The company which bore her name, the Queen's Men, did occasionally perform at court, but they were essentially a touring company performing popular history plays such as *The True Tragedy of Richard the Third* and *The Famous Victories of Henry the Fifth* in the provinces.[1] It was the companies under the patronage of two of her chief Privy Councillors, the Lord Chamberlain's Men and the Lord Admiral's Men, which came to dominate court theatricals in the latter years of the sixteenth century.[2] The first extant record of court performance of Shakespeare's company, the Lord Chamberlain's Men, is in the Chamber Accounts, which record payment to 'William Kempe, William Shakespeare and Richard Burbage, servants to the Lord Chamberlain' for two comedies performed on St Stephen's Night (26 December) and Innocents' Day (28 December).[3] After the Jacobean accession in 1603 and the promotion of the Lord Chamberlain's Men to the King's Men, the company performed regularly during the Christmas Revels and often at All Hallows, or Hallowmass. *Measure for Measure*, for example, was performed on St Stephen's Night in 1604, *King Lear* on the same feast day in 1606; at All Hallows in 1604 *Othello* was performed, and in 1611 *The Tempest*. Secular as well as religious rites were occasions for theatrical performance, and there is a record in the Chamber Accounts of the Chamberlain's Men performing at the wedding of the Earl of Derby and Lady Elizabeth Vere on 26 January 1595, which has given rise to the reasonable conjecture that the play chosen for this occasion was Shakespeare's *A Midsummer Night's Dream,* which opens and closes with projected weddings.

In his essay Tian Yuan Tan observes that, whilst Chinese legal documents indicate what was forbidden to be represented on stage, knowledge of who or which agency implemented censorship is lacking. In England, before and after 1616, we do have more specific detail and evidence of theatrical censorship. From the mid-sixteenth century, court revels were supervised by the Master of the Revels and the plays the companies performed as part of court festivities were in theory chosen by the Master. We have no way of knowing, though, what kinds of mediation there might have been. In an entry in the Revels Accounts of 1572, for example, it is noted that six plays were 'chosen out of many and found to be the best that then was to be had; the same also being often perused and necessarily corrected and amended by all the aforesaid officers'.[4] This entry pre-dates the extensive powers given to the Master of the Revels in 1581, but there is little reason to doubt that the contents of plays chosen for court performance would have been subject to careful scrutiny. We may note, for instance, the emphasis in the quoted entry: 'chosen out of many', '*often* perused', '*necessarily* corrected', 'amended by *all* the aforesaid officers' (my italics). The little we know about the plays performed at the Elizabethan court points to a preference for comedy. Shakespeare's romantic comedies of the 1590s, comprising part of the repertoire of the Lord Chamberlain's company, may have helped to set this agenda, although equally these comedies follow the dictates of earlier court comedy made fashionable by John Lyly and performed by boy actors. Lyly's comedies, however, with their implicit celebration of the queen's chastity, are exclusively designed for a court or aristocratic audience, while Shakespeare's are more dual-purpose, catering as well for popular theatre audiences at one of the earliest public playhouses, the Theatre, and later at the Globe.

The authority of the Master of the Revels, an office created originally to oversee and coordinate entertainment for the monarch and the court, was considerably extended in the late sixteenth century into the public and commercial realm. With the appointment of Edmund Tilney to the position of Master in 1579 sweeping changes were introduced to the production and licensing of plays. In the Queen's commission granted to Tilney in 1581, the role is enlarged from that of supervisor of court revels to a licensor and censor of plays to be performed outside the court:

we have and do by these present authorize and command our said Servant Edmund Tilney Master of our said Revels by himself or his sufficient deputy or deputies to warn, command, and appoint in all places within this our Realm of England as well within franchises and liberties as without, all and every player or players with their playmakers either belonging to any noble man or otherwise bearing the name or names of using the faculty of playmakers or players of comedies, tragedies, interludes [...] to appear before him with all such plays, tragedies, comedies or shows as they shall have in readiness or mean to set forth and them to present and recite before our said servant or his sufficient deputy whom we ordain, appoint and authorize [...] to order and reform, authorize and put down as shall be thought meet or unmeet unto himself or his said deputy in that behalf.[5]

Quite new to the Office are the powers vested in Tilney to license and suppress plays at his discretion and the right to imprison both actors and playwrights who disregard his authority. Unlike the dictates of the Great Ming Code, first issued in 1397, which stipulates that 'actors shall not be permitted to dress up as former emperors, empresses, or other imperial consorts, loyal ministers, martyrs, sages, or worthies', on the crucial matter of what the censor is to censor Tilney's commission is vague. The Master is 'to order and reform, authorize and put down as shall be thought meet or unmeet unto himself or his said deputy'. In leaving the substance of censorship open and indeterminate, the commission empowers the Master of the Revels to decide where the line should be drawn from case to case, in relation to current political concerns.[6] The evolution of the role of the Master of the Revels during Shakespeare's working life to encompass not only the material production of court entertainment but the licensing and censorship of all plays prior to performance is indicative of how seriously the Elizabethan and Jacobean state took its pastimes.

Tilney's commission stipulated that players should recite their plays before the Master, a practice which must soon have proved impractical and which no doubt must on some occasions have been replaced by reading the play manuscript (the so-called 'book'). Play manuscripts which were perused and marked by the Master of the Revels offer irrefutable evidence of state censorship. In reconstructing theatrical censorship during the late sixteenth and early seventeenth centuries, we are fortunate that a number of play manuscripts have survived which show the interventions, objections and occasional rewritings of the

Master of the Revels. One of the most well-known cases is that of Tilney's censorship of the manuscript of an unpublished play about the humanist scholar and statesman, Thomas More. The play telescopes two disparate narratives: the May Day riots of 1517 against foreigners in London which Thomas More helped to quell, and the Reformation politics of Henry VIII's break with Rome leading to More's execution in 1534. Both these narratives are politically provocative in so far as they represent alleged acts of treason. The insurgents are seen as traitors because their uprising is directed against foreigners who came from countries friendly to the king (they are referred to as 'Frenchmen' and 'strangers', but in the manuscript Tilney changes the reference to 'Lombards'). The other act which may have been regarded as treasonous and therefore not to be represented on stage is contained in a scene in which More denies the King's supremacy in matters spiritual and resigns his office. Tilney has marked the scene for omission and has written the marginal note 'All Alter'.

Throughout the manuscript Tilney consistently registers his objection to representing and referring to riots against foreigners who had taken refuge in London and who were blamed by many for causing economic disadvantage to the indigenous population. The entire first scene of the play in which rowdy citizens protest against the rights and privileges of the 'strangers' in the city has been marked for omission, indicated in the margins by rules and crosses. Signing a marginal note, Tilney wrote:

> Leave out the insurrection wholly and the cause thereof, and begin with Sir Thomas More at the Mayor's sessions, with a report afterwards of his good service done being Sheriff of London upon a mutiny against the Lombards – only by a short report, and not otherwise, at your own perils.[7]

Tilney's directive indicates a shift in emphasis from the actual rebellion and its causes to the suppressing of it. There is more piecemeal censorship later – two of the nobles, for example, comment on the restiveness of the Commons, using words such as 'dangerous times', 'frowning vulgar brow', 'distracted countenance of grief', 'displeased commons of the city'. Tilney has written in the margin 'Mend this'. Censors are not of course interested in what constitutes a good play and this is very much in evidence in Tilney's imperatives – entire scenes are to be omitted and replaced simply by reports of the events they represent. It is evident that Tilney intended the play to be revised and rewritten, not suppressed altogether, and indeed parts of the play were revised and the revisions form part of the manuscript as we have it. Yet there is no evidence that the play was ever acted and there is no printed text. It may be that his interference was so extensive that the play was not viable for performance.

Certain other dramatic manuscripts attest to the authority of the Master of the Revels, but display less detail of dramatic censorship. In 1611, Tilney's successor, George Buc, perused an anonymous, untitled tragedy which concludes with the politically sensitive act of tyrannicide. After Buc had read the play, making corrections as he went, he authorized on the final leaf the performance of the play, but with certain conditions:

This Second Maiden's Tragedy (for it hath no name inscribed) may with the reformations be acted publicly. 31 October 1611. G. Buc.[8]

George Buc's presence is felt more heavily in the play manuscript which came before him in 1619, that of *The Tragedy of Sir John Van Olden Barnavelt* which represents the opposition of the Advocate of Holland, Johan van Oldenbarnevelt, to the Stadtholder, the Prince of Orange.[9] James I supported the House of Orange and had little sympathy for Dutch Republicanism. One of the evident purposes of Buc's censorship is to protect the reputation of the Prince of Orange. In one scene, guards refuse the Prince of Orange entry into the Council Chamber. Buc was evidently disturbed by such physical opposition to a prince, and a potential act of treason, and places crosses and rules in the margin, signifying omission, writing 'I like not this: neither do I think that the prince was thus disgracefully used. Besides he is too much presented.' One very telling intervention by Buc relates to a speech by Barnavelt in which he compares the Netherlands under Orange to Rome and its transition from republic to empire under Octavius Caesar. He has made the marginal note 'cut off his opposites' displaying a censor's wariness towards historical parallels and analogues. All in all, the censor's interventions recorded in the manuscript indicate censorship in line with the interests of the English crown.

During the period of Shakespeare's working life considerable changes occurred in the popularity of specific genres of plays. As Helen Cooper has demonstrated in her essay in this volume, English history plays were popular in the 1590s; in the early seventeenth century, so was satire of urban and court life. The preoccupations of the Master of the Revels, as dramatic censor, changed in response to such changes in the subject matter of plays and as these subjects related to the politics of the moment. What might have been judged seditious or offensive theatre at one time did not necessarily remain so. In the 1590s, with an ageing and childless monarch on the throne, matters relating to succession and dynastic change were topical, indeed dangerously topical to the extent that it was forbidden to discuss openly the question of the succession. Composed in the mid-1590s, Shakespeare's *Richard II,* presenting opposition to the weak and corrupt Richard, was potentially treasonable in its depiction of the successful deposition of a legitimate king. There is no record of this, or indeed of any of Shakespeare's English history plays, being performed at the Elizabethan court, although the play may have been performed privately as well as in the public playhouse.[10] To readers and audiences, used to interpreting texts analogously, the similitudes of the childless Richard II and the childless Elizabeth I could not have gone unnoticed. Richard's deposition and murder brought to an end the Plantagenet dynasty, and with the death of the ageing queen would come the end of the Tudor line. Perhaps it was this which prompted Elizabeth's much quoted remark, 'I am Richard II know ye not that'.[11] Moreover, the dethroning of a legitimate king went quite contrary to the dominant ideological position that obedience was due even to a bad ruler. No manuscript play book has survived to indicate what the Master of the Revels might have objected to in *Richard II*. However, as with the differences between palace and non-palace editions of Ming plays, discrepancies between published editions of plays can be revealing. When *Richard II* came to be published in 1597 and again in 1598, the long scene – familiar to modern audiences – in which Richard is forced to surrender his crown to his cousin Henry Bolingbroke is not included in the text. The deposition scene first appears in an edition of *Richard II* printed in 1608. Once James I had peacefully acceded to the English throne, the succession was no longer controversial and the scene could be played and read with impunity.

In the final section of this essay, I want to return to the performance of Shakespeare's plays at the Jacobean court in the years immediate to 1616. As noted earlier, *Measure for Measure* – probably the first of Shakespeare's plays to be produced for his new patron – was performed on St Stephen's Night, 1604.[12] *King Lear* was performed on the same day two years later and *The Tempest,* probably Shakespeare's last play, was performed at Hallowmas in 1611. Were these plays chosen for the occasion and were they often perused, corrected or amended? Or was Shakespeare, as leading playwright of the King's Men, so adroit at identifying the interests of his royal patron that little surveillance of his texts took place? One would like to know.

What we do have, however, is two texts of *King Lear*: one published in 1608 during Shakespeare's lifetime, and the other published in 1623, in the posthumous Folio edition of his works. It seems reasonable to suppose that the 1608 text is closer to the court performance of 1606 advertised on its title page. Attention to the discrepancies between the texts might suggest some of the political pressures operative on the court performance. The 1608 text of *King Lear* describes itself not as a tragedy but as a chronicle history, a curious description for a play which leaves most of the main characters dead. The death toll includes King Lear, his three daughters, his son-in-law, two of his leading noblemen and probably his Fool. Of the survivors, there is Edgar, now Duke of Gloucester, who has spent most of the play disguised as a Bedlam beggar, and the Duke of Albany, Lear's 'good' son-in-law. It is Albany, ruler of Albania, Scotland, who emerges as Lear's probable successor, unifying a fractured kingdom. At the play's close, Albany turns to Edgar and Kent: 'Friends of my soul, you twain / Rule in this kingdom, and the gored state sustain' (5.3. 315–16),[13] a proposition which is invalidated by Kent's premonition of death. In uniting the 'gored state,' Albany brings his marginalized dukedom from the periphery to the national centre. In the 1608 text, Albany, accepting the obligation to rule, speaks the final words recognizing the ordeals of the passing generation:

> The weight of this sad time we must obey,
> Speak what we feel, not what we ought to say.
> The oldest have borne most; we that are young
> Shall never see so much, nor live so long.

> (5.3.319–22)

In its packed allusions to feeling and saying, truth and decorum, youth and age, real and vicarious suffering, the speech gives great moral heft to the play's ending. It also summarizes what it is like to live in this sad time which is why the lines can be so readily switched to Edgar in the Folio text. The Quarto text, however, based on the court performance, chooses to enhance Albany's role, a not insignificant or arbitrary textual detail, given the provenance of the text. The Dukedom of Albany, dating from 1398, was recreated by Mary, Queen of Scots, for her husband Henry Stuart, Lord Darnley. James inherited his father's title.[14]

Shakespeare's last play, *The Tempest*, was performed at court as part of the festivities of Hallowmas. It is a play about brotherly perfidy, exile, the supernatural, revenge and forgiveness, in a 'New World' location. It is also a play self-conscious of its identity as a show, transitory as any court revels put on to amuse the prince. Whether it was 'chosen out of many', as we know happened in preparation for occasional court theatricals, or whether it was composed with a view to court performance, there is no doubt that in its use of music, dance and spectacular effects *The Tempest* fits the occasion. Prospero, magus, ruler and theatrical impresario, stage manages an entertainment – what he describes as a 'vanity' of his art – to mark the betrothal of his daughter to Prince Ferdinand of Naples. They may be on an island far away from supposedly civilized Europe, but Prospero celebrates the betrothal as in any court with a masque. When forced to break off his show at the news of a revolt on the island, he gives eloquent voice to the transitory nature of revels and their spectacular opulence:

> Our revels now are ended. These our actors
> As I foretold you, were all spirits, and
> Are melted into air, into thin air,
> And, like the baseless fabric of this vision,
> The cloud-capped towers, the gorgeous palaces,
> The solemn temples, the great globe itself,
> Yea, all which it inherit, shall dissolve,
> And like this insubstantial pageant faded,
> Leave not a wrack behind.

(4.1.148–56)

Prospero's speech would seem to resonate with Bacon's recognition that masques are but toys, graced with eloquence. At the end of his career Shakespeare seems to acknowledge the original function of court revels as princely, occasional and ephemeral pastimes even though *The Tempest* – a richly allusive play – has gone much beyond such occasional limitations.

In examining the relationship between theatre and state in Ming China around the year of 1616, Tian Yuan Tan has deduced much from the 'court archive' of plays diligently copied and collated by Zhao Qimei, a court official. We have no such archive of court theatre for Elizabethan and Jacobean drama, for none existed. Plays performed at court were drawn from the repertories of the acting companies who acted in and about London. On the other hand, documents of control are more extensive, if less explicit, for Shakespeare's theatre than similar records appertaining to Ming court theatre. For each culture we can deduce something about the preoccupations of censorship. But, given the disparity between these cultural dispensations – Ming and Jacobean – specific parallels and conclusions are bound to be elusive. What is evident is that the censorship had an undoubted impact on the artistry of plays, shaping them morally, as in Ming China, or politically, as in Jacobean Britain, to conform with and protect the interests of the ruler.

Notes

1   See Scott McMillin and Sally-Beth MacLean, *The Queen's Men and Their Plays* (Cambridge: Cambridge University Press, 1998), pp. 170–88. Records details place of performance and accounts of payment, but not which plays were performed.

2   See Roslyn Lander Knutson, *Playing Companies and Commerce in Shakespeare's Time* (Cambridge: Cambridge University Press, 2001), pp. 21–47.

3   See E. K. Chambers, *The Elizabethan Stage*, 4 vols (Oxford: Clarendon Press, 1923), vol. IV, pp. 164–5. See Chambers's Court Calendar in this volume for records of plays performed at court referred to in this essay.

4   See E. K. Chambers, *Notes on the History of the Revels Office Under the Tudors* (London: A. H. Bullen, 1906), p. 23.

5   See A. Feuillerat, *Documents Relating to the Office of the Revels in the Time of Queen Elizabeth* (Louvain: Uystpruyst, 1908), pp. 51–2. Spelling has been modernized.

6   It was tacitly understood that the living monarch was not represented on the stage. A play in which Elizabeth I was represented, Ben Jonson's *Every Man Out of his Humour*, was censored; see Janet Clare, *'Art made tongue-tied by authority': Elizabethan and Jacobean Dramatic Censorship* (Manchester: Manchester University Press, 1999), pp. 103–4.

7   See *Sir Thomas More*, ed. John Jowett, the Arden Shakespeare (London: A&C Black Publishers Ltd., 2011), p. 5.

8   British Library MS Lansdown 807, Folio 65r, see also *The Second Maiden's Tragedy*, ed. Anne Lancashire (Manchester: Manchester University Press, 1978). Spelling modernized.

9   British Library MS Add. 18653. See also *Sir John van Olden Barnavelt*, prepared by T. H. Howard-Hill for the Malone Society (1980), pp. vi–x.

10   See *Richard II*, ed. Andrew Gurr (Cambridge: Cambridge University Press, 1984), pp. 1–3, 44.

11   See J. Nichols, *Progresses of Queen Elizabeth*, 2 vols (London, 1788), vol. II, p. 41. The remark was made to the antiquary William Lambarde.

12   I have argued elsewhere that *Measure for Measure* is a radical adaptation of Whetstone's *Promos and Cassandra* designed to express political morality and scrutinize theological ideas 'in the air' at the Jacobean accession: see Janet Clare, *Shakespeare's Stage Traffic: Imitation, Borrowing and Competition in Renaissance Theatre* (Cambridge: Cambridge University Press, 2014), pp. 195–210.

13   Quotations are from *The First Quarto of King Lear*, ed. Jay L. Halio (Cambridge: Cambridge University Press, 1994).

14   The play's genealogy has been well explained by John W. Draper in 'The Occasion of *King Lear*', *Studies in Philology*, 34(2) (1937), pp. 176–85.

5

The circulation of dramatic texts and printing

1616 marked a significant year in the publication of drama in both China and England. How were plays being published and in what forms? Who was publishing them? Who were their audiences? What do these publications tell us about early modern reading practices, business strategies and the status of drama texts and playwriting?

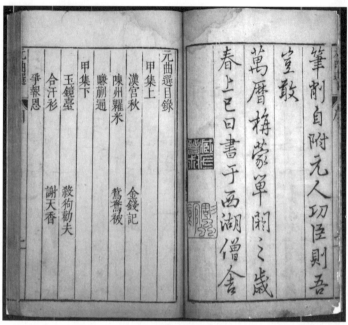

FIGURE 4 *The end of Zang Maoxun's first Preface (dated 31 March 1615) and the start of the Table of Contents (mulu* 目錄, *'Catalogue') of* A Selection of Yuan Plays *(Yuanqu xuan* 元曲選, *1615–16). No. 15167, National Central Library, Taiwan.*

5.1 Tired, sick, and looking for money: Zang Maoxun in 1616

Stephen H. West

In 1616 Zang Maoxun was at the zenith of his career as an entrepreneur in editing and printing texts and as a critic and anthologist of performance literature. But the story of that year must be set against the surrounding years of 1613–18, when he gathered and edited not only his famous *Selection of Yuan Plays* (Figure 4), but also Tang Xianzu's *Four New Plays from the White Camellia Hall*.[1] He was in the throes of some kind of intermittent illness from 1613, contracted when he returned in the spring to Zhejiang from taking his grandson to Ru'nan to enter into an arranged marriage.[2] This illness took nearly six months to recover from, would recurrently plague him for the rest of his life, and seems to be a factor in his complaints about over-tiredness and lack of energy that one often sees in his later letters. In the summer of 1613, the illness took a turn for the worse, as he remarked to his friend Li Weizhen 李維楨 (1570–1627) in 1617:

> When in the past I was mooring at the Old Stone City,[3] I was very honoured by your visit, and very much appreciated the gift of the fan inscribed with verse. The next morning I quickly released the lines and headed eastward, without being able to make my proper goodbyes. Please forgive this breach. That summer, after I had been struck with illness, I could barely rise and became an invalid. My footprints could not go outside of the inner gate.[4]

Upon his return to the Songjiang area (in the southwestern part of modern Shanghai municipality), Zang nurtured his health for another five months. In the years leading up to 1617, he expressed recurrent desires to travel, but it seems that for the most part he was housebound, or at least garden-bound,[5] by his constant lack of energy or desire. One of the benefits – if illness can indeed be beneficial – was that he turned his attention from a wide range of texts from classics on military strategy to Tang poetry solely to dramatic texts. His return stop at Macheng, where he acquired the drama manuscripts, was, in fact, one of several stops he made on that trip with his grandson and he took the opportunity to collect texts wherever he could. In his description of his trip, he takes pains to point out that he not only gathered drama scripts (among others), but that he also made use of his bout of 'heat sickness'[6] to begin to anthologize and edit dramatic texts.

Earlier [i.e., 1610] I had gathered together verses from the poets of the Late Tang, and had assembled about eighty to ninety per cent of what I needed. In the winter of the year *gengxu* (1610–11) about half were stolen by some crooked good-for-nothing. All of the effort I had put into gathering and collating the texts was destroyed in a day. Each time I think about it I get so filled with anger and hatred my stomach almost splits open.

Last winter, I took my young grandson to be married into the family of the Magistrate of Ru'ning, and because of that passed by Langling, where I visited Chen Huibo's[7] home to look at his library as it remains. I found actually that the books that he cites in his works, the *Record from Tianzhong Mountain* (*Tianzhongji* 天中記)[8] and the *Daylily and Gaosu Tree of the Garden of Learning* (*Xuepu xuan su* 學圃蕙蘇)[9] were actually not in his house. My return was by way of Macheng, and I attained more than three hundred manuscripts of *zaju* from the household of Liu Yanbo, of the Imperial Guard. What the people of the world denote the best of the musical drama of the Yuan were complete in these. It was Tang Xianzu who originally selected these, but only twenty of them were of adequate quality. The rest were so vulgar that they were not worth looking at. Contrary to what might be expected, they were not the equal of the various commercial xylograph editions, which are the most craftsmanlike.

Lately I have been in state of senescent weariness, and for fun I take the various *zaju* and cut away or rub out what is superfluous or messy in them. As for those things that should not have been done, I change them according to my own ideas, and I can say of myself that I have pretty much gotten the secret knack of the Yuan writers.[10]

It was also precisely during this period that he also began to annotate Tang Xianzu's dramas. And it is in his comments that we see a practical application of a theory of drama that Zang had been formulating over these years and finally expressed in the prefaces he wrote to accompany the instalments of his *Selection of Yuan Plays* – which appeared in 1615 and 1616 along with each set of fifty plays. As he wrote in the last part of his preface to the *Plays from the White Camellia Hall*:

After I was sick, I abandoned all [high literature] books and historical records, and in leisure took up the four *Stories*, and repeatedly excised and corrected them. The matters in each must be beautiful and emotionally affective, the sound must accord with the musical tune so it makes those who hear it full of joy and those who see it forget their weariness. If so, they can be considered fine music poetry that can be passed side by side with the various dramas from the *Western Wing*. Even if this is so, the current day is the height of southern musical tunes; mistake follows mistake, error leads to error. Let alone authors, a single person who can appreciate the rules of sound (i.e., rhyme, tonal prosody, singing style, etc.) can never be found. This is why Boya broke his strings for Ziqi and why craftsman Shi put away his axe for the man from Ying. Now that the cutting of the texts is finished, I stroke them with appreciative sighs.[11]

We also know, from a poem by Zang Maoxun's good friend, Wu Mengyang 吳夢暘 (d. 1616), that Zang also made an attempt to set sixteen 'unofficial histories'[12] from the Tang period to *tanci*, a form of musical ballad popular in southern China.[13]

1616 witnessed the publication of Zang's final instalment of his *Selection of Yuan Plays*, which he was forced to produce over two consecutive years because of his lack of funds. In 1615, he wrote to Huang Ruheng 黃汝亨 (1558–1626), seemingly in a response to a request for Zang to visit him in Nanjing, where Huang held a post in the Board of Rites:

I have been lodging in the Zhaoqing Temple,[14] and have received three of your letters, and it was only with the last one that I am finally able to respond. I am very embarrassed about this, as well as not being able to send you the Yuan dramas that I have had cut for publication. It is precisely that Chang'gan[15] is a place of historical significance during the Six Dynasties, and I am definitely a person who takes delight in roving as a way to forget my age. But now I am worn out and weary, and the desire to do this is fitful: sometimes it is there, sometimes it is blocked. So what to do? Your achievements as an official grow by the day; put this together with all of the writing and wine that must circulate in that circle and the well-known friends and fine disciples that gather around you as thick as clouds, then that I would be the only one not to be in attendance at your literary gathering is precisely what the Grand Historian raised his face to heaven to sigh about when he was stuck in Zhounan.[16]

In cutting the blocks for the Yuan dramas, I had envisioned a total of one hundred, but I still lack half of that. It was no easy task to gather and edit them, so I have first put fifty into circulation, and it turns out now I have empty pockets, nothing with which to hire woodblock cutters, so I am temporarily borrowing this small amount to alleviate the pressing needs. I have also sent off a servant to send them to bookstores, and am first sending one set to you for your perusal. It would be to my good fortune if you were to promote these among your acquaintances – this would be an act no less than 'Bo Le's appreciation'[17] and it would provide me a way to purchase paper. If there is something you still require, I will certainly send it your way, but dare not try to entice you by this.

[P.S.:] Wu Yunzhao has been fortunate enough lately to have no illness, but a half month earlier he had already entered his gates to write out *The Lotus Sutra*.[18]

The second instalment was issued in 1616, and accompanied (as the first had been) by a preface in which Zang Maoxun laid out what we might call his 'theory of drama', a set of principles that define what a good play is.[19] This was not a *sui generis* theoretical stance, but one that was the culmination of several decades of critical writing that had tried to rationalize regional styles to a universal model, the differences between performance and reading text, and also had to deal with the age-old problem of poetics: the problem of content and language, which they understood as a correct balance struck between 'flower' and 'fruit' (*huashi* 花實), between beautiful language for its own sake (elegant, florid, weak) and substance (fortuitously the same word as 'fruit').[20] Zang was writing when the older northern drama was passing from the textual stage of the literati, and he was deeply frustrated by the increasing non-performability of southern *chuanqi*. In his preface to his recension of Tang Xianzu's plays (cited above), he wrote:

Tang Yireng [Tang Xianzu] of Linchuan wrote the four plays that included the *Peony Pavilion*. Those who discussed them said, 'These are desktop books, they are not *qu* for the feast mat.' But, once you have already been designated as *qu* and yet they cannot be performed at the feast, then what is the point in selecting them? Furthermore, what about considering Linchuan's talent, which can be considered no less than that of the Yuan writers, still inadequate in terms of the *qu*? Now in Yuan times, it was merely northern drama in which writers were skilled. Only Shi Junmei's *Hidden Boudoir* and *The Lute* of Gao Zecheng [Gao Ming] were near to the southern in terms of their sound, and these were selected as models by later writers who had no idea that *Hidden Boudoir* was at least half an indiscriminate forgery, and had already lost its authentic features.[21]

He goes on to further criticize Tang Xianzu:

[he] did not step into the gates of Wu [i.e. follow the errors perpetrated against drama by Wu musicians]; his learning has yet to pry into rules of prosody and rhymes; he has glorified the reputations of the former wise ones and displayed a prodigious range of literary splendour [i.e. ornate language], he is constrained by what he has seen in his own home area, and he sets his songs to music that has no rhythm – can he not be laughed at by Yuan writers?[22]

We see here, and in the 'Preface'[23] to the second instalment, a set of rigorously applied rules that he will exercise in all facets of his editing of dramatic texts, not only his anthology of one hundred *zaju*, but also his annotations and recensions of Tang Xianzu's and Tu Long's plays.[24]

First, the language of drama is promiscuous in its eclecticism: classical texts, history and philosophy, religious language and oral stories captured in text of various kinds. These include both classical and colloquial registers that are to be 'strung together without flaw'. This 'stabilizes and balances' feeling and language. The focus here is on the appropriate matching of linguistic register to social register.

Second, the actual lyrics of the song must be true to character, including being able to express the regional dialect of the characters. The affairs expressed in the song must have a ring of authenticity to them, miming what he calls 'true reality'. This reality is not empirical mimesis, but a revelation of the propositional philosophical truth that authenticates each situation. The setting of the play – not its sets or designs, but the ambience created through language and music – must be self contained and developed without tangent, just as the language cannot introduce anything from outside. This last statement is difficult to deal with; I take it to mean that language cannot introduce or refer to anything that is not present in each unique combination of character, incident, emotion and 'truth' onstage. These are the keys to his understanding of plot.

Third, it must capture the rules of prosody and rhyme appropriate to a model based on Yuan texts.

Finally, plays must be eminently performable, and they must rely on highly skilled actors who can utilize what the playwright has provided to transport the audience to a state in which the reality of the stage overcomes the reality of their ordinary perception of the rhythms of life. The audience must immerse themselves in the world of the play through the medium of the actor, finding their full emotional range within.

It is tempting of course to see these as purely dramatic criteria, but there are also other factors at play. The primary underlying cause was clearly economic. Zang was an indefatigable traveller, looking for manuscripts and texts at prominent households.[25] These he frequently revised, edited, collated or published. Although he came from a prominent Changxing family and was the fourth generational *jinshi* in a row, his dismissal from office for carrying on with his catamite in public led to hard times in his later years. As he wrote to Yao Siren 姚思仁 (c. 1550–1640)[26] in 1606:

After I was cashiered I then encountered bad harvest;[27] then I was encumbered by a series of arranged marriages [for female and male children and grandchildren] and the inheritance from my father was gone with the wind. I wandered widely over river and lake, selling my writing to support myself,[28] until I was shedding tears on a dead-end road. Who would not pity me, seeing this? During ordinary days I would constantly think about your powerful name and your pure reputation, a radiant presence at court that would eventually come to hold the tally and ceremonial axe of office as you oversaw some critical regional area. At that time I should pay my respects to your regional offices, walking staff in hand, with a desire to have my worth as an official debated – I wonder if I would have been countenanced?

I, your younger colleague, have a fetish for carving insects, which has not diminished with age, and in my spare time, I have edited some old-style poems and several volumes of the early and high Tang poets, which I have called *Poetry's Proper Place*. I have latched onto the idea of 'Elegancia and Court Odes each finding [their proper place]' and I am sending them for your perusal.[29] I have also sent a servant to take them to booksellers, hoping to collect enough from their prices to provide funds to 'kill the green'[30] for the Mid- and Late-Tang poets. I hope to be fortunate enough that you, sir, will bruit the work about among the noblemen and officials from the provinces who come to Chang'an. This would be a great giving of alms to the forest of poetry, and it is not only I, your impoverished junior, who will be moved by this.[31]

As a former Erudite in the National Academy, Zang had a large network of friends, particularly in Zhejiang and Nanjing. 'Noblemen' in the above passage, to use Yung Sai-shing's definition, 'designates people of the upper class, such as the wealthy merchants and court officials.'[32] He used this network to get his published material into general circulation. Although he seems to have been able to sustain his large family, he was clearly in circumstances that were diminished from his father's time. As the letter above suggests, he was also aware that his chances of returning to the civil bureaucracy were nil. In the end he opted to be a gentleman-publisher, and in his later years to become a critic of drama and other forms of performing literature.

Moreover, his critical moves can be seen as devices to increase the popularity of his editions of texts. As reading texts (*Selection of Yuan Plays*), he tightened the plots, brought a more elegant style to the arias and reduced the repetitive prose sections of the palace editions. In his changes to *chuanqi* drama, he reduced the number of acts, changed arias, stripped out sections that he deemed peripheral, and all to make these long pieces performable. The economic motive of these changes is clear: he wanted to make popular editions that would be a pleasure to read or to listen to in performance. At this confluence of economic want, recurring illness and his new interest in editing and publishing dramatic texts, he was able to secure his status as critic and publisher in the years 1615–18. In his own eyes he saw himself as a 'loyal minister' to authorial power.[33] His *Selection of Yuan Plays* is, indeed, a remarkable rewriting of text to fit a literati taste, and it has withstood the test of time, canonized as the finest collection of Yuan drama. His editions of Tang Xianzu's works, however, have been largely forgotten.

Notes

1　His edition is known as *Four New Plays from the White Camellia Hall, Collated and Set by the Hall of Carving Insects* (*Diaochongguan jiaoding Yumingtang xinci sizhong* 雕蟲館校定玉茗堂新詞四種). See Zhao Hongjuan, 'Preface', in Zang Maoxun, *Zang Maoxun ji*, Zhao Hongjuan (ed.) (Hangzhou: Zhejiang guji chubanshe, 2012), p. v; and Zhu Hengfu, 'Lun Diaochongguan ben Zang Maoxun pinggai *Mudanting*', *Xiju yishu*, 16 (2006), pp. 40–8.

2　The grandson was married and entered his wife's family, taking that family's surname, a practice that ensured the continuation of a surname lineage. He married into the family of Min Zongde 閔宗德 (1576–1629), who was the prefect of Ru'ning, in modern Runan, Henan. Like Zang Maoxun, Min was a native of Wucheng. See Xu Shuofang, 'Zang Maoxun nianpu', in *Zang Maoxun ji*, p. 297.

3   Metonymy for Nanjing; stemming from the use of the name of the Six Dynasties' city wall, which came to be called the 'old stone wall'. The Chinese term *cheng* 城 can be used to refer both to a wall and to a city.

4   See 'Answering a Letter from Li Benning', in Zang, *Zang Maoxun ji*, p. 149. See also 'Answering a Letter from Magistrate Pu', ibid., p. 144: 'Because I am suffering from heatstroke, I have long been abed, and it has been more than half a month since I have been able to eat.'

5   See 'Answering a Letter from Lu Bosheng', ibid., p. 143.

6   The term *shangshu* 傷暑, which is the modern term for heatstroke, was used to refer to a variety of summertime illnesses. The fact that the illness lingered so long and that it was recurrent and debilitating suggests that he may have contracted some disease like malaria along the Yangzi River basin on his return.

7   Chen Yaowen 陳耀文, *zi* Huibo 晦伯 (or 誨伯), c. 1520–70.

8   A book of categorized documents (*leishu* 類書), this text, according to the editors of the *Essential Summaries of the Complete Collection of the Four Treasures* (*Siku tiyao* 四庫提要), is a rather disorganized set of citations. While critical on this point, the editors obviously did not show due diligence when researching the sources of this text. As opposed to Zang's onsight investigation, they were of the opinion that 'For the most part Ming dynasty *leishu* do not provide sources for their citations. This work has copious citations, and in every case lists from whence they come.' See *Siku tiyao* 136.10b–11a.

9   A compendium of neologisms and new phrases in texts, uncategorized. The title stems from the phrase, 'Daylilies make one forget cares, *gaosu* trees release one from weariness 蘐草忘憂, 皋蘇釋勞'. See *Siku tiyao* 131.20a–b.

10   From a letter to Xie Zhaozhi (c. 1560–1620). See 'Ji Xie Zaihang shu', *Zang Maoxun ji*, p. 151.

11   'Yumingtang chuanqi xu', *Zang Maoxun ji*, p. 121.

12   That is, unverified accounts of events and people that could range from gossip to fiction to actual events. I take this to refer

to stories related to the Tang emperor Xuanzong, Yang Guifei and other court ladies.

13 Wu Mengyang, *Shetang shichao* (undated Ming dynasty ed.), 1.16b–17a, in *Siku quanshu cunmu congshu*, vol. 194 (Jinan: Qi Lu shushe, 1997), pp. 448–9.

14 Located northwest of Changxing on the western shore of Lake Tai.

15 The name of a famous lane in the Six Dynasties' city of Jiankang (modern Nanjing); here metonymy for Nanjing itself.

16 Zhounan is an archaic name for Luoyang. The incident involves the Grand Scribe Sima Tan (165–110 BC), who had been left behind when Han Wudi departed from Mt Tai to perform the Feng sacrifices there. At this crucial moment, just as Sima Tan was about to die, he entrusted the position of Grand Scribe to his son, Sima Qian, and exhorted him to carry on his legacy. His plaint was, 'Now the emperor … has gone to make investiture at Mt. Tai. That I am not able to follow in his retinue is fate, indeed. Fate, indeed!' See Sima Qian, 'Autobiographic Preface of the Grand Scribe', *Shiji,* vol. 10 (Beijing: Zhonghua shuju, 1959), 70.3295.

17 Bo Le was one of a number of noted physiognomers in China's ancient past. To be a Bo Le was to be someone who could find, nurture and promote fine talent. Also a compliment to Huang Ruheng, from the famous lines of the early Song poet, Shi Jie (1005–45), 'If there is no Bo Le in the world, no one knows horses, / Eyes judge the fine steed Qiji as no more than a jaded hack.'

18 'Ji Huang Zhenfu shu', *Zang Maoxun ji*, pp. 143–4.

19 'Yuanqu xuan houji xu', *Zang Maoxun ji*, pp. 115–16.

20 See West, 'Text and Ideology: Ming Editors and Northern Drama'.

21 'Yumingtang chuanqi xu', *Zang Maoxun ji*, p. 121.

22 Ibid.

23 'Yuanqu xuan houji xu', *Zang Maoxun ji*, pp. 115–16.

24 For an excellent discussion of the changes Zang wrought on the plays of Tang Xianzu, see Zhu Hengfu, 'Lun Diaochongguan'.

25 See Xu Shuofang, 'Zang Maoxun he tade *Yuanqu xuan*', in *Xu Shuofang ji* (Hangzhou: Zhejiang guji chubanshe, 1993), vol. 1, p. 33.

26 Yao did not accrue the title of Assistant Commissioner of the Transmission Office until 1618, which suggests that the title of the poem has been changed by the editors to match the most recent title held by Yao.

27 A famine and pestilence swept Shanxi, Shaanxi, Henan, the Nanjing area, and Zhejiang in 1616–17. 'Shizong benji', in Zhang Tingyu et al., *Mingshi*, vol. 1 (Beijing: Zhonghua shuju, 1974) 20.272, and Zang Maoxun, 'Ji Wang Xiaolian wen', *Zang Maoxun ji*, p. 164.

28 That is, writing funerary epitaphs, birthday congratulations, etc. Judging from the number left in his collection, he did not seem to be too successful. See Xu Shuofang, 'Zang Maoxun', p. 36.

29 From *Analects* 9.15, 'When I returned to Lu from Wei, then music was rectified, and the Elegancia and Court Odes each found their proper place.' That is, each was in its proper category and was used in the appropriate place.

30 To 'kill the green' is to prepare bamboo slips to write on; here of course anachronistic.

31 'Ji Yao Tongcan shu', *Zang Maoxun ji*, p. 147.

32 Yung Sai-shing, 'A Critical Study of *Han-Tan Chi*' (PhD dissertation, Princeton University, 1992), p. 200.

33 See closing lines to his first Preface to *A Selection of Yuan Plays* (Figure 4) and his commentary to the changes he wrought to the tune *Yujia deng* (漁家燈) in Scene 28 of *Peony Pavilion*, 'If Tang Xianzu had known about these [changes], he would absolutely have considered me his loyal minister.' Cited in Zhu Hengfu, 'Lun Diaochongguan', p. 47.

5.2 Status anxiety: Arguing about plays and print in early modern London

Jason Scott-Warren

The year 1616 stands for two key events in English theatre history: the death of William Shakespeare and the publication of Ben Jonson's *Workes*. The Jonson folio has long been recognized as a landmark publication that proclaimed for drama a high literary status, insisting that plays deserved a place on the library shelf alongside the classics, the *Opera omnia*, of Graeco-Roman authors. It has also been seen as a vital precursor to that later act of immortalization, the 1623 'First Folio' of Shakespeare's *Comedies, Histories and Tragedies*, in which Jonson was prominently involved, not least in writing the poem 'To the Reader' that faced the title page.[1]

But if Jonson's publishing strategies helped to legitimate the posthumous canonization of Shakespeare, they also – so we have always thought – served to emphasize the unbridgeable gap between the two authors. Jonson's Folio was designed to stake a claim for his plays, but it was underwritten by anti-theatricalism, a fundamental intolerance of the messy compromises that playwrights were forced to make in their day-to-day work.[2] The plays, poems and masques were scrupulously presented with great authorial care, in typography that emphasized their links with classical models; plays written in collaboration with other writers were either rewritten or left out; omitted too was Jonson's riotous evocation of Smithfield, in his most exuberantly theatrical work, *Bartholomew Fair*. Shakespeare, in stark contrast, was a man of the theatre who took no part in the printing of his plays. When plague closed the London playhouses in 1593 and 1594, he wrote and published two narrative poems, *Venus and Adonis* and

Lucrece, which were printed with care and prefaced with dedicatory letters signed by the author. But the plays seem to have escaped into print without their author's involvement, in copies that were often (as the editors of the First Folio put it) 'stolne and surreptitious'.[3] The small-format (quarto) editions of Shakespeare's plays did not always reveal the author's name because the handwritten texts belonged not to the author but to the playing company that commissioned them; it was the theatre, not the writer, that intermittently released texts for publication. Shakespeare did not have the proprietary interest in his plays that we assume authors should have.

The implications of this polarization of Shakespeare and Jonson are massive. On the one hand, Shakespeare's involvement in the living business of theatre and his indifference to the ossified record of print can be understood as one source of his greatness, an adjunct to the 'Negative Capability' that Keats ascribed to him. Just as Shakespeare was able to write in the midst of 'uncertainties, Mysteries, doubts, without any irritable reaching after fact & reason', so he was capable of giving himself up fully to the collaborative business of theatre, while Jonson remained aloof.[4] On the other hand, the Jonson/Shakespeare dyad licenses the familiar view that Shakespeare wanted to be performed and forgotten about, that 'he never meant to be studied'. As if you could never study something that didn't positively intend you to study it – which would rule out most academic work, especially in the sciences.

Recently, however, this vision of Shakespeare and of the broader relationship between theatre and print in early modern England has been challenged from several directions. This has happened mainly via a debate over the earliest, small-format editions of Shakespeare's plays, the quartos. Over the course of the twentieth century, scholars turned to the quartos mostly for the purpose of establishing an authoritative text. By comparing different quarto texts, where they existed, with texts in the Folio, and by analysing the habits of particular publishers, printers and typesetters, bibliographers hoped that they could purge the printed record of errors and retrieve the words that Shakespeare actually wrote. Over the last twenty years, however, attention has shifted significantly, and the quarto texts have begun to be studied instead for what they can tell us about the social, political and cultural situation of early printed drama.[5] Surviving copies have been intensively scrutinized in terms of their size, their paper, their typography and mise-en-page and the ways in which they were annotated by readers, while renewed attention has been paid to the careers of the printers who brought these texts into being. At stake in the discussion is our sense of the location of the literary in early modern England, which is significantly also a discussion about the place of literary studies in the interdisciplinary maelstrom.

This is clear from the intervention that kick-started the current debate, an article by the bibliographer Peter Blayney on 'The Publication of Playbooks'. Blayney argued that, contrary to the assumptions of many literary scholars, playbooks formed only a very minor part of the output of the London presses, and they were often not a profitable line for those who published them. In order to establish this, Blayney did a lot of counting, thanks to which he demonstrated that in the average year in the period extending from 1582 to the closing of the theatres in 1642, only about six new plays appeared, out of perhaps 460 titles. Furthermore, the most popular playbooks received only eight or nine reprints in twenty-five years, whereas the most popular devotional books received between ten and thirty-six reprints.[6] Fewer than 50 per cent of plays, on average, even ran to a second edition, and (as Blayney established through a detailed reconstruction of the economics of print) it was only in the second and later editions that playbook publishing really became profitable.[7] Puncturing the fantasies of literary scholars still further, Blayney pointed out that Shakespeare's most reprinted plays (*Henry IV, Part I, Richard II and Richard III*) were outperformed by the anonymous *Mucedorus*, Marlowe's *Doctor Faustus* and Kyd's *Spanish Tragedy*. If closet and academic plays were admitted to the list, Shakespeare would not even make it into the top five. What is more, 'Shakespeare's best-selling work, *Venus and Adonis*, outsold his best-selling play by four editions'.[8]

Blayney's work, based on a lifetime of familiarity with the printed trade in plays, was influential and has been built upon by Peter Stallybrass and Roger Chartier, among others.[9] Stallybrass and Chartier draw attention in particular to the flimsy physical form of the playbook and to what we might infer from it. In quarto format plays typically occupy only about ten sheets of paper, with each sheet folded in four and cut to make the book. Like most early modern books, they would have been sold unbound, though their sheets might have been crudely sewn together to facilitate reading. Their physical insubstantiality means that 'playbooks' may not even count as books. Instead, Stallybrass and Chartier suggest, we should think of them as pamphlets, ephemeral publications that would have been read avidly and then discarded.[10] The testimony of William Cornwallis, who wrote that he kept 'Pamphlets and lying Stories, and News, and two penny Poets' in his privy, 'which when I have read, I use in that kind, that waste paper is most subject to', gives some idea of how cheap print might be regarded.[11] According to Stallybrass and Chartier (who diverge here from Blayney), some playbooks may have been popular – although they note that Shakespeare's name was made by his poetry, not his plays. But plays were always catchpenny publications that had few aspirations to high cultural status, let alone literary immortality. Print and performance here start to look rather similar: dubious, rough-edged, pulling in the crowds for a temporary spectacle.

The narratives advanced thus far might be said to suit a historicist temperament. They put drama in its place, reminding us that it was a small part of the early modern social world. And such a move may be salutary; just as new historicist critics have claimed that the marginality of drama – its place in the liberties and at the edges of the early modern city – gave it its power to critique society, so we might value the playbook precisely for its precarious position in the marketplace.[12] But a more recent wave of commentators is having none of that.

The reaction began with Alan B. Farmer and Zachary Lesser's article entitled 'The Popularity of Playbooks Revisited'.[13] Here they returned to Blayney's statistics and recalculated them using what seemed to them more reasonable assumptions – excluding all examples of non-speculative printing (for which sales may not indicate popularity) and all patented or monopolistic books (which may have been sold to captive audiences), and eventually books not published in English ('as were all professional playbooks') from the annual publication figures. At the end of their number-crunching, drama bulks much larger in the literary marketplace: 'in peak years, about one in every eleven editions in this market was a professional play'.[14] Farmer and Lesser divide the period into boom years, such as those from 1598 to 1613 and from 1629 to 40, and periods when the market was in decline. And they give Shakespeare a significant place in creating the first of these booms: between 1594 and 1600, 'not only was Shakespeare England's first best-selling playwright ... but the success of the printed editions of his plays also helped to establish the playbook market itself'.[15]

This pro-drama, pro-Shakespearean approach was picked up by Lukas Erne. Erne contends that, in focusing on the eighteenth-century canonization of Shakespeare as national playwright, we have lost sight of his popularity in his own day. This he demonstrates partly through a proliferation of graphs and tables, which extend and to some extent challenge the statistical work initiated by Blayney. But Erne also undertakes a good deal of cultural bibliography, looking at Shakespeare's presence in the marketplace in terms of the number of plays that were mistakenly attributed to him, considering who published Shakespeare and why, and exploring the question of who read Shakespeare.[16] Erne's conclusions are startling. At the very least, he thinks that Shakespeare would have known and approved of his presence in the literary marketplace. But his strong insinuation is that Shakespeare must have had some involvement in that growing presence, whether that meant taking his manuscripts to the publishers or – later in his career – withholding them from publication in anticipation of a collected edition that for some reason failed to materialize in his lifetime.[17] Yet for all of the circumstantial detail that Erne amasses, the smoking gun – a single piece of hard evidence proving that Shakespeare was personally involved in the printing of just one of his plays – is nowhere to be found.

Like Farmer and Lesser, Erne moves the statistical goalposts in his work, including the indisputably successful *Venus and Adonis* and *Lucrece* in several of his calculations, and so rolling Shakespeare up into a poet/playwright with a formidable presence in the bookshops. Thus, Erne is able to demonstrate that Shakespeare outsold Robert Greene, whose name is today a byword for early modern 'popular' authorship; but this is only because Greene lacks a pair of bestsellers like *Venus* and *Lucrece*.[18] In fact, if you look across the run of Shakespeare's publications, their success rate looks quite as erratic as does those of Greene. Some works (like *Richard II*, *Richard III* and *Henry IV*) do quite well; others fail spectacularly. Why was Part I of *Henry IV* (first published in 1598) a steady seller (six editions within twenty-five years) while Part II (first published in 1600) enjoyed no reprints until the Folio of 1623?[19] Why was a major play like *Much Ado* not reprinted once between 1600 and 1623?[20] Why did *Shakespeare's Sonnets*, which put its author's name up in large capitals on the title page when it was first published in 1609, sell so badly, attracting no reprints until the poems were comprehensively revamped by John Benson in 1640?[21] It may well be that we have lost editions of these works, just as we have (probably) lost the first edition of *Love's Labour's Lost* and (possibly) lost the whole of a play now known only by its title, *Love's Labour's Won*.[22] But even taking such losses into account, we are still left with an impression of the unevenness of the early modern print marketplace, of how much remains utterly imponderable about it.

Imponderability also governs the question of who published Shakespeare and why they did so. Publishers, it seems, were prone to be skittish. Richard Field, like Shakespeare a native of Stratford, and someone who might be glancingly remembered in *Cymbeline*'s reference to 'Richard du Champ', printed *Venus and Adonis* in 1593. But Field rapidly transferred the rights and, aside from printing *Lucrece* for John Harrison in 1594, had almost nothing to do with Shakespeare thereafter.[23] James Roberts, who printed playbills and therefore had a direct link to the London theatre companies, entered several of Shakespeare's plays in the Stationers' Register but then sold his rights to others, apparently because as a specialist in religious works he 'simply did not want to publish plays'.[24] Erne suggests that he left such work to his associate Andrew Wise, a minor publisher who may have benefited from the success of *Richard II*, *Richard III* and *Henry IV, Part I*, while also suffering from the failure of *Henry IV, Part II* and *Much Ado*.[25] Cuthbert Burby published Shakespeare, Greene, Nashe and other 'literary' authors in the 1590s but published only religious works after 1601.[26] John Busby published poetry and prose in the 1590s but changed his focus to news pamphlets and drama after 1598; among his publications were *The Merry Wives of Windsor*, *King Lear* and *Henry V*.[27] Nicholas Ling specialized in literary titles and in literary anthologies such as *England's Helicon* and *England's Parnassus*; he published the first and second quartos of *Hamlet* in 1603 and 1604, and *The Taming of the Shrew* in 1607, but (as Marta Straznicky comments) 'his play publications are surprisingly few'.[28] Meanwhile a great many stationers published just one or two of Shakespeare's playbooks. Most of the promoters of drama in print seem to have been eking out a living through heterogeneous publications, and not pinning much hope of profit on their theatrical output.[29]

Although the fact of Shakespeare's authorship undoubtedly became more visible across the period, here too we are presented with puzzles. Judging by the evidence of title pages, some publishers did not know they were publishing Shakespeare when they were, and others believed they were publishing Shakespeare when they were not (so we get *Thomas Lord Cromwell*, *Locrine* and *The Puritan* by 'W. S.', *A Yorkshire*

Tragedy by 'W. Shakespeare' and *The London Prodigal* by 'William Shakespeare'). If Shakespeare had cared about his standing in print, we might expect him to have kicked up a fuss about these publications, as he reportedly did about one poetic miscellany – *The Passionate Pilgrim* – that took his name in vain, so that it had to be reissued with a cancel title page that omitted his name.[30] But there is no evidence that he did protest against these misattributions. Erne believes that Shakespeare engaged in a form of non-possessive authorship that stood in contradistinction to Jonson's possessive brand, and sees this as testimony to Shakespeare's faith in his readership.[31] But Shakespeare's brand of dramatic publishing was *so* non-possessive as to leave virtually no trace. We are back at square one, with a Shakespeare who let his printed plays take care of themselves.

And what of readers? We know perilously little about who bought and read drama in print, and what we do know is predictably skewed towards social elites. But evidence that the nobility and the gentry read printed drama might be taken as sufficient proof in itself that, far from being rough-and-ready pamphlets, printed plays had some status, and that they counted as 'literature' for their early readers rather as they might do for us today.[32] The reality is probably rather more complicated than this. Take Edward Dering, whose accounts show him buying copies of Jonson's and Shakespeare's collected works in the 1620s, and who also itemizes the cost of seeing plays, buying plays in quarto and binding the playbooks up.[33] Dering even went so far as to create his own compressed version of the two parts of *Henry IV*, which survives in a manuscript at the Folger Shakespeare Library.[34] All of this activity might seem quite 'literary', and it certainly appears that playgoing and playreading counted as fashionable activities in Dering's social circle. But it is likely that Dering's main aim was not closeted reading but household performance; he frequently bought multiple playbooks, sometimes specifying that these were multiples of a single title ('3 playbookes of ye Woman-Hater', '6 playbookes of Band Ruff and Cuff') and he invested in wigs and false beards for the actors.[35] The distinction between the play as performed and the 'literary' play as transmitted in print thus breaks down as soon as it is made. Another elite reader, Frances Wolfreston, presents a slightly different case. This Staffordshire gentlewoman bought plays by authors including Chapman, Ford, Heywood, Shakespeare and Shirley, along with works of poetry and prose, devotion and medicine.[36] But although one analysis estimates that just under half of Wolfreston's library was made up of 'English Literature', in practice a good part of this 'literature' is made up of pamphlets that might have come fresh from the pedlar's pack. These include such works as *Good Counsell to be Hadd at a Cheap Rate* (1663), the sixteen pages of which urge their readers to forbear cursing and swearing and to make patience their constant companion. Wolfreston also bought several works by John Taylor, the Water-Poet, and jest-books such as *Mirth in Abundance* (1659), *The Pleasant Conceits of Old Hobson, the Merry Londoner* (1640?) and Robert Armin's *Foole upon Foole* (1605). Far from allowing us to speak of the elevation of playbooks to 'classic' status, therefore, Wolfreston's collection suggests that they may have continued to be perceived as part of a capacious popular culture.

The more we learn about early modern reading, the more we are forced to realize that modern divisions between the literary and the non- or sub-literary did not apply in any straightforward way in this period. Even William Cornwallis, who read pamphlets in his privy, reported that he valued the insight they gave into 'the difference of wits, and dispositions, the alterations of Arguments pleasing the world, and the change of stiles'.[37] The status of early modern playbooks looks set to remain unsettled for many years to come.

Notes

1   David L. Gants and Tom Lockwood, 'The Printing and
     Publishing of Ben Jonson's Works', in David Bevington,
     M. Butler and I. Donaldson (eds), *The Cambridge Edition of*

the Works of Ben Jonson (Cambridge: Cambridge University Press, 2012), vol. I, pp. clxiv–clxxxvi; Douglas Brooks, From Playhouse to Printing House: Drama and Authorship in Early Modern England (Cambridge: Cambridge University Press, 2000), pp. 104–7.

2   Jonas Barish, The Antitheatrical Prejudice (Berkeley: University of California Press, 1981), pp. 132–54; Timothy Murray, Theatrical Legitimation: Allegories of Genius in Seventeenth-Century England and France (New York: Oxford University Press, 1987), pp. 39–63. For a revisionist view see Laura Levine, Men in Women's Clothing: Anti-Theatricality and Effeminization, 1579–1642 (Cambridge: Cambridge University Press, 1994), pp. 2–3, 73–107.

3   For the influential division of the quartos into 'good' and 'bad', see A. W. Pollard, Shakespeare Folios and Quartos: A Study in the Bibliography of Shakespeare's Plays, 1593–1685 (London: Methuen, 1909), pp. 64–80. See further David Scott Kastan, Shakespeare and the Book (Cambridge: Cambridge University Press, 2001), pp. 14–49.

4   John Keats, Selected Letters, ed. Robert Gittings, rev. John Mee (Oxford: Oxford University Press, 2002), pp. 41–2. For the wider ramifications of the contrastive treatment of the two playwrights, see Ian Donaldson, 'Jonson and the Tother Youth', in idem, Jonson's Magic Houses: Essays in Interpretation (Oxford: Oxford University Press, 1997), pp. 6–25.

5   See, for example, Scott Kastan, Shakespeare, pp. 14–49; Brooks, From Playhouse to Printing House, pp. 14–65; Marta Straznicky (ed.), The Book of the Play: Playwrights, Stationers, and Readers in Early Modern England (Amherst: University of Massachusetts Press, 2006).

6   Peter W. M. Blayney, 'The Publication of Playbooks', in John D. Cox and David Scott Kastan (eds), A New History of Early English Drama (New York: Columbia University Press, 1997), pp. 385, 388.

7   Ibid., pp. 387, 412–13.

8   Ibid., p. 388.

9   Peter Stallybrass and Roger Chartier, 'Reading and Authorship:

The Circulation of Shakespeare 1590–1619', in Andrew Murphy (ed.), *A Concise Companion to Shakespeare and the Text* (Oxford: Blackwell, 2007), pp. 35–56.

10 Stallybrass and Chartier, 'Reading and Authorship', pp. 40–2.

11 William Cornwallis, *Essayes* (London: Edmund Mattes, 1600), p. I7r.

12 Steven Mullaney, *The Place of the Stage: License, Play and Power in Renaissance England* (Chicago: University of Chicago Press, 1988).

13 Zachary Lesser and Alan B. Farmer, 'The Popularity of Playbooks Revisited', *Shakespeare Quarterly*, 56 (2005), pp. 1–32.

14 Lesser and Farmer, pp. 13–18 (17, 18).

15 Ibid., p. 11.

16 Lukas Erne, *Shakespeare and the Book Trade* (Cambridge: Cambridge University Press, 2013), chs 2, 4 and 5.

17 'Insinuation' because Erne stops short of stating this (see, for example, p. 19, where he proposes that Shakespeare was 'complicit with – albeit not directly involved in – his dissemination by the book trade'). Stationers who printed Shakespeare none the less become 'Shakespeare's publishers' in Chapter 4, and we are assured that 'he was neither oblivious nor indifferent to the books they published' (p. 185).

18 Erne, *Book Trade*, pp. 30–5.

19 Erne, *Book Trade*, p. 12: 'Despite the failure of *2 Henry IV* to reach a second edition, Shakespeare's history plays were easily the most popular of the three genres into which the First Folio divided Shakespeare's plays.' Douglas Bruster has argued that the success and failure of Shakespeare in print relates to the proportion of prose and verse in each play; 'Shakespeare the Stationer', in Marta Straznicky (ed.), *Shakespeare's Stationers: Studies in Cultural Bibliography* (Philadelphia: University of Pennsylvania Press, 2013), pp. 112–31. We are invited to believe that *Henry IV, Part II* was a flop because it was 52 per cent prose, despite the fact that *Henry IV, Part I* was a roaring success with 45 per cent prose (pp. 121, 124–7).

20 Erne, *Book Trade*, pp. 12, 82 (where Erne observes that 'the

reasons for a playbook's popularity or lack of popularity are often difficult to recover'). Bruster, 'Shakespeare the Stationer' (p. 125), argues that *Much Ado* was unpopular with readers because it was 72 per cent prose.

21   Erne, *Book Trade* (p. 97), observes that 'the only quarto which gives Shakespeare's name even greater prominence [than the 1608 quarto of *King Lear*] is the 1609 *Sonnets*, which not only has Shakespeare's name in large letters on the title page as part of the title ... but also prints his name in the header of the left-hand page ... of every opening'. This is later taken to suggest that Thorpe 'invested in Shakespeare because he believed in the drawing power of his name'. On the evidence of the publication history of the *Sonnets* this appears to have been a misplaced belief.

22   Pervez Rizvi, 'The Bibliographic Relationship between the Texts of *Troilus and Cressida*', *The Library*, 14 (2013), pp. 271–312, proposes that textual problems in that play can be resolved if we infer the existence of a 'Q0' (published in 1603) of which no copies now survive. For *Love's Labour's Won*, see Erne, *Book Trade*, p. 17, which affirms the likelihood that this was an alternative title for a comedy that still survives today.

23   See Adam G. Hooks, 'Shakespeare at the White Greyhound', *Shakespeare Survey*, 64 (2011), pp. 260–75. Field later printed Robert Chester, *Loves Martyr: Or Rosalins Complaint* (London: Edward Blount, 1601), which contained Shakespeare's poem 'The Phoenix and the Turtle'.

24   Erne, *Book Trade*, p. 161.

25   Erne, *Book Trade*, pp. 161–4; Straznicky (ed.), *Shakespeare's Stationers*, pp. 302–5.

26   Erne, *Book Trade*, pp. 165–6 calls this 'a sudden and astonishing conversion' (166).

27   Ibid., pp. 170–1.

28   Straznicky, *Shakespeare's Stationers*, p. 266.

29   Erne, *Book Trade*, pp. 179–82. See also the analysis of Holger Schott Syme, 'Thomas Creede, William Barley, and the Venture of Printing Plays', in Straznicky, *Shakespeare's Stationers*, pp. 28–46.

30 Erne, *Book Trade* (p. 89), concludes his survey of authorial misattribution to Shakespeare by stating that a lack of evidence does not mean that Shakespeare was indifferent to the abuse of his name. None the less, it remains problematic that this kind of evidence for Shakespeare's popularity can also be taken as further evidence of his insouciance about print.

31 Ibid., 128–9.

32 Ibid., ch. 5. The insistent and in my view simplistic alignment of the text-as-read with 'the literary' is a feature of Erne's earlier study, *Shakespeare as Literary Dramatist* (Cambridge: Cambridge University Press, 2003).

33 Laetitia Yeandle (ed.), 'Sir Edward Dering, 1st bart., of Surrenden Dering and his "Booke of Expences" 1617–1628' (published online at www.kentarchaeology.ac/authors/020.pdf, accessed 4 July 2015). See further Laetitia Yeandle, 'Sir Edward Dering of Surrenden Dering and his "Booke of Expences", 1617–1628', *Archaeologia Cantiana*, 125 (2005), pp. 323–44.

34 A facsimile edition of this manuscript was prepared by G. W. Williams and G. Blakemore Evans: *The History of King Henry IV; As Revised by Sir Edward Dering, Bart* (Charlottesville: University Press of Virginia, 1974).

35 See Yeandle, 'Booke of Expences', entries for 16 March 1623/4; 4 December 1623, 10 December 1623, 18 February 1622/3.

36 Paul Morgan, 'Frances Wolfreston and "HorBouks"': A Seventeenth-Century Woman Book-Collector', *The Library*, 6th series, 11 (1989), pp. 197–219; Arnold Hunt, 'Libraries in the Archives: Researching Provenance in the British Library', in Giles Mandelbrote and Barry Taylor (eds), *Libraries within the Library: Aspects of the British Library's Early Printed Collections* (London: British Library, 2009), pp. 363–84.

37 William Cornwallis, *Essayes*, p. I7r.

6

Dramatic authorship and collaboration

How had dramatic authorship come to be understood by 1616 and to what extent were authorial intention and presence relevant in the two cultures? What concepts and practices of collaboration were available to the composition of drama?

6.1 Is there a playwright in this text? The 1610s and the consolidation of dramatic authorship in late Ming print culture

Patricia Sieber

The typical Ming literatus wrote dramas either before the onset of his career as a scholar-official or when he was nearing retirement or after voluntary or involuntary withdrawal either from the realm of examination preparations or the world of officialdom.[1] For instance, in 1516, at the age of nineteen whilst preparing for the imperial examination, Lu Cai 陸采 (1497–1537) authored, with some assistance from his older brother, *The Story of the Bright Pearl* (*Mingzhu ji* 明珠記), a romance that not only became a staple in writings about Ming drama, but remained a fixture in the theatrical repertoire. Similarly, as a newly-wed before he reached the age of twenty, Zhang Fengyi dashed off a successful drama, *The Story of Hongfu* (*Hongfu ji* 紅拂記) in 1545.[2] Several decades passed before Zhang discontinued his repeated attempts to pass the imperial examination and resumed his playwriting activities at least in part in exchange for remuneration. Having completed the highest level of examinations, Tang Xianzu ran foul of the powers that be, and, repeatedly beset by political difficulties, he composed his most famous and enduring play, *The Peony Pavilion* (c. 1598); all this when he was on the verge of retiring from official life.

In its precarious positioning in a writer's life cycle, drama occupies a potentially multivalent place within the literary output of mid- and late Ming literati. It is the purpose of this brief essay to explore some of the salient attributes of such authorship in order to determine not only how the choice of that particular literary genre created meaning within the literary field of the Ming as a whole, but to what extent such extra-official endeavours contributed to the creation of an alternative literary world nested within the interstices of the state-sanctioned orthodox culture. As we shall see, the debate over drama as a literati form coalesced around a number of flashpoints. Was drama a vehicle for publicly minded self-expression, for public vengeance or for literary games? Did plays aspire to be literary drama, operatic theatre or both? Was the realm of the theatre designed for collective communion or an arena for the individual transcendence of social convention?

A closer look at the chronology of drama-related literati imprints will reveal, however, that the 1610s conspired to give literati authorship in the realm of drama unprecedented visibility. In rapid succession, a number of landmark publications appeared that demarcated dramatic authorship as a newly viable form of literati composition. In 1613, Lü Tiancheng's *Evaluative Classification of Drama* (*Qupin* 曲品) organized itself around the individual authors and their dramatic oeuvre. In 1614, Wang Jide pioneered the concept of the literati edition of drama geared towards appreciative connoisseurs of a vernacular and highly eroticized philology. The Yuan text *The Register of Ghosts* (*Lugui bu* 錄鬼簿), which had most likely inspired Lü's *Evaluative Classification of Drama*, was excerpted in Zang Maoxun's 1615/16 edition of what would become the definitive anthology of heavily redacted but ostensibly authentic Yuan-dynasty drama, *A Selection of Yuan Plays*. Around 1618, *The Plum in the Golden Vase* (*Jin Ping Mei* 金瓶梅), the seminal novel of manners in China, made extensive references to songs and drama in its encyclopedic gesturing towards the whole of late Ming print culture. That same year, Zang Maoxun adapted and anthologized his recently deceased friend Tang Xianzu's four *chuanqi* plays under the title *Four New Plays from the White Camellia Hall* (*Yuming xinci sizhong* 玉茗新詞四種), soon to be followed by Feng Menglong's reworking of Tang's masterpiece *The Peony*

Pavilion in 1623. While such competing renditions point to the fervour of the literary discussions over drama at the time, nevertheless the 1610s mark the moment when literati – regardless of their partisan preferences – coalesced around the notion of plays as a deliberately authored and publicly significant art form worthy of being carefully orchestrated in print. In what follows, we will examine some of the salient aspects of the author function as it came to deploy itself in the lead-up to this crucial decade.

Historical fact vs. sympathetic fiction

In the wake of Roland Barthes, we may consider the author merely a zombie creation of yesterday's literary critics, but in China the author never died. Authorial intent was a prime concern for writers of every stripe precisely because they were writing to be read. Writing was a mark of idealized masculinity, a self-fashioning that I have tried to capture with the neologism 'attestatory authorship'.[3] As such, writing was a self-consciously social pursuit – audiences both near and far in time and space were never far from the writer's mind as they thought to inscribe themselves in the collective memory. Conversely, readers were immensely interested in the 'public aspirations and moral intent' (*zhi* 志) lodged either overtly or tacitly in any piece of writing in keeping with the Mencian notion of being able 'to know the man' through what was transmitted of their verbal expression.[4]

By the early sixteenth century, literary communities in Shaanxi and Shandong, two regions with deep historical roots in northern song and drama, precipitated the emergence of drama as a literati form.[5] The circles surrounding Kang Hai (1475–1541) and Wang Jiusi 王九思 (1468–1551) in Shaanxi as well as Li Kaixian 李開先 (1502–68) in Shandong were instrumental in fashioning arias – both in song and dramatic form – into instruments of self-expression. After their dismissal from the Ming court, these men created plays out of their interest in literary experimentation, access to local musical traditions and imaginative self-fashioning in the tradition of the most exalted of recluses.[6] In their prefaces to song-based forms, they explicitly acknowledged that they harbored 'intent',[7] an implicit gesture towards a public and political meaning of their literary works. A generation later, Wang Shizhen (1526–90), the towering arbiter of things literary in the second half of the sixteenth century, was perhaps the first critic to explicitly pinpoint a connection between Wang Jiusi's political fortunes and the genesis of Wang's play *Du Fu Buys Wine and Roams in the Spring* (*Du Zimei gujiu youchun ji* 杜子美沽酒遊春記, 1510s).[8]

Increasingly, plays could be deployed to attempt to set the historical record straight. Most famously perhaps, Wang Shizhen, himself a known theatre enthusiast and acknowledged author of arias, probably had a hand in the composition of the most poignant political play of the Ming dynasty, *The Crying Phoenix*.[9] Remarkable for its historical accuracy on the topic of contemporary affairs long before topical plays became commonplace in the seventeenth century,[10] the play treated one of the *causes célèbres* of the sixteenth century, that is, the confrontation between upright and outspoken officials and a ruthless grand secretary, Yan Song (1480–1567). Having seen his own father die as a result of Yan's machinations and having written ballads on Yan's stranglehold on imperial favour and bureaucratic leverage in terms similar to those found in the drama, Wang staged the play in the presence of the district magistrate at the precise moment of Yan's fall from power. Alive to the political implications of the play, the district magistrate paled and rapidly excused himself.[11] However, over the course of the next century, the parties executed and injured by Yan were eventually vindicated and Yan Song himself relegated to the category of 'traitorous minister' in the official *History of the Ming*.

This interventionist practice of attestatory playwriting eventually became so widespread that when Li Yu 李漁 (1611–80), the irrepressible *causeur*, impresario, playwright and publisher, looked back upon the rise of the *chuanqi* drama tradition in his *Casual Jottings of Idle Feelings* (*Xianqing ouji* 閒情偶寄, 1671), he took his fellow literati to task for viewing and employing plays as vehicles for venting personal and public grievances. By way of an example, he sought to rescue *The Lute* (*Pipa ji* 琵琶記) from the 'baseless innuendo' that it had been written to settle private scores between the author and an acquaintance. Insisting on the coincidental nature of all similarities of actual events in his own plays, Li Yu hoped not to abet the trend of 'writing plays to vent one's spleen' (*tianci xiefen* 填詞洩憤),[12] but instead to lay a foundation for drama as a challenging aesthetic form in its own right.[13] In discussing language, rhyme and performance at length, Li Yu sought to synthesize some of the partisan debates that had roiled in late Ming literati circles over what constituted the principal aesthetic peculiarities of drama and the corollary demands on dramatic authorship.

Literature vs. music

From its inception, Chinese literary drama was a form of musical drama that sought to ingeniously pair unique lyrics with commonplace tunes. However, while public and private schools were in place to teach male children the rudiments of polite prose, no corresponding institutional framework fostered literati acquisition of musical competence. Instead, musical performance was primarily cultivated at court as part of imperial music programmes closely tied to dynastic legitimacy on the one hand and through hereditary musical families in the service of governmental organizations at all levels on the other. While literati traditions favoured certain musical instruments such as the qin 琴 (zither), these tended not to be ones used in theatrical performance. Thus, the acquisition of musical proficiency – in particular the ability to write pleasing lyrics that were singable – was a rare skill among literati. Apart from innate talent or family tradition, musical competence on the part of literati bespoke social contact beyond the charmed circles of literati peers, and as such had traditionally been viewed as a mark of social and moral abasement despite the fact that music enjoyed a central place in regulating emotion in the Confucian scheme of things. However, in the late Ming, musical proficiency could be newly read as a sign of aesthetic distinction and unconventional learning.

In his foundational *A Record of Southern Drama* (*Nanci xulu* 南詞敘錄), Xu Wei constructs the transformation of southern theatre from an anonymous popular entertainment to an identifiable individual art form as a dual process of literary and musical excellence.[14] In Xu's view, Gao Ming, the author of what came to be seen as the foundational southern play, *The Lute*, served as an important touchstone for the emergence of dramatic authorship. In Xu's telling, Gao Ming 'used beautiful phrasing (清麗之詞) and thus washed away the vulgarity of earlier writers ...' Hence, from a literati perspective, a play that no longer merely formed part of 'the minor entertainments of the villages and the boroughs' and instead conformed to 'ancient standards' (古法)[15] could not only constitute literature, but also established an author's reputation. At the same time, Xu Wei also reported on a legend surrounding the genesis of the play that revolved around the author's solitary musical experiments: 'Gao Ming worked and slept in a small residence and completed the play within three years. The floorboards where he tapped out the rhythm were worn to the point of having holes. He often sat through the night singing to himself.'[16] However, Gao Ming was the rare playwright who was credited with simultaneous literary and musical competence; most late Ming playwrights either professed to favour one over the other or were accused by others of promoting one at the expense of the other.

Music was a highly technical art and consequently part of the challenge in successfully blending musical and literary elements involved access to musical learning and practice. Many of the renowned literati playwrights – Kang Hai,

Li Kaixian and Wang Shizhen, for example – maintained in-house theatrical troupes. In light of the greater appreciation of technical skills among late Ming literati and the diversification of valid domains of elite knowledge in general, musical expertise among literati stood a greater chance of being viewed either as a form of conspicuous consumption or as a mastery of an unconventional body of knowledge rather than as a form of sexual and social dissipation. Thus, when Lü Tiancheng designated his two most outstanding playwrights, he lauded Shen Jing 沈璟 (1553–1610) for his unparalleled musical understanding. Even with regard to his other top choice, the literarily unrivalled Tang Xianzu, Lü did not fail to point out how the regular music-drama performances at Tang's estate provided sublime inspiration for his lyrics.[17] Social tensions between the high and low strata of society informed another aspect of dramatic authorship in the late Ming, namely the drama's purported effect on audiences. In so far as such effects were thought to emanate from the lyrics more than the music, the dramatic author was thought be accountable over whether or not his works fostered community values or whether he chose to flaunt such conventions in the name of ethical or aesthetic renewal.

Convention vs. transcendence

Literary production in Ming China was inherently social, but the authoring of drama was complicated by the presumption that the consumption of drama straddled different social groups. In the late Ming, in the wake of Wang Yangming's 王陽明 (1472–1529) 'innate knowledge', the moral capacity of the lower orders underwent a pronounced upward appraisal. However, despite the equalizing tendencies among thinkers, literature was still recruited in the service of moral pedagogy. As Wang Yangming was noted to have said, 'the language of the *Mulian* opera is not as flowery as that of the *Western Wing*, but it contains more filial piety and righteousness than the *Western Wing*.[18] At the same time, however, some critics viewed all theatre as a source of moral corruption and instead encouraged the dedicated and exclusive pursuit of the Confucian canon. However, precisely because a greater number of aspirants from non-elite families began to pour resources into the acquisition of classical learning, the intellectual vanguard championed unconventional writings such as drama as a sign of genuine sophistication and as a potential force for moral recalibration in the face of the pervasive monetization of human bonds. Thus, authorship was embroiled in redefining the role of literature in the social compact and, because drama was understood as a literary art that could reach the literate and the illiterate alike, the stakes were particularly high. At the same time, with the burgeoning interest in drama as a print product among commercial publishing houses and literati publishers, it also offered new economic opportunities among the 'overeducated and underemployed' strata of aspirants to elite status and could not be divorced from the commercialization of late Ming society.[19]

As Tanaka Issei, Harriet Zurndorfer, Anne McLaren and others have shown, drama had long had a lively communal life across many regions of late imperial China. For example, in late imperial Huizhou, the affluent merchants organized regular theatrical performances in lineage halls for the public. As part of religious festive occasions, these celebrations would last for several days and nights and called for edifying materials. It was in this context that Zheng Zhizhen 鄭之珍 (1518–98), a local literatus who had failed the imperial examination, reworked the sprawling corpus of tales surrounding the originally Buddhist figure of Mulian, who saves his immoral mother from hell, into a Confucian play cycle overlaid with a syncretistic discourse of 'encouraging goodness and punishing evil' in keeping with the beliefs current in the local lineage culture. Innovative in its synthesis of Confucian ethics, divine retribution and commercial morality, Zheng's *Mulian Rescues His Mother: A Drama for Goodness* (目連救母勸善戲文, 1582) was widely adopted in the region, and he himself became the focal point of observances on occasion in his village. Moreover, located in a major centre of expert printing for export to other regions, Huizhou publishers marketed Zheng's drama with attractive designs, helping to promulgate the cult of female chastity that took hold during this period.

Even among acknowledged innovators in the realm of drama, the concern with social convention was not moot. As Sophie Volpp has argued, in *Peony Pavilion*, Tang Xianzu methodically lambasted the social imposture made possible by the routine citation of canonical Confucian classics.[20] In addition to calling into question the rote use of literary tropes by nouveau literati, Tang also experimented with the admixing of vastly different linguistic registers in his own plays. As Cyril Birch has pointed out, Tang admixed the sublime and the grotesque in a quest for emotional authenticity.[21] However, despite Tang's impatience with hackneyed clichés and his daring plot device of an unmarried woman's sexual fantasy as the main conceit for a play, he nevertheless subscribed to the idea that the power of drama rested on its ability 'to reinforce firm devotion of subjects to the emperor, to mediate compassion between father and son, to cultivate fraternity among brothers, to generate love between husband and wife, and to develop faithfulness among friends'.[22] Thus, in this view, drama was designed to breathe new life into the Confucian canon rather than to do away with it.

In other cases, the repackaging of old plays under the auspices of what I have termed 'reproductive authorship' could serve to suppress or to bring out the hidden and ultimately subversive potential of such works in print.[23] Not only did such rewritings redraw the boundaries between originality and plagiarism in defining who could be a dramatic author, but they hinted at the protean potential of theatre to exceed the orthodoxy of an examination-centred literary value system. In some cases, such reinscriptions explicitly transcended the framework of customary Confucian relations. Wang Jide's work as critic and playwright, for instance, points to the foundational nature of eroticism as a basis for hetero- or homoerotic bonds for a circle of similarly minded connoisseurs, giving pride of place to the sympathetic imagination at the expense of a historical literalism. In his *Selection of Yuan Plays* (1615/16), Zang Maoxun ingeniously engaged in literary mythmaking. Despite the fact that he had first-hand knowledge of the Yuan historical record, Zang brazenly claimed that the Yuan dynasty had selected its officials through examinations that featured the writing of arias (*qu* 曲).[24] Such a deliberately counterfactual claim eked out a space for playwriting that tapped into and yet exceeded contemporary imperial patronage for gifted, yet wayward author-editors such as himself. Taken together, such authors took drama beyond the realm of didacticism and conjured up, however ephemerally, a glimpse of an imaginary world where imperial authority no longer held the key to socio-literary validation.[25]

Conclusion

In summary, the late Ming was a period when drama emancipated itself from the confines of court performance and communal rites and came within the purview of highly literate individuals, who, when faced with the varied traditions of drama and the new dilemmas of self-fashioning, ushered in a second boom for literary drama in the history of Chinese literature. The process was uneven and fraught with risks large and small as the breakdown of sumptuary practice, the ready access to print and the diversification of literary standards converged to produce new opportunities and new dangers for literary authorship. Situated in a unique force field riven with particular audiences, aesthetic demands and social tensions inherent in the genre, the authorship of drama became a contested site fraught with new possibilities for authorship and the corollary literati identity formation. By the end of the seventeenth century, the social energy that powered the formation of the late Ming/early Qing corpus found new theatrical outlets, but at that point it was no longer the author that dominated dramatic production, but patrons and actors came to occupy centre stage. The intermittent efflorescence of dramatic authorship that culminated in the publication of key texts of both the southern and northern drama traditions in the 1610s disabuses us of any notion of historic inevitability and instead invites us to consider what institutional factors conspired to make drama an attractive field of endeavour for literary authors during this period.

Notes

1   Xu Shuofang, *Wan Ming qujia nianpu* (Hangzhou: Zhejiang guji chubanshe, 1993), vol. 1, p. 173.

2   Ibid., p. 181. Zhang is said to have completed the play within a month.

3   Patricia Sieber, *Theaters of Desire: Authors, Readers, and the Reproduction of Early Chinese Song-Drama, 1300–2000* (New York: Palgrave Macmillan, 2003), pp. 74–8.

4   Ming Dong Gu, *Chinese Theories of Reading and Writing: A Route to Hermeneutics and Open Poetics* (Albany: SUNY Press, 2005), pp. 19–20.

5   One might be tempted to use the term 'revival', but in contrast to *sanqu*, very few Yuan scholar-officials wrote plays. Hence, the embrace of *zaju* by former scholar-officials can be considered a first. Cf. Xu Zifang, *Ming zaju shi* (Beijing: Zhonghua shuju, 2003), pp. 10–13.

6   Sieber, *Theaters of Desire*, pp. 91–101 and Tian Yuan Tan, *Songs of Transgression and Contentment: Discharged Officials and Literati Communities in Sixteenth-Century North China* (Cambridge, MA: Harvard University Asia Center, 2010), pp. 52–4.

7   Tan, *Songs of Transgression and Contentment*, pp. 60–1.

8   Wang Shizhen, *Quzao*, in *Zhongguo gudian xiqu lunzhu jicheng* (Beijing: Zhongguo xiju chubanshe, 1959), vol. 4, p. 35; Douglas Wilkerson, 'Shih and Historical Consciousness in Ming Drama' (PhD dissertation, Yale University, 1992), p. 243.

9   See further discussion on *The Crying Phoenix* in Ayling Wang's essay (Section 3.1) in this volume.

10   For another early play that retold a local suicide and sought to enshrine the woman at the heart of the story as a form of social intervention, see Tan, *Songs of Contentment and Transgression*, pp. 107–10.

11   Wilkerson, 'Shih and Historical Consciousness in Ming Drama', p. 238.

12   Li Yu, 'Jie fengci', *Xianqing ouji*, p. 8.

13   See Patricia Sieber, 'Seeing the World through *Xianqing ouji* (1671)', *Modern Chinese Literature and Culture*, 12 (2000), pp. 1–42.

14   See also the discussion on Xu Wei's *A Record of Southern Drama* in the essay by Regina Llamas (Section 9.1) in this volume.

15   Xu Wei, *Nanci xulu, Zhongguo gudian xiqu lunzhu jicheng* series (Beijing: Zhongguo xiqu chubanshe, 1959), vol. 3, p. 239.

16   Xu Wei, *Nanci xulu*, pp. 239–40. As Xu proceeds to note, despite Gao Ming's best efforts to make the plays singable, the theatrical entertainment bureau had to make further adjustments to make it performable at court.

17   Lü Tiancheng, *Qupin jiaozhu* (Beijing: Zhonghua shuju, 1990), pp. 30, 34.

18   Quoted in Guo Qitao, *Ritual Opera and Mercantile Lineage: The Confucian Transformation of Popular Culture in Late Imperial Huizhou* (Stanford: Stanford University Press, 2005), p. 102.

19   Kai-wing Chow, *Publishing, Culture and Power in Early Modern China* (Stanford: Stanford University Press, 2004), p. 92.

20   Sophie Volpp, *Worldly Stage: Theatricality in Seventeenth-Century China* (Cambridge, MA: Harvard University Asia Center, 2011), pp. 89–128.

21   Cyril Birch, *Scenes for Mandarins: The Elite Theater of the Ming* (New York: Columbia University Press, 1995), p. 152.

22 Tang Xianzu, *Tang Xianzu ji*, vol. 2, p. 1127, quoted in Guo, *Ritual Opera and Mercantile Lineage*, p. 146.

23 Sieber, *Theaters of Desire*, pp. 168–71.

24 Ibid., pp. 109–11.

25 From a comparative perspective, Chow observes that the 'strong tension between the habitus and the practice of the literati's *shishang* (cultural merchant) career ... was not strong enough to endow the literary field with the level of autonomy witnessed in Europe since the eighteenth century'. See Chow, *Publishing, Culture, and Power in Early Modern China*, p. 145.

6.2 'May I subscribe a name?': Terms of collaboration in 1616

Peter Kirwan

If the redating by Martin Butler and the team behind the *Cambridge Edition of the Works of Ben Jonson* is to be believed, then the theatrical season of 1616 began with the dancing of Ben Jonson's masque *The Golden Age Restored* in the Whitehall Banqueting House on 1 January.[1] The goddess Pallas descends in order to introduce Astraea and establish the Golden Age, representing the just age of James I. In order to achieve this, she calls forth poets:

> You far-famed spirits of this happy isle,
> That for your sacred songs have gained the style
> Of Phoebus' sons, whose notes the air aspire
> Of th'old Egyptian or the Thracian lyre,
> That Chaucer, Gower, Lydgate, Spenser hight,
> Put on your better flames and larger light
> To wait upon the age that shall your names new nourish,
> Since virtue pressed shall grow, and buried arts shall
>   flourish.
>
> (ll. 103–10)

The poets reply collectively that 'Our best of fire / Is that which Pallas doth inspire' (lines 112–13) and join together with her to awake the masquers who represent the returned Golden Age.

In the opening days of 1616, then, Jonson (in collaboration with the designer Inigo Jones, whose designs for this masque are not extant) offers a vision of authorial collaboration. His selection of four poets laureate is significant in itself, adding the Tudor poet Edmund Spenser to a conventional grouping of the medieval poets Geoffrey Chaucer, John Gower and John Lydgate. Yet despite identifying and naming these four poets laureate, they never speak individually. Instead, their individual voices are subordinated to a collective expression, as they speak and sing only in pairs or as a group of four. They are simultaneously remembered individually for their 'sacred songs' and required to 'put on [their] better flames and larger light' in communal service of James's Golden Age.

That the year 1616 began with an image of named authors working in collaboration is fitting, given the importance usually accorded to 1616 in established narratives of the development of dramatic authorship in England. By the end of 1616, Jonson had produced his first folio, the first major collection of works in English to feature predominantly dramatic entertainments. This book also, infamously, effaced collaboration by excluding plays written with other authors such as *Eastward Ho* and/or writing out the contributions of others to plays such as *Sejanus, His Fall*.[2] It is also, perhaps, interesting to note the coincidences of a year in which several of the age's great collaborative forces died. On the date of the second performance of *The Golden Age Restored*, 6 January, Philip Henslowe – coordinator of a vast number of collaborative plays and the man whose papers provide the best evidence for the extent of dramatic collaboration in the period – passed away. Later in the year followed Francis Beaumont, one half of the celebrated 'Beaumont and [John] Fletcher' partnership that would be immortalized in a 1647 folio, and William Shakespeare, of whose works between a quarter and a third are now generally understood to contain the work of multiple creative agents.

It would be tempting to support a narrative in which 1616 illustrates in microcosm a shift from the collaborative milieu of early dramatic writing to the emergence of the modern author; but this is of course too neat a narrative. Wendy Wall, intervening in debates about the nature of authorship in the early modern period, argues that 'the facts about the conditions of writing and publishing still seem sketchy and ambiguous', and that the major interventions in the field have instead involved 'revisiting and arranging evidence' to suit preferred narratives of sole authorship or collaborative production; as she notes, the evidence for both narratives suggests that both were functional modes of production in the period.[3] Rather than seek a neat emergence of the author in 1616 (or, indeed, 1623), Wall advocates the treatment of these narratives as 'psychologically and socially provocative fictions ... [that] prompt us to ask more questions', an approach I pursue here.[4] This chapter focuses closely on the dramatic publications of 1616 to argue that print representations of dramatic authorship demonstrate a multivalent and complex picture. The terms of collaboration do not develop unilaterally, and in some cases seem to move counter to the broader historical sweep. In fact, dramatic authorship in 1616 illustrates a much wider and more diverse range of definitions of collaboration that blur, rather than reinforce, the distinctions between collaborators, authors and 'co-authors'.

Print authorship

The Database of Early English Playbooks (DEEP) lists some forty-three playbooks published in 1616.[5] Twenty-seven of these are those included in Ben Jonson's *Works* of 1616, and another four in William Alexander's collection of closet drama, *The Monarchic Tragedies*. The rest, issued individually, are listed in Table 6.1.

The data of these quartos can be interpreted in several ways, and Wall's caution about clear, all-encompassing narratives is justified. Yet there are several points of interest. Of the twelve plays and entertainments listed here, three are understood to be collaborative and two more (*Faustus* and *Mucedorus*) are issued with new additions which postdate the original author's work. Despite this, only one title page out of twelve (*The Scornful Lady*) makes explicit reference to collaboration or

Table 6.1 Twelve playbooks published in 1616 and issued individually.

Authorship	Title	Title page attribution
Anonymous	*Mucedorus*	'Amplified with new Additions'
John Marston	*Jack Drum's Entertainment (Katherine and Pasquil)*	'Newly corrected'
Thomas Dekker, Thomas Middleton	*1 The Honest Whore*	'Tho. Dekker'
Christopher Marlowe (and others?)	*Doctor Faustus (B-text)*	'Written by Ch. Marklin'
Edward Sharpham	*Cupid's Whirligig*	[no information]
Thomas Middleton	*A Trick to Catch the Old One*	'By T. Midleton'
Lewis Machin, William Barkstead, John Marston	*The Insatiate Countess*	[no information]
Francis Beaumont, John Fletcher	*The Scornful Lady*	'Written by FRA. BEAUMONT and JO. FLETCHER, Gent.'
Anthony Munday	*Chrysanaleia: The Golden Fishing, or Honor of Fishmongers*	'Deuised and written by A.M. Citizen and Draper of LONDON'
William Haughton	*Englishmen for My Money, or A Woman Will Have Her Will*	[no information]
S.S.	*The Honest Lawyer*	'Written by S.S.'
Thomas Middleton	*Civitatis Amor*	[no information]

co-authorship. Jonson's folio, which appeared in November 1616, seems to consolidate rather than create practices of attribution in which assertions of single authorship override the fine details of collaboration. Second, the authorial attributions are decidedly scattered. Four are attributed explicitly to known authors, although one – 'Ch. Marklin' – appears in an unfamiliar form and may well cause confusion. Two more title pages employ initials to stand for the author, with one set of initials (those on *Chrysanaleia*) pieced out by the civic rather than personal identity of the author, credited as 'Citizen and Draper of LONDON'. The dedication inside the book identifies the author more explicitly as 'An. Mundy', just as the dedication to *Cupid's Whirligig* adds the initials 'E.S.' to a volume with no attribution on its title page. The other title pages make no mention of authors, but two of the plays are explicitly revised: *Mucedorus* is 'amplified with new additions' and *Jack Drum's Entertainment* is 'newly corrected'. The four dramas with no information on their title pages include a civil entertainment, two plays for a children's company and one for an Elizabethan adult company, but the authors are not credited.

These publications collectively demonstrate the unpredictability of print representations of early modern dramatic authorship. Collaborative plays are represented as sole authored; sole-authored plays are represented as anonymous; authors themselves are renamed or misnamed. The inconsistency and inaccuracy of authorial attributions on dramatic title pages tend to be treated as a lack, as in Michel Foucault's identification of the impulse to 'locate the space left empty by the author's disappearance'.[6] Certainly this is the aim of attribution studies that seek to identify authors and categorize plays into authorial canons, and this is an aim aligning neatly with the strategies of Shakespeare and Jonson's contemporaries in Ming China, who 'explicitly acknowledged that they harboured "intent"'.[7] Yet where the writers of the scholar class created their song-dramas outside of their official duties, their contemporaries in England wrote within a series of overlapping systems and institutions that at times take precedence on title pages. The obvious example is the general preference for acknowledging theatre companies over authors on title pages, as for *Cupid's Whirligig* and *Jack Drum's Entertainment* (both performed by the Children of the Queen's Revels) and *Mucedorus* (attributed to the King's Men). This is not to deny the presence of real individual authors in writing the plays, but the culture of print prioritizes in these cases the social and collaborative milieu of performance over the circumstances of writing.

While across the early modern period there is a clear emergence of a modern author figure in print attribution, from predominantly anonymous printing in the 1570s to the regular appearance and articulation of authorial self-assertion in the 1630s (more reminiscent of Ming dramatists, particularly in the use of prefaces to assert intent), I suggest that critics should attend to how individual books articulate their own circumstances of production, rather than lamenting 'missing' information. For this, I am inclined to stress Mark Robson's utilization of a model of 'signature' and 'countersignature', in which 'an anonymous text might … be thought of as the "without-signature," in which the unsigned is figured in terms of an attitude towards the unknown that retains the possibility of an ethical relation'.[8] I find this a particularly useful way to conceptualize, for example, Thomas Middleton's *Civitatis Amor*, a civic entertainment celebrating the investiture of James's heir, Charles, as Prince of Wales on 4 November 1616. This title page makes no mention of the authorship of the entertainment, and its anonymity arguably functions as a form of countersignature that draws attention away from authorial identity towards its authorizing figure, Prince Charles himself, whose name is capitalized and set prominently on its own line. The same might be said of the title page of *Chysanaleia*, where Anthony Munday's name is alluded to only by initials, yet his civic identity 'Citizen and Draper of LONDON' appears in full. Here, the occasion is the admittance of a new Lord Mayor of London and the city's name, capitalized and repeated, dominates the title page. In both cases the author is speaking as representative of a larger institution, the City of London itself. The paean to the celebrated subject is legitimized not by an individual sentiment but in the capturing by a poet of a collective voice, as in *The Golden Age Restored.*

To extract the author from this social context is, I suggest, to defeat the purpose of these title pages. Unlike Wang Shizhen and other Ming dramatists whose interventions offered an individual and even oppositional voice, the dramas created here are dependent on their alignment with, and their authorship subordinate to, the formal voice of the city. This does not mean that the individual, named author is little more than a vehicle. Tracy Hill discusses the significance of Munday's reworking of patriarchal models of authorship (traditionally, the idea of 'begetting' or 'fathering' a text) through his deferral to London, referred to elsewhere as 'tender mother and Nurse'. In *Chrysanaleia*, Munday figures his own masculine authorship as birthed by another institution conceived of as female, the Fishmongers' Company, and speaks of himself as an orphan. Hill argues:

> The Fishmongers' Company perform in a metonymic fashion the maternal role that London more generally often does for Munday. In contrast to the usual representation of the City 'Fathers', the Fishmongers are presented as a mother figure in relation to those who seek employment with them, who Munday ... likens to 'Rivers' directing themselves naturally towards 'their nursing Mother the Sea'. The master, warden and assistants of the Fishmongers, he claims here, had been entirely responsible for his birth and upbringing and even in adulthood he still places himself as dependent on their collective ability to nurture him.[9]

The act of authorizing the text here brings into play both 'countersign' (the partial accreditation of the name 'A.M.' that draws attention to what is lacking) and 'sign' by bringing into the authorial partnership a series of social and civic institutions to which Munday considers himself beholden. The performance of authorship in this particular instance is enabled by Munday's subordination of his own name. Print authorization signifies much more than a simple attribution (or lack of the same). It mediates modes of authorial representation that situate the text to a greater or lesser extent within the social circumstances that gave occasion to it. I suggest that what is happening in this year – and by extension, the period – is less an emergence of the modern authorizing author than a complex mediation of the potential agencies of authorization that shape texts. The trope of the begetting father figure becomes unsustainable because of the complexity of authorial relationships.

Effacing collaboration

Jonson's folio is usually considered an exemplar of the modern process of authorizing a body of work, but it was not the only dramatic publication of 1616 that effaced collaboration. The 1616 quarto of Christopher Marlowe's *Doctor Faustus* was the first to incorporate the 'new additions' of what is commonly known as the 'B-text'. Interestingly, however, these additions are not referred to until the next quarto of 1619, which announces the new material. Also, the 1616 quarto proclaims itself uniquely to be written by 'Ch. Marklin'. Marklin is a fascinating figure, who in print takes sole responsibility for the entire, newly extended play of *Doctor Faustus*, with no reference made to previous versions or distinctions within the text. The 1619 quarto 'corrects' the authorial attribution to 'Ch. Mar' and adds notice of the new additions. Whether the 'Mar' of 1619 refers to 'Marklin' or 'Marlowe' is perhaps irrelevant, as variant spellings of names in the period are common. But both quartos present information that jars with modern understandings of authorship. 'Marklin' certainly did not write the whole of the play, and the additions announced as 'new' by the 1619 quarto are in fact at least three years old, if not older, and postdate Marlowe's death by more than two decades. Similarly, the 'new additions' to *Mucedorus* proclaimed on the 1616 quarto had in fact been in every publication of the play since 1610, and are already in this sense at least six years 'old'. The fact that, as MacDonald Jackson and others have recently claimed, the additions to *Mucedorus* may well have been by the King's Men's resident playwright, William Shakespeare, goes unmentioned.[10] The new text is subsumed into the old without further comment, creating yet another situation in which multiple anonymous voices contribute to the 'larger light' of the play.

The consistency here is inconsistency. Title pages are at odds with the information implied by the newly expanded texts, and the interventions of 1616 do not necessarily advance the clarification of authorship. In 1615, Beaumont and Fletcher's *Cupid's Revenge* had been published attributed to John Fletcher alone. In 1616, following Beaumont's death, the same company's *The Scornful Lady* followed with attribution to both Beaumont and Fletcher, reviving the author in fame even as his physical body died, in what may be a deliberate tribute to the dramatist's passing. While collaborative authorship is correctly established in accordance with modern standards here, the reverse was true for the Thomas Middleton and Thomas Dekker partnership. The pair's *Roaring Girl* was attributed to both authors on the title page of that play's 1611 quarto, but collaboration was effaced from *1 The Honest Whore*, attributed to Dekker alone when it was printed in 1616.

Attribution studies have, since the late nineteenth century, fine-tuned the details of early modern dramatic collaborations, ascertaining both the identities of authors and the precise responsibilities of those authors within dramatic texts. In the early years of the twenty-first century, this has led to the introduction of the term 'co-author' (or the elided form 'coauthor') as in the work of Brian Vickers and Jeffrey Knapp, adopting a model that prioritizes individual authorial responsibility and the 'correct' assignation of literary property.[11]

Ongoing debates in the field dispute how far such a model is appropriate to a genre that depends on the effacement of collaboration; as Jeffrey Masten argues, the role of the dramatic collaborator is to elide difference as far as possible in the service of an end product that is experienced as a unified whole.[12] At stake here are a set of fundamental questions about the stake authors had in their own dramatic authorship. Did collaborating authors expect or anticipate credit for specific contributions, beyond payment? Did an author retain a sense of proprietary right over the words they had contributed, or did the unity of the play take precedence? Would authors want to be individually identified within a play, and is this an appropriate critical question to be asking? David Nicol's recent work on the canon of Thomas Middleton and William Rowley takes a middle ground, arguing that critics need to be attentive to the varieties and individual manifestations of collaborative authorship. In the case of the pair's *A Fair Quarrel*, first performed in 1616 and printed in the following year attributed to both authors, Nicol argues:

> Studying *A Fair Quarrel* as a collaboration rather than simply as a Middleton play reveals the ways in which both authors were playing to their different strengths: paradoxically, the play's unity emerges directly from the disjointed nature of its conclusion. Simply seeing the play as constructed by a unified voice called 'Middleton-and-Rowley' is misleading: the play's ideas and structure can only be appreciated by recognizing that it was written by playwrights whose styles developed in different social contexts and whose resulting friction was creatively used in this play.[13]

The important distinction I would like to make here is between the acknowledgement of 'Middleton' and 'Rowley' as separate and identifiable identities within the work, and 'Middleton-and-Rowley' as a combined entity. In the case of *A Fair Quarrel*, Nicol argues for the importance of understanding

FIGURE 5 *The title page of Thomas Middleton and William Rowley,* A Faire Quarrell *(London, 1617), with the authors' names bound together in parentheses. STC 17911a, Houghton Library, Harvard University.*

a creative conflict within the play that aligns with authorial identities. While this conflict may not have appeared so explicit to early audiences, Nicol argues that the retention of both Middleton's customary satire and Rowley's flare for romance enables a creative conflict that, if we were to assume title-page authorizations carry particular meaning, justifies the inclusion of both names on the 1617 title page. Here, the names are bound in parentheses in a way that simultaneously separates and yokes together the two authors in support of the whole. This may be coincidence, but a relatively rare acknowledgement of collaboration on a title page fits in this instance with a play that Nicol argues is dependent on the juxtaposition of two distinct voices and ideologies.

The wider importance of Nicol's work for this period, however, is that it argues for an attuned and individual response to instances of collaboration, which in other cases might prioritize the authorial influence of actors, genres, repertories, politics and so on, while continuing to pay close attention to divisions between sections of writing. This does not contradict calls for attention to text over authorship such as those of Jeffrey Masten, and indeed Masten specifically calls for exactly the kind of study that Nicol offers.[14] Nor does it deny the importance of establishing co-authors and individual style, as long as this does not happen at the cost of examination of specific authorial strategy. In this period, a consensus seems to be emerging that authors can neither be disappeared entirely into a text nor considered as autonomous of the circumstances within which they write. Reading title pages attentively may reveal much more about the text's self-conception than is usually noted, and we need to accord them this kind of nuanced attention.

Conclusions

Returning to the key text of 1616, Jonson's folio, the opening and closing contents of the volume complicate the presentation of sole authorship. The volume's first commendatory poem in the vernacular begins, simply, 'May I subscribe a name?'[15] Ed. Heyward's poem proposes to subscribe a name to an individual, Jonson:

> Of all I know thou onely art the man
> That dares but what he can:
> Yet by performance shows he can do more
> Than hath bene done before,
> Or will be after.

Heyward's poem offers a confident and bold statement of assertive authorship concluding with the evocative image of a monument to Jonson:

> These are thy lower parts. What stands above
> Who sees not yet must love,
> When on the Base he reads BEN. IONSONS name,
> And heares the rest from Fame.

At the beginning of Jonson's monumental book, his authorship and authority are simultaneously inscribed through the identification of a single name, presented here in block capitals. Yet within this poem there is another quill working from the first line: 'May I subscribe a name? Dares my bold quill / Write that or good or ill'. The poem begins, conventionally, with Heyward musing on his own authorship before his own identity is subordinated to the volume's praise of Jonson. As with all commendatory poems, this serves a double purpose of praising the poem's addressee while also foregrounding the talent of the author. At the beginning of Jonson's sole-authored volume, therefore, a collaborator in the literary construction identifies and promotes his own influential hand.

At the other end of the 1616 volume appears the masque with which the calendar year began, *The Golden Age Restored*. This masque appears in two different states in different copies of the folio, both of which can be viewed on Early English

Books Online, and the differences affect the words with which the masque ends. Some copies conclude the masque with a powerful speech by Astraea, who brings the masque to a celebratory conclusion in praise of the Golden Age of James.

> This, this, and only such as this,
> The bright Astraea's region is,
> Where she would pray to live,
> And in the midst of so much gold,
> Unbought with grace or fear unsold,
> The law to mortals give.

(ll. 188–93)

This is the ending preferred by earlier editors of Jonson as giving a stronger ending to the Folio. An individual voice imposes law on mortals, arguably even articulating Jonson's own voice in bringing the masque to an ordered close. However, other copies following printing house corrections instead close with a Choir singing collectively:

> To Jove, to Jove, be all the honour given,
> That thankful hearts can raise from earth to heaven.

(ll. 214–15)

This ending, preferred by the Cambridge edition, reverses the direction in which the final words are spoken, replacing the sole authorial voice with collaborative acclamation. Where Astraea descends from Heaven to Earth, here the voices return 'from earth to heaven'.

The juxtaposition of these two alternative endings in different copies of the book is striking: the one coming from the 'author' of the Golden Age who has subsumed poets laureate to a broader cause and now asserts her own voice of order and control; the other a collective voice, that of a large body of singers and actors, responding to the authorial figure in joy. It is fitting, perhaps, that these two sets of voices co-exist at the end of Jonson's Folio, published in November 1616, complicating the power dynamics of authorship and vocalization within this apparently sole-authored work even as the year drew to its close. The co-existence of the two different states of this ending serves as a fitting synecdoche for the model of authorship demonstrated throughout 1616: contingent, social and suited to the occasions and institutions that shape the purpose of the works.

Notes

1   Martin Butler, 'The Golden Age Restored', in David Bevington, Martin Butler and Ian Donaldson (eds), *The Cambridge Edition of the Works of Ben Jonson*, vol. 4, p. 447.

2   The preface to the first quarto of *Sejanus* suggests – perhaps disingenuously – that Jonson has replaced the contributions of a 'second Pen' with 'lesse pleasing' material of his own. Ben Jonson, *Sejanus, His Fall* (London, 1605).

3   Wendy Wall, 'Early Modern Authorship in 2007', *Shakespeare Studies*, 36 (2008), pp. 61–2.

4   Ibid, p. 66.

5   *DEEP: Database of Early English Playbooks*. Eds Alan B. Farmer and Zachary Lesser. Created 2007. Available online: http://deep.sas.upenn.edu/cite.html (accessed 6 February 2015).

6   Michel Foucault, 'What Is An Author?' (1969), trans. Josué V. Harari, in *The Foucault Reader*, ed. Paul Rabinow (London: Penguin, 1984), p. 115.

7   See Patricia Sieber's companion piece to this essay in this chapter.

8   Mark Robson, 'The Ethics of Anonymity', in *Anonymity in Early Modern England*, eds Janet Wright Starner and Barbara Howard Traister (Farnham: Ashgate, 2011), p. 170.

9   Tracy Hill, *Anthony Munday and Civic Culture* (Manchester: Manchester University Press, 2004), pp. 23–4.

10   See Will Sharpe, 'Authorship and Attribution', in *William Shakespeare and Others: Collaborative Plays*, eds Jonathan

Bate and Eric Rasmussen (Basingstoke: Palgrave, 2013), pp. 710–16.

11   Brian Vickers, *Shakespeare, Co-Author* (Oxford: Oxford University Press, 2002); Jeffrey Knapp, 'Shakespeare as Coauthor', *Shakespeare Studies,* 36 (2008), pp. 49–59.

12   Jeffrey Masten, *Textual Intercourse* (Cambridge: Cambridge University Press, 1997), esp. pp. 14–20.

13   David Nicol, *Middleton & Rowley* (Toronto: University of Toronto Press, 2012), p. 118.

14   Masten, *Textual Intercourse*, p. 20.

15   Ben Jonson, *The Workes of Beniamin Ionson* (London, 1616).

7

Audiences, critics and reception

What kinds of interactions are evident between stage and audience? How did playwrights and actors produce or adapt plays to fit their audiences' varied tastes? Did audience reception match the playwrights' expectations? How did the audiences in the public and commercial theatres differ from the private, elite ones?

7.1 Revising *Peony Pavilion*: Audience reception in presenting Tang Xianzu's text[1]

Shih-Pe Wang

Literati-playwrights' revisions as audience reception in theory

In the late Ming period, the prosperous printing culture accelerated the circulation of drama; the more widespread a play text was, the more diverse were the responses it received from readers and audience. With regard to the case of Tang Xianzu's *Peony Pavilion*, the differing and sometimes conflicting reception of the play is demonstrated in the phenomenon of multiple revisions and adaptations of the play that appeared soon after its publication in 1598.

Peony Pavilion was a stroke of genius which earned loads of admiration among the contemporaneous audience, such as Shen Defu's 沈德符 (1578–1642) comment, 'As soon as Tang Xianzu's *Peony Pavilion* came out, it was transmitted and recited in every household, which almost diminished the popularity of *The Story of the Western Wing*.'[2]

However, despite this praise, the contemporary literati were also very critical of the inharmonious match between Tang's music and his literary text. For example, Shen Defu commented that 'Tang was not familiar with musical notations, so he arranged the rhymes just randomly, completely relying on his gifted talent'.[3] Because of the brilliance of the play text on one hand and its musical flaws on the other, some connoisseurs of both drama and music were inspired to revise this play to make it more correct and perfect. In their opinion, Tang's lack of attention to tunes and rhymes would cause difficulties in singing and render this masterpiece only a desktop book for reading rather than a stage play for performance.[4]

As a result of such criticism, some of Tang's contemporary literati-playwrights attempted to revise *Peony Pavilion* from immediately after its publication till after his death in 1616. Among them, four revisions are worthy of brief mention. The first was Tang's friend Lü Yusheng's, though this version no longer exists.[5] Tang was enraged by this corrected rewriting, justifying his original version by saying it was a matter of literary taste:

> My *Peony Pavilion* has been severely distorted by Lü Yusheng to be sung in the language and tunes of Wu region. I could not help laughing mutely. Once upon a time, there was someone who disliked Wang Moujie's (Wang Wei's courtesy name; 701–61) painting of the plantain in snowy winter, hence he cut off the plantain and replaced it with the plum blossom. Yes, it showed the realistic winter landscape; however, it was not Wang Wei's winter landscape any more, which was filled with spiritual abundance beyond the principles of writing.[6]

Lü's modified work, in Tang's opinion, changed the spirit as well as the rich imagination of his original text, just as Wang Wei's famous painting should not be viewed as a realistic scene but instead as a lyrical expression of colours, a contrast of opposites and a display of unrestrained talents.

Almost at the same time, a famous musical theorist Shen Jing also revised *Peony Pavilion* as *The Story of the Equivalent Dream* (*Tongmeng ji* 同夢記). As Shen was a master of musical notation as well as dramatic format, his lost manuscript is likely to have focused on reviewing Tang's tunes and rhymes. In addition, he changed the plot sequence to clarify an ambiguous point in the original play, that is, in making the dreams of male and female protagonists the same. Again, Tang was extremely angry and very critical of it: '[Shen's] musical notations and other theoretical essays are quite good; however, indulging in them long, he could not elaborate too much. ... I regard myself as one who knows the meanings of music. Sometimes I was just lazy with checking tunes and adjusting rhymes; if so, why not bend and distort the singers' throats to fit my words?'[7]

It is obvious that in Tang's opinion a genius could break away from the limits of formulary rules. The conservatives, however, took it as an act of disrespect, so criticisms and arguments from his contemporary literati arose. The dispute between Tang and Shen, or to be more precise, between words and tunes, hereafter was greatly elaborated by academic scholars in the late twentieth century.[8]

In 1618, after Tang's death, Zang Maoxun published his complete revisions of Tang's four plays including *Peony Pavilion*, as Stephen H. West has discussed in his essay earlier in this volume (Section 5.1). Zang's reason for rectifying the musical errors in Tang's works was the needs of the audience and actors.

As Tang had passed away at the time Zang's revisions were published, he could not jump up from the grave to oppose Zang, but another famous editor and compiler obviously was not happy with the current revisions, including Zang's. This was Feng Menglong 馮夢龍 (1574–1646), who compiled the three anthologies of short stories collectively known as *Three Words* (*Sanyan* 三言) during the period from 1620 to 1627 and who was also a connoisseur of dramatic adaptation. As Feng explained in his preface, he revised *Peony Pavilion* in 1623 based on Shen Jing's version: 'The inherent relationship of Liu Mengmei and Du Liniang was originated in each other's one shared dream, so Shen Jing titled his revision as *The Story of the Equivalent Dream*, and I called mine *The Story of the Romantic Dream* (*Fengliu meng* 風流夢).'[9]

In addition to the cutting down and rebuilding of the plots, Feng also criticized Tang's errors and tried to correct them. 'Only one [big flaw in *Peony Pavilion*] is that Tang filled in the words without considering its rhyme, and used the sounds not according to the notations ... if the actors would like to put it into performance on stage, it is impossible to do so without revising or adjusting the words more or less.'[10]

From the above four cases of Lü Yusheng, Shen Jing, Zang Maoxun and Feng Menglong, it is evident that some contemporary literati-playwrights were biased in criticizing Tang's music flaws and plot defects, hence their revisions were focused on correction, deletion and reconstruction. Their intention was to make *Peony Pavilion* available as a well-made play for performance, but their theory did not work in practice. It is ironic that their method of adaptation was soon proved to be a failure; none of their revisions could satisfactorily replace Tang's original text, either on the desk or on stage.

Performers' revisions as audience reception in practice

Performers, meaning either actors or singers or both in the context of Chinese drama, seem always to have preferred Tang Xianzu's original version. During the same period, a totally different form of dramatic texts were published. They are the 'miscellanies' of selected plays (*xuanben* 選本). These miscellanies were collections of 'excerpts' (*zhezixi* 折子戲) or 'arias of individual song or song suite'. A *zhezixi* could be regarded as one scene selected from the full-length play, which was often treated as an independent, one-act play. Readers and audiences would not understand *zhezixi* if they were not already familiar with the stories, plots or backgrounds of the full-length play; also, they needed to appreciate the actors' performances in order to get greater enjoyment from the piece. The compiler of the 'aria and aria-suite' always selected the most tuneful and popular songs, or those suitable for spectacular occasions. The appearance of *zhezixi* in the miscellanies shows that audiences' preferences had shifted away from the performance of complete works to the performance of individual scenes, and the significance imbued in them by specific performers. In this way, a *zhezixi* reveals an alternative method of revision, created from the viewpoint of the actors and singers. In the case of the selections of *Peony Pavilion*, it could be viewed as a subtle way of adapting Tang's original text whereby it was abridged or particular scenes were selected for performance, instead of changing the whole play.

Some good examples of miscellanies published around 1616 which include excerpts or songs from *Peony Pavilion* are: *A Collection of Corals* (*Shanshan ji* 珊珊集, prefaced in 1616), *Sounds like Dew under the Moonlight* (*Yue lu yin* 月露音, prefaced in 1616), *Extraordinary Voices of Song Forest* (*Cilin Yixiang* 詞林逸響, prefaced in 1623) and *Brocade of Spring Delight* (*Yichun jin* 怡春錦, printed in the *Chongzhen* period, 1628–44).[11] The first two are miscellanies of songs, while the latter two are miscellanies of excerpt texts. Table 7.1 shows the selections of *Peony Pavilion* in these miscellanies.

A close examination of the miscellanies scene by scene will demonstrate that almost all of them followed the original text of Tang Xianzu without any changes except for one or two omissions or additions of words on a few occasions. Only the second half of Scene 12 in *Brocade of Spring Delight* shows some minor differences from Tang's text, but it does not follow the major kind of revisions made by those literati mentioned above. In other words, the miscellanies reflected a remarkable phenomenon around 1616: the performers could display Tang's text word by word, in spite of the difficulties caused by the errors in his tunes.

In addition to the above-mentioned four miscellanies, there is a 1655 (early Qing) edition of musical notations of individual arias titled *New Manual of the Southern Arias* (*Nanci xinpu* 南詞新譜, hereafter *New Manual*), edited by Shen Jing's nephew, Shen Zijin 沈自晉 (1583–1665).[12] Shen Zijin was a famous *qu* musician and he compiled this book based on his uncle's original manuscript to supply song writers and playwrights with formulary rules for southern *qu* music. Probably out of consideration for the relationship with his uncle as well as the literati nature of this book, Shen Zijin

Table 7.1 Excerpts of Peony Pavilion *in four miscellanies.*

Miscellanies	Volume	Number and title of scenes in *Peony Pavilion*
A Collection of Corals	Vol. 4	Scene 2 'Declaring Ambition'
Sounds like Dew under the Moonlight	Vol. 1	Scene 53 'Interrogation under the Rod'
Sounds like Dew	Vol. 2	Scene 10 'The Interrupted Dream'
Sounds like Dew	Vol. 2	Scene 12 'Pursuing the Dream'
Sounds like Dew	Vol. 2	Scene 26 'The Portrait Examined'
Sounds like Dew	Vol. 2	Scene 28 'Union in the Shades'
Sounds like Dew	Vol. 3	Scene 14 'The Portrait'
Sounds like Dew	Vol. 3	Scene 20 'Keening'
Sounds like Dew	Vol. 3	Scene 27 'Spirit Roaming'
Brocade of Spring Delight	Vol. Li 禮集	Scene 10 'The Interrupted Dream'
Brocade of Spring Delight	Vol. She 射集	Scene 12 'Pursuing the Dream'
Brocade of Spring Delight	Vol. She 射集	Scene 28 'Union in the Shades'
Extraordinary Voices of Song Forest	Vol. Yue 月卷	Scene 10 'The Interrupted Dream'
Extraordinary Voices of Song Forest	Vol. Yue 月卷	Scene 12 'Pursuing the Dream'

included a few songs from the revisions of Shen Jing, Zang Maoxun and Feng Menglong, as shown in Table 7.2.[13]

Generally speaking, *Sounds like Dew under the Moonlight* and the three other miscellanies represent the perspectives of performing actors and singers, while *New Manual* represents those of the literati, or rather, a reconciliation between the ideal and the practical situation, or between the revisions and the original. That is why Shen Zijin did not change Tang's text. Furthermore, Tang's arias occupied even more space in *New Manual* than the sum of the three revisions in Table 7.2. Let's look at the citation of Tang's original words without changes in *New Manual* in Table 7.3.

Table 7.2 Arias of Literati's Revisions (of Peony Pavilion) in New Manual.

Miscellanies	Volume	Cited revised edition	Selected aria (original scene in *Peony Pavilion*)
New Manual	Vol. 16	Shen Jing's *Tongmeng ji*	To the tune of *Manshan yi* (蠻山憶) (Scene 48)
New Manual	Vol. 22	Strung-together version of *Peony Pavilion* (*chuanben Mudan ting* 串本牡丹亭)[14]	To the tune of *Zhenzhu lian* (真珠簾) (Scene 2)
New Manual	Vol. 18	Feng Menglong's *Fengliu Meng*	To the tune of *Yingti ji yulin* (鶯啼集御林) (Scene 35)
New Manual	Vol. 22	Zang Maoxun's *Gaiben Huanhun* 改本還魂	To the tune of *Zhoujin huamei* (晝錦畫眉) (Scene 32)[15]

Table 7.3 *Arias of* Peony Pavilion *in* New Manual.

Miscellanies	Volume	Individual Aria (Scene in *Peony Pavilion*)
New Manual	Vol. 12	To the tune of *Chaotian lan* (朝天懶) (Scene 28)
New Manual	Vol. 14	To the tune of *Wanxian deng* (翫仙燈) (Scene 25)
New Manual	Vol. 16	To the tune of *Fanshan hu* (番山虎) (Scene 48)[16]
New Manual	Vol. 16	To the tune of *Fanshan hu* (another example) (番山虎（又一曲）) (Scene 48)[17]
New Manual	Vol. 18	To the tune of *Huangying yuduer* (黃鶯玉肚兒) (Scene 20)
New Manual	Vol. 22	To the tune of *Xiaobai ge* (孝白歌) (Scene 8)
New Manual	Vol. 23	To the tune of *Guiyue suo nanzhi* (桂月鎖南枝) (Scene 13)

Theoretically, Tang's musical flaws might have compromised the singing; in practice, however, they do not appear to have posed any major problems for the performers. When his contemporary literati attempted to make *Peony Pavilion* more performable on stage, the actors just found a creative way of performing it as close to Tang's original as possible, even though a literatus musician like Shen Zijin still struggled to preserve the increasingly weak voice of his community in the more 'elite' form of a book of notations. How then shall we judge the goodwill of the literati who criticized in vain?

Audience reception in critics' comments, playwrights' mimesis and composers' notations

In order to understand the discrepancy between literati's and actors' standpoints, as well as their causes and consequences, we might seek the opinions of certain critics, playwrights and composers. Around 1616, some literati critics read and watched Tang's play with great enthusiasm and apparently without too much bias; their notes recorded the readers' and audience's preferences, which implicitly expressed their supportive attitude towards *Peony Pavilion* and its reception.

One critic's record is taken from the playwright Zhang Dafu about the true story of a contemporary female reader Yu Niang 俞娘. Yu loved *Peony Pavilion* and wrote a dense commentary on the script, but soon after completing it, with a destiny similar to that of the protagonist Du Liniang, she died at the age of seventeen, and her commentary was lost forever.[18] Yu Niang's commentary spoke of female readers' passion for *Peony Pavilion*, attracted by Tang's fascinating words.

Another anecdote comes from an early Qing man of letters, Shen Mingsun 沈名蓀, who describes a late Ming legendary female actor Shang Xiaoling 商小玲.[19] Shang was famous for her beauty and excellent performances, especially her playing of Du Liniang. She would become so involved with the emotional intensity of the role that she eventually died heartbroken on stage while playing the *zhezixi* of 'Pursuing the Dream'. In this case, Shang embodied the female actor's infatuation with Tang's words, and probably, through her passionate performance, the audience would be infected with it as well.

As Anjna Chouhan says, in her companion piece in this chapter, 'plays themselves offer important insight into audience management from the stage-end'. Another valuable source in documenting the audience's reaction comes from late Ming playwright Wu Bing's 吳炳 (1595–1648) play *Jealousy-Curing Stew* (*Liaodu geng* 療妒羹), which tells the popular legend of a talented beauty Xiaoqing 小青. Xiaoqing is the concubine of a rich man, who was treated miserably by his jealous wife and then died young. One scene of the full-length play, also a famous *zhezixi* performed on stage, 'Tiqu' 題曲 (Commentary on the Play), could be viewed as a eulogy to *Peony Pavilion*. During a sleepless night, Xiaoqing reads *Peony Pavilion*. Closely identifying with the sorrow it depicts, she makes detailed comments on the play text in this scene.[20] 'Tiqu' describes a female reader's fascination with Tang's words, while its play text by Wu Bing could be regarded as a male reader's comment on and mimesis of *Peony Pavilion*, since he simply followed Tang's original version in playwriting rather than any other literati's revisions. In this way, 'Tiqu' could be interpreted as a metaphoric 'drama review' or a miniature 'abridged adaptation' of *Peony Pavilion*.

Another critic, Pan Zhiheng, a friend of Tang and an avid theatregoer, discussed lots of actors and their performances in his anecdotes. He made comments on a performance of *Peony Pavilion* by a family troupe:

> Wu Yueshi, a fellow member of my club, owns a family troupe of young actors. Once Wu ordered his actors to perform the play [*Peony Pavilion*]. The actor's figure, swaying and flickering, stirred my vision in most tiny ambiguous motions, my sorrows drifted beyond the tones. His singing and performing was so perfect, without one word lost, without any detail overlooked.[21]

Clearly, as both a member of the audience and a critic, Pan and the actors on stage all enjoyed each word and each detail of Tang's text. Pan tried to convey the most astute observation; for him, *Peony Pavilion* could inspire the souls of the actors and their audience in part through the interplay between the sublime lyrics and the performance. Pan's essay was titled 'Qingchi' (the man who was obsessed with passion) and the source of *qing* 情 (passion) in this case comes from the performance of Tang's powerful words.

No wonder the literati's revisions were doomed to failure. Another critic, Mao Yuanyi 茅元儀 (1594–1640), expressed the following opinion on Zang Maoxun's revision: 'Reading Zang's revision, I was annoyed with its mediocre words put in the original extraordinary plots, its mediocre tunes put in the original extraordinary words, and its mediocre rhymes put in the original extraordinary tunes. The playwright's [Tang Xianzu's] delicate design was totally spoiled; to the extent that it cannot even compare to most ordinary works.'[22] Obviously, any person who dared to revise Tang's words would be challenged on the level of literariness, as well as on the level of elegance, passion and rhetoric skill. It is amazing that actors, critics and audiences all stand on the side of literary value, rather than Zang's preference for stage value.

The tension between words and music continued and was not resolved until decades after Tang's death. A musical connoisseur, Niu Shaoya 鈕少雅 (1564–after 1651), composed a work titled *Corrected Musical Tunes of Peony Pavilion* (*Gezheng Huanhun ji cidiao* 格正還魂記詞調, posthumously prefaced in 1694). Here only arias (song texts) are printed and dialogues and stage directions are not included.[23] Niu focused on amending the errors by amending the tunes but not the words. After Niu, the most successful and influential composer was Ye Tang 葉堂 (1724?–97?), a legendary musician in the history of Chinese drama who published all of the entire 'adjusted' music notations of Tang's *Four Dreams* in 1792 and solved the controversies among Tang's opponents through his professional skill of composing. His strategy was to emend the musical errors by following Tang's original words. Since Ye Tang did his work, there is no longer any problem in singing *Peony Pavilion*. His book of music notation is significant in affirming the priority of Tang's text over the other literati's endeavours at revision. As Ye Tang explains in his rules of notation, 'because of the excellence of Tang's text, I did not dare to change it casually, so I change the tunes in various ways to fit in his words'.[24]

Ye Tang also embodies the opinions of singers and actors through the ultimate method of expression. In contrast to some of the literati's revisions, those who actually performed Tang Xianzu's work revealed more of its literary value. Selected pieces in miscellanies maintained Tang's original taste for the delicacy of each scene or aria, while Ye Tang's full-length notations re-established a way in which Tang Xianzu's words could be fulfilled musically. These different kinds of audience reception suggest that it was almost impossible to revise or imitate a work of genius satisfactorily. Any rules or laws that are applied to it seem inferior to the work itself. Hence, around 1616, we find the best playwright in the history of Chinese drama, and also the most talented actors, readers and critics as audience in the history of theatre. The interplay which took place between the playwright and his audience, both his opponents and his supporters, gives us a glimpse of the unlimited exploration on Tang Xianzu and the theatrical landscape of his times.

Notes

1   This essay was inspired by Catherine C. Swatek, *Peony Pavilion Onstage: Four Centuries in the Career of a Chinese Drama* (Ann Arbor: The University of Michigan, 2002).

2   Shen Defu, *Wanli yehuo bian* (Beijing: Zhonghua shuju, 1997), p. 643.

3   Ibid.

4   See, for example, Zang Maoxun's preface to his recension of Tang Xianzu's plays as quoted in Stephen West's essay (Section 5.1) in this volume.

5   Xu Shuofang thought Lü's revision was actually Shen Jing's: Lü sent Shen's revision to Tang Xianzu after deleting the author's name, so Tang mistakenly thought it was Lü's work. See Xu Shuofang, 'Guanyu Tang Xianzu Shen Jing guanxi de yixie shishi', in idem, *Xu Shuofang Ji* (Hangzhou: Zhejiang guji chubanshe, 1993). On the contrary, Zhou Yude supported the actual existence of Lü's revision. See Zhou Yude, 'Lüjia gaide ji qita', in idem, *Tang Xianzu lungao* (Beijing: Wenhua

yishu chubanshe, 1991), pp. 303–8. Since both Lü's and Shen's complete revisions are no longer extant, this is still a controversial issue today.

6   Tang Xianzu, 'Da Ling Chucheng', in Xu Shuofang, ed., *Tang Xianzu quanji*, p. 1442.

7   Tang, 'Da Sun Siju', ibid., p. 1392.

8   The most representative argument on this issue is Zhou Yude, 'Yetan xiqushi shang de Tang Shen zhizheng' 也談戲曲史上的湯沈之爭, in idem, *Tang Xianzu lungao*, Beijing: Wenhua yishu chubanshe, 1991, pp. 264–80.

9   Feng Menglong, 'Xiaoyin', in *Feng Menglong quanji*, ed. Wei Tongxian (Nanjing: Jiangsu guji chubanshe, 1993), pp. 1047–8.

10   Ibid, p. 1047.

11   All these four woodblock, late Ming edition miscellanies have been published in the form of photocopies, collected in a series compiled by Wang Ch'iu-kuei et al., *Shanben xiqu congkan* (Taipei: Xuesheng shuju, 1984–7).

12   Shen Zijin 沈自晉 (comp.), *Nanci xinpu* 南詞新譜, photolithographic reprint in *Shanben xiqu congkan* 善本戲曲叢刊 (Taipei: Taiwan xuesheng shuju, 1984), vols 29–30.

13   The form of notations in this book is marked by tonal patterns (*pingze* 平仄) through the examples of individual arias, unlike the notations of musical scores (*gongchi pu* 工尺譜) as in the later period.

14   This is an alternative title of Shen Jing's *Tongmeng ji*.

15   In Zang Maoxun's version, this aria was under the tune pattern *Jintang fan*, but Shen Zijin in his book corrected it to the tune pattern *Zhoujin huamei* and changed quite a few words within it.

16   Shen Zijin used Tang's original words of this aria *Fanshan hu* in Scene 48 'Mother and Daughter Reunited', but then on the next page he used Shen Jing's revision in this aria as a contrast (changing the tune title to *Manshan yi*).

17   Shen Zijin gave two examples of Tang's aria *Fanshan hu*, so the second one would be marked as 'another *qu* (another example of this aria)'.

18 Zhang Dafu, 'Yuniang', in *Meihua caotang bitan quanshu*, vol. 7 (Beijing: Quanguo tushuguan wenxian suowei fuzhi zhongxin, 2006), pp. 470–3.

19 Shen Mingsun's words are recorded in *Jianfang eshutang xianbi*, which could only be found partially in Jiao Xun's *Jushuo*. See *Jushuo*, in *Zhongguo gudian xiqu lunzhu jicheng* series (Beijing: Zhongguo xiqu chubanshe, 1959), vol. 8, p. 197.

20 Wu Bin, 'Tiqu' 題曲, in *Liaodu Geng* 療妒羹, in Liu Shiheng (ed.), *Nuanhongshi huike Canhuazhai wuzhong* (Yangzhou: Guangling guji Keyinshe, 1982), pp. 33a–37a.

21 Pan Zhiheng, 'Qingchi: guanyan Mudanting huanhunji shuzeng erru', in Wang Xiaoyi (comp. and annot.), *Pan Zhiheng quhua* (Beijing: Zhongguo xiju chubanshe, 1988), p. 72.

22 Mao Yuanyi, 'Pidian Mudan tingji xu', cited from *Tang Xianzu quanji*, p. 2574.

23 Niu Shaoya, *Gezheng Huanhun Ji Cidiao*, in Liu Shiheng (ed.), *Nuanhongshi huike Linchuan Simeng* (Yangzhou: *Guangling* guji keyinshe, 1981).

24 Ye Tang, 'Fanli' 凡例 of *Nashuying simeng quanpu*, in *Xuxiu Siku Quanshu* edition (Shanghai: Shanghai guji chubanshe, 2002), p. 170.

7.2 'No epilogue, I pray you': Audience reception in Shakespearean theatre

Anjna Chouhan

Citizen   *I will have a citizen, and he shall be of my own trade.*
Prologue   *Oh, you should have told us your mind a month since.*
Our play is ready to begin now.

FRANCIS BEAUMONT, *THE KNIGHT OF THE BURNING PESTLE,*
'INDUCTION', LL. 30–3

In Tanya Pollard's essay on audience reception in *The Oxford Handbook of Shakespeare*, she argues that records of audience responses in this period come from extreme ends of the spectrum, what she calls 'anti-theatricalists' and theatre 'defenders', with this significant caveat: 'of course, neither anti-theatricalists nor defenders of the theatre are necessarily *reliable* witnesses of how audiences responded to plays'.[1] Pollard's observation is also applicable to the reverse situation – playwrights' responses to their audiences. Plays themselves offer important insights into audience management from the stage-end, as well as playwright interpretations of audience conduct and function, though they are self-evidently biased. Andrew Gurr suggests that 'the complex interactive communication between stage and audience [...] depends as much on the audience's state of mind as it does on the author's and players' expectations of what, mentally, their audience will be prepared for'.[2]

Using audience or consumer expectations as an anchor – and with a focus on, but not limited to, Shakespeare – this essay explores how the people frequenting playhouses in the early 1600s were at the forefront of playwrights' imaginations and anxieties. The distinction between audience and author, and their respective influences on any given play, is one that echoes concerns in Shih-pe Wang's companion piece to this essay about audience reception of textual adaptations of Tang Xianzu's play *Peony Pavilion* in early seventeenth-century China. By the term 'audience reception' I am asking whether audiences shaped and influenced what was being performed on stage. And by 'audience' I mean frequenters of playhouses, rather than other playwrights or actors.

There were two ways in which an audience could legitimately influence a play: at the writing stage and at the performance stage. The first is perhaps the most obvious. That playwrights had to consider, create and presumably direct players with an audience in mind can be taken for granted. In 1620, the printer introducing C. J.'s *The Two Merry Milkmaids* stated that every writer 'must govern his pen according to the capacity of the stage he writes to, both in the actor and the auditor'.[3] Though the players are part of the raw materials available to the early modern playwright, the audience was considered, at least in this case, vital to the writing process.[4]

Audiences – though simultaneously the consumers and critics of any play – were considered limiting, restrictive and a body of people for whom artistic integrity would have to be sacrificed. Pleasing those audiences had to be a priority as Webster, Dekker and Jonson lamented at various points in their careers. Gurr's study of terminology within the early modern theatrical world has revealed different ways in which playwrights conceptualized their audiences: namely as spectators, hearers or auditors.[5]

So how is this reflected in Shakespeare's work? In the early part of his career, he imagines his audience as a body capable of commenting on, interrupting and engaging with a play – without much sympathy for the actors. In *Love's Labour's Lost* (c. 1594) the amateur actors perform the 'Pageant of the

Nine Worthies', but not one of the actors is able to complete his performance for the constant interruptions of the audience. Here, the play's consumers are at liberty to mock, interfere with and change the performance proper. At the other end of Shakespeare's career, in around 1610, he reconsiders this audience agency in *The Tempest*. Here, the word 'audience' is not used. Instead, Prospero instructs the play's observers thus: 'no tongue! all eyes! be silent!' (4.1.59). This suggests that audience expectations, desires and responses came to represent something unwelcome rather than useful to the actors and even the playwright – in this case, Prospero, the creator of the entertainment. We shift, in a very crude way, over the course of Shakespeare's career as fictional audience creator, from hissing to silent audience members: from verbal to visual.

How playwrights chose to distinguish between the visual and aural was indicative of their attitudes towards the consumers of their work. For instance, Jonson listed the usual make-up of an audience in his induction to the 1614 comedy *Bartholomew Fair*, first performed at the Hope theatre by Lady Elizabeth's Men:

> it is covenanted and agreed, by and between the parties abovesaid, and the said spectators and hearers, as well the curious and envious, as the favouring and judicious, as also the grounded judgments and understandings, do for themselves severally covenant, and agree to remain in the places, their money or friends have put them in, with patience, for the space of two hours and a half, and somewhat more.[6]

Jonson asks that audiences remain in their allotted positions – spectators and hearers alike. Gurr points out that Jonson associates the hearers with favour and judiciousness, while the spectators are envious. The groundlings here are judgemental and prone to formulate their own 'understanding' of the play, rather than consider the playwright's motive, for instance. Such assumptions about the groundlings seem invariably dismissive, not just from Jonson but also much earlier in the period. Puttenham, in his *Art of English Poesie* (1589), claimed that comedies, in particular, are intended 'much for the solace and recreation of the common people by reason of the pageants and shows'.[7] Again the emphasis is on the visual nature of theatre as ocular, recreational entertainment over and above being thoughtful or intellectually engaging. Shakespeare too laments the desire of groundlings for laughter at the expense of the play in *Hamlet* (c. 1600). He notes that the groundlings are for the most part 'capable of nothing but inexplicable dumb-shows and noise' (3.2.11–13). Together with his call for silence from the audience in *The Tempest*, it is tempting to claim that Shakespeare thought quiet, visually and aurally engaged audience members were ideal.

Theatre historians have observed that while playwrights wrote for different companies of players throughout their careers, from Lyly and Marlowe to Shakespeare and Fletcher, they did become associated with specific theatres and, by extension, the audiences who frequented those playhouses. This forms the most striking parallel between Chinese and English audience–playwright relationships in the period, because traditional Chinese plays were written by and performed for the learned. Scholars were producing work for other scholars: stories of students falling in love with beautiful courtesans, and musical composition, were calculated to be recognizable by repeat audiences in spaces that were not, by definition, theatres. Plays in England were suited to the play*house* and plays in China were for one unique audience.

Audiences in England came in different shapes and sizes. And we do know that audiences had reputations at specific playhouses. Marston's epilogue to *Jack Drum's Entertainment* in 1600 mentions the types of people frequenting the Paul's company, calling them 'a good gentle audience':

I'faith I like the audience that frequenteth there
With much applause: a man shall nor be choked

> With the stench of garlicke, nor be pasted
> To the barmy jacket of a beer-brewer.[8]

A play written for performance in the open-air Red Bull, for instance, was not considered fit for central London Blackfriars audiences. Equally, Jonson's plays produced for the Children of the Chapel boy players were not suitable for public amphitheatre audiences at the Globe, at least in theory.

While it is tempting to draw a clear demarcation between plays designed for indoor and public audiences, in real terms the shifting of a single play between the two locations is hard to trace through the texts themselves, most obviously because surviving texts were published after revisions were made. Alexander Leggatt explains this problem more eloquently:

> stylistically individual scripts do not always follow the traditions associated with their playhouses. If we did not know that one was performed at the Globe and the other at the Swan, we would think of *The Revenger's Tragedy* and *A Chaste Maid in Cheap Side* as private-theatre plays. … after 1617 the former repertoire of the public Red Bull would be seen at the private Cockpit. Even within the public tradition, plays did not stay in one place.[9]

Since plays and players moved around, it is natural to assume that playwrights or even the actors themselves adjusted, edited and adapted their plays for different spaces.

But the problem was that an audience was never a passive entity: their involvement and reactions were a necessary aspect of the playhouse experience. And audience experience differed according to playhouse. Theatre historian Tiffany Stern argues that the actual process of observing and hearing a play in a private theatre would have felt less whole or complete than in an amphitheatre, open-air performance. The frequent breaks and interludes fragmented the otherwise linear narrative story-telling, making the plot less complete for both audience and player. This is just one problem requiring, presumably, specific methods of audience management according to each playhouse.

Another, more perplexing, matter for playwrights was the issue of in-house interruptions from the audience. In Beaumont's satire *The Knight of the Burning Pestle*, performed in 1607 in a private theatre, most likely transferring later to Blackfriars, representative audience members in the forms of a grocer and his wife turn director and writer, collectively. Here Beaumont draws attention to the centrality of any given audience in any given playhouse. The players and their play are overshadowed by the new plot imposed on them by the audience. In spite of the play at hand, all our hypothetical audience members seem to desire is a story about a grocer who kills a lion with a pestle. Though satirical, the play reveals authorial concerns about audience interaction, interpretation and, ultimately, adaptation of plays. Beaumont's satire, as well as ridiculing the agency hall plays apparently gave to their audiences, expresses anxiety about pleasing those same customers at face-level, during the performance itself.

In real terms, though, this is all fictional. The audience in *Love's Labour's Lost*, the silent couple watching the masque in *The Tempest* and the grocer's family in *Pestle* are not real: they are representations of what is or is not to be expected from live audiences. So how did audiences actually respond to what they were observing/hearing onstage? One striking, and frankly unusual, record of audience reaction is a letter written in Latin by a student, Henry Jackson, at Oxford in 1610 in response to a performance of *Othello* (1603–4) by the King's Men. As well as complaining about impious dialogues and actors, Jackson explains that the players performed *Othello* with movement, facial expressions and speech so striking that they became emotive, moving audience members to tears.

At vero Desdimona illa apud nos a marito occisa,
quanquam optime semper causam egit, interfecta tamen

magis movebat, cum in lecto discumbens spectantium misericordiam ipso vultu imploraret.[10]

In Tillotson's translation, it was Desdemona's dying face that 'implored the pity of the spectators'.[11] Such emotional reaction does not compare with the extreme example Shih-pe Wang offers of Shang Xiaoling who died of heartbreak while performing the role of love-struck Du Liniang. However, Jackson's letter provides useful insight into the *audience* experience. He does not refer to the actor playing a character, but writes about Desdemona and *her* sorrow, *her* experience. In this case, it is the spectator and auditor being moved to tears, rather than the actor him or herself.

Notwithstanding Jackson's record of distress at Desdemonda's plight, what the average individual thought about any given performance cannot be assumed to be representative of 'audience' attitude or experience in the early 1600s. Gurr notes that the astrologer Simon Forman in particular 'thought of each play as if it were a drama-tized romance narrative, with incidental lessons that could be drawn by a naive individual from the activities of tricky characters'.[12] The student John Manningham's diary entry for 1602 recalls a performance of *Twelfth Night* (1601) at a feast which, rather infamously now, he seems to have misre-membered – prioritizing the character of Malvolio above all others, mistaking Olivia for a widow rather than a grieving sister and misquoting Italian comedy.[13] In addition, Forman's notes about a performance of *The Winter's Tale* (1609–10) at the Globe, for example, indicate that the most memorable detail was the character of Autolycus. Clearly, the banishment of Hermione and subsequent grief of Leontes were not worth noting down. Similarly, from the performance of *Macbeth*, Forman noted the appearance of Banquo's ghost, the slaughter of the Macduff children and the doctor writing down Lady Macbeth's midnight utterances. Gurr's phrase 'incidental lessons' seems apt here, but it is curious that these 'romance narrative' interpretations came from the uninterrupted public performances at the Globe, rather than from the indoor playhouses with their broken, staggered plots. Yet even with a linear narrative, Manningham and Forman seem to have recalled only minor plot details as part of their play-going experiences.

To complicate matters further, audience experience seems to have been affected by the presence of students. Frequent rows broke out between students (invariably from the Inns of Court) and actors. Evidently, young men had a lot to say and interject into performances – both public and private. A list of rules distributed to students at Cambridge upon the occasion of a royal visit bans the use of tobacco, prohibits any standing or loitering about at the beginning of the play, as well as stating that no 'rude or immodest exclamations be made; nor any humming, hawking, whistling, hissing, or laughing be used, or any stamping or knocking, nor any such other uncivil or unscholarlike or boyish demeanour, upon any occasion; nor that any clapping of hands be had until the *Plaudite* at the end of the Comedy'.[14]

Such an extensive list of items is indeed revealing, for while these were loud, boisterous young men, they were also presumably mimicking usual public audience behaviour, categorized here as 'unscholarlike'.

Presumably, if new plays were being performed for such occasions, playwrights and players would be conscious of trigger points with their audiences. One can't imagine a silent playhouse filled with students at *Henry VI, Part II* when Dick the butcher exclaims 'let's kill all the lawyers' (4.2.74). In fact, as far as Tiffany Stern can make out, plays were adapted according to audience responses. According to Stern, 'plays were written in long form first and potentially shortened in the light of performance; one reason for long versions of published plays is that they may be in first-performance state; shorter texts may show that cutting has been made in the light of audience criticism'.[15]

Naturally, playwrights were in the business of entertaining audiences. But given that audience responses are immediate, contagious and irreversible, the texts in their 'first performance' state, to borrow Stern's terminology, may not resemble the post-performance texts that circulated in print after revisions. It is preferable, and logical, to do as much as possible beforehand (i.e. at the creative stage) so as to avoid unpleasant responses in the playhouse. There is some fascinating speculation about first-performance tricks to ensure audience cooperation. The 'Induction' to John Day's ill-fated political satire *The Isle of Gulls* (1606) seems to suggest that playwrights actively planted their companions in the audience to rally and cheer the players in an attempt to stir up audience spirit:

> 2 GENT. Hath he not a prepared company of gallants, to applaud his jests, and grace out his play?
>
> PROLOGUE None, I protest. Do poets use to bespeak their auditory?
>
> 2 GENT. The best in grace do ...[16]

Are we to conclude that audience members were planted amid the crowds to cheer and laugh at appropriate moments to encourage others to enjoy the performance? It seems an alluring assumption.

Of course, such actions are indicative of authorial anxiety about audiences disapproving or misjudging the play itself. Hence, Stern argues, the frequency of prologues and epilogues throughout the period. Shakespeare's own plays often express anxiety about audience responses; even *A Midsummer Night's Dream* (1595), a play about fairies and love-juice, is fitted with an apologetic epilogue to appease potentially disappointed spectators. Over a decade later, anticipating audience responses, Jonson wrote in his 'Induction on the Stage' to *Bartholomew Fair* (1614): 'It is further covenanted, concluded and agreed, that how great soever the expectation be, no person here, is to expect more than he knows, or better ware then a fair will afford: neither to look back to the sword-and-bucklerage of Smithfield, but content himself with the present.'[17]

By this logic, audiences should not treat playhearing/observing/going as a comparative activity; rather, each play must be judged according to its own merits and weakness. This is why so many frameworking narratives in the forms of prologues and epilogues exist: they approach, warn and apologize to the audience for what they are about to or have just seen. They operate like a pre-theatre agreement or disclosure intellectually and artistically to withhold responsibility for any dissatisfaction. This is not surprising, especially in the light of Jason Scott-Warren's essay in this volume (Section 5.2) on early modern play publication and Shakespeare's, in particular, apparent indifference to it. If a play was neither profitable nor widely circulated in print form, then a playwright's success had to be determined by audiences.

This explains why audience reputations gave playwrights flexibility to blame their less successful works on reception. Webster famously complained about his Red Bull audience in the epistle to *The White Devil*, published in 1612: 'most of the people that come to that playhouse, resemble those ignorant asses who visiting stationers' shops, their use is not to inquire for good books, but new books ...'.[18] For Webster, the only thing wrong with the performance was the lack of 'a full and understanding auditory'.[19] In this case he transitioned to print, thereby gaining a new kind of audience: a readership rather than auditors. Here, the play was in no way altered or edited to please the theatre audience. Fortunately for Webster, later Jacobean audiences of the finer indoor playhouses acquired a taste for *The White Devil*, thereby securing its place in the canon of great early modern tragedy.

The most tangible example of adaptation or revision comes from the few examples of post-performance complaints and lawsuits, which indicate that factual errors and offensive references could be edited out of plays. This is where the editing and rewriting, or in the case of Shakespeare, renaming came into play. Most famously, in the mid-1590s, Shakespeare was forced to rename his historical character, Sir John Oldcastle, creating the ever-popular Sir John Falstaff in his place. The less documented kind of revision comes from the nature of playing companies as repertory players. Gurr notes that with growing playing companies, playwrights were increasingly prolific, meaning that audiences came to expect new offerings on a weekly, sometimes daily basis. In turn, new plays were mingled with older plays to create a repertory unique to each company. Roslyn Knutson's study of repertory systems in the early 1600s indicates that, in Shakespeare's case, the acquisition of Blackfriars informed both the writing and choice of plays undertaken by the King's Men. But the Revels Account for court performances in spring 1604 includes *Measure for Measure*, *Othello*, *The Comedy of Errors*, *Love's Labour's Lost*, *The Merchant of Venice*, *The Merry Wives of Windsor* and *Henry V*. Most of these were old plays, revived and possibly adapted for court.[20] Any number of revisions could have been made to these plays, in some cases ten years after their first performances. But, as Gary Taylor notes, the cost of hiring the playwright to produce additional scenes or make alterations, or even a stand-in playwright to adapt an older work, coupled with the expense of replacing worn-out costumes and props, would suggest that only the popular plays were worth reviving.[21] In short, not new, specially commissioned works, but the familiar plays were what audiences wanted.

So while this does not alter current thinking about audience reception in the early 1600s, it does place emphasis on the agency that audiences – in whatever shape and size – had in the writing and performing of a play, in a way that highlights the more scholarly concerns of Chinese theatre at the time. Whereas in China adaptation and revision were matters for learned argument, they were, in England, an ongoing dialogue between playwright and audience. Stern concludes her chapter on prologues and epilogues by arguing that 'in performance (at least after c. 1600) stage-orations broadcasted a play's virginity and its author's fear, and were therefore a site of tension between author and play'.[22] Fear and tension are terms that conceptualize one aspect of a playwright's relationship with his audience. But I would argue that with this fear came a degree of admiration for an audience's ability to reserve such objective judgement for any performance. Playwrights like Shakespeare needed audiences and were dependent on them, but simultaneously were cautious and even manipulative. So when, in A Midsummer Night's Dream, Theseus claims that he wants neither an excuse nor an epilogue for the short piece 'Pyramus and Thisbe', and when Beaumont's grocer and his wife interpolate Rafe into their performance, it is the audience and not the players dictating the performance: its content, length and even the peripheral entertainments. The irony is that these playwrights have *written* those audiences and their responses, regaining their authorial and authoritative position, and manipulating true audience members into believing that every play is designed for and directed towards them. For all the lamentations and trepidations of the playwrights, it seems that playgoers in London by 1616, whether they were ignorant asses or learned ears, were led to believe that they were the real test of a play's quality and endurance. Though this was most likely the case, it is amusing that in spite of Theseus's call to skip the epilogue to the play-within-the-play, Shakespeare proceeded to bolt one onto the end of his, along with something approaching an apology: 'Gentles, do not reprehend. / If you pardon, we will mend' (5.1. 423–4).

Notes

1   Tanya Pollard, 'Audience Reception', in Arthur Kinney (ed.), *The Oxford Handbook of Shakespeare* (Oxford: Oxford University Press, 2012), pp. 458–73, 466.

2   Andrew Gurr, *Playgoing in Shakespeare's London*, 3rd edn (Cambridge: Cambridge University Press, 2004), p. 6.

3   C. J., *The Two Merry Milkmaids. Or, The Best Words Weare The Garland*, George Harold Metz (ed.) (New York: Garland, 1979), p. 3.

4   See Gary Taylor, 'Shakespeare Plays on Renaissance Stages', in Stanley Wells and Sarah Stanton (eds), *The Cambridge Companion to Shakespeare on Stage* (Cambridge: Cambridge University Press, 2002), pp. 1–20.

5   Gurr, *Playgoing in Shakespeare's London*, pp. 102–24.

6   Ben Jonson, *Bartholomew Fair*, in David Bevington, Lars Engle, Katharine Eisaman Maus and Eric Rasmussen (eds), *English Renaissance Drama: A Norton Anthology* (London: W. W. Norton & Co. Inc., 2002), p. 973.

7   George Puttenham, *The Arte of English Poesie*, A Facsimile of the Edition of 1589 (Menston: Scolar Press, 1968), p. 47.

8   John Marston, *Jack Drum's Entertainment*, quoted in Gurr, *Playgoing in Shakespeare's London*, p. 259.

9   Alexander Leggatt, *Jacobean Public Theatre* (Abingdon: Routledge, 1992), p. 3.

10   Latin letter of 1610 by Henry Jackson, translated in Geoffrey Tillotson, '*Othello* and *The Alchemist* at Oxford', *Times Literary Supplement* (20 July 1933), p. 494.

11   Ibid.

12   Gurr, *Playgoing in Shakespeare's London*, p. 135.

13   John Manningham, *The Diary of John Manningham*, Robert Parker Sorlien (ed.) (Hanover: University Press of New England, 1976), p. 48.

14   Quoted in Gurr, *Playgoing in Shakespeare's London*, p. 288.

15   Tiffany Stern, *Documents of Performance in Early Modern England* (Cambridge: Cambridge University Press, 2009), p. 92.

16   John Day, *John Day's Isle of Gulls: A Critical Edition*, Raymond S. Burns (ed.) (New York: Garland, 1980).

17   Ben Jonson, *Bartholomew Fair*, in Bevington et al., *English Renaissance Drama*, p. 973.

18   John Webster, *The White Devil*, in Bevington et al., *English Renaissance Drama*, p. 1664.

19   Ibid.

20   Roslyn L. Knutson, 'Repertory System', in idem, *The Oxford Handbook of Shakespeare*, ed. Arthur Kinney (Oxford: Oxford University Press, 2012), pp. 404–19, 416–17.

21 Taylor, 'Shakespeare Plays on Renaissance Stages', pp. 17–19.

22 Stern, *Documents of Performance in Early Modern England*, p. 117.

8

Music and performance

What was the role of music in theatre productions? Arias and songs which were integral to the dramas also circulated separately and readily migrated from play to play. How was theatrical music structured, styled and received in the two cultures?

8.1 Seeking the relics of music and performance: An investigation of Chinese theatrical scenes published in the early seventeenth century (1606–16)

Mei Sun

An indirect but necessary approach

The most difficult part about exploring Chinese theatrical and musical performance of the early seventeenth century is the paucity of relevant information. First of all, there are no audio-visual records of Chinese theatre in the seventeenth century, and the performances of generations of performers have vanished in the long process of history. Second, there is an insufficiency of written records, since little information regarding theatrical practices in China has ever been written down. In particular, any *xiqu* 戲曲 (literally 'theatre of song') scores from this period that may have been written are no longer extant. *Xiqu* is a generic term covering a wide variety of theatrical forms that synthesize singing, acting, reciting, acrobatics and martial arts in stylized and conventionalized performances. The earliest surviving texts are a number of *kunqu* 崑曲 (literally 'songs from Kunshan') scores dated 1720.[1] *Kunqu* is a *xiqu* form with a history of around five hundred years. In 2001, for the first time, the United Nations Educational, Scientific and Cultural Organization (UNESCO) awarded the title of 'Masterpieces of the Oral and Intangible Heritage of Humanity' to nineteen outstanding cultural spaces or forms of expression from the different regions of the world. *Kunqu* is on the list.

Fortunately, we may obtain some relevant information through a close reading of the extant lines and stage directions of various *chuanqi* 傳奇 (literally 'transmission of the marvellous') scenes, the most popular *xiqu* form during the early seventeenth century. A *chuanqi* play consists of dozens of scenes, so many that it had to be performed over the course of several days and nights. Therefore, complete *chuanqi* plays were rarely presented; most *chuanqi* performances included only the most brilliant scenes. During the Ming Wanli period (1573–1620), a number of collections of popular *xiqu* scenes were compiled and commercially published by bookshops.[2] However, for the most part these popular scenes were not directly extracted from the original plays in their entirety. Instead, they were very likely passed down from one generation of performers to the next, during the course of which various changes were introduced. By carefully comparing the scenes in these collections with their counterparts in the earlier and complete versions of the plays in question, we are able to acquire some useful information on the theatrical performances of the early seventeenth century.

The texts discussed

Among the collections of popular scenes published during the Ming Wanli period, four appeared between 1606 and 1616. They are: *The First Branch in the Lyric Forest* (*Cilin yizhi* 詞林一枝, hereafter abbreviated as *CLYZ*), published in 1606 or 1607;[3] *An Anthology of Brocaded and Splendid Songs* (*Zhaijin qiyin* 摘錦奇音, hereafter abbreviated as *ZJQY*), published in 1611;[4] *Assembling Elegant Songs in Suzhou* (*Wuyu cuiya* 吳歈萃雅) published in 1616;[5] and *Sounds like Dew under the Moonlight* (*Yue lu yin* 月露音), also published in 1616.[6] Unfortunately, the latter two 1616 examples do not provide much information on how the theatrical performance was actually carried out, since they are anthologies of sung arias without any spoken lines or stage directions.

It is not possible to examine every scene in both *CLYZ* and *ZJQY*, so I shall look at the scenes originally from *The Lute*

(*Pipa ji* 琵琶記) as representative samples,[7] and compare these with their counterparts in the earliest complete edition of *The Lute* yet known. During the Ming and Qing dynasties, *The Lute* was printed or hand-copied numerous times in various editions, around forty of which have survived.[8] However, the original edition of *The Lute* was lost several hundred years ago, and the earliest edition found to date is a hand-copied version of *The Newly Printed Yuan Edition of 'Cai Bojie and the Lute'* (*Xinkan yuanben Cai Bojie pipa ji* 新刊元本蔡伯喈琵琶記, hereafter abbreviated as the *Yuan Edition*) dated 1548. Based on textual analysis, most Chinese scholars believe that this text has largely preserved the essential features of the original edition of this masterpiece.[9]

As regards the number of scenes from *The Lute* included in *CLYZ* and *ZJQY*, I found that the former contains five, while the latter includes nine, only two of which are common to both collections. One of these is the scene where the female protagonist longs for her newly-wed husband who has gone far away from home; the other is the scene where the male protagonist misses his first wife and his elderly parents at the Mid-autumn Festival (the Moon Festival), traditionally an important time for family reunions.

Before presenting the comparative study, I will first provide a synopsis of *The Lute*. At the outset of the play Cai Bojie – the male protagonist – prefers to stay at home with his newly-wed wife and take care of his elderly parents. However, his father, eager to bring glory to the family, forces him to take the imperial examination. As a filial son, Bojie complies and leaves home for the capital. As it turns out, the talented young scholar passes the imperial examination, thereby becoming a *zhuangyuan* 狀元 (top-ranking scholar), and the emperor soon orders him to marry the prime minister's daughter. Bojie endeavours to decline the marriage, but fails. While enjoying a comfortable life with his second wife, the daughter of the prime minister, he secretly worries about his parents and his first wife back in his home town. Zhao Wuniang – Bojie's first wife – endures all manner of hardship while looking after her invalid parents-in-law, who long for their only son. After the old couple die during a famine, she leaves home penniless and sets out for the capital. In the course of her journey, Wuniang earns a living by playing her *pipa* 琵琶 (lute). After several setbacks, she finally reunites with her husband.

Annotating obscure literary allusions

In the scene depicting Wuniang longing for her husband, the *Yuan Edition* contains five *qupai* 曲牌 (tune titles), each including a passage of sung arias. A *qupai* is a fixed melody and prosodic pattern. Each of these patterns has a fixed number of lines, but these lines vary in length. Extrametrical syllables known as *chenzi* 襯字 (padding words) may be added to these lines without changing the basic prosodic pattern. According to musical logic, individual *qupai* are organized into a *taoshu* 套數 (song suite). The musical structure used in *The Lute* is called *lianqu ti* 聯曲 體 (joined-song form) by modern scholars. Obviously, melodies are reused in the joined-song form. Coincidentally, a roughly similar situation can also be seen in the theatre of the English Renaissance as discussed by David Lindley in the companion piece to this essay. *ZJQY* includes all five of these *qupai*. However, in *CLYZ* this scene begins with the second *qupai*, omitting the first *qupai* and a long monologue.

In the scene depicting Cai Bojie at the Mid-autumn Festival, the *Yuan Edition* consists of nine *qupai*. In this scene *CLYZ* again begins from the second *qupai*, but *ZJQY* preserves all nine. Moreover, all the sung arias in both collections are almost exactly the same as those in the *Yuan Edition*, but a great deal of spoken lines have been added. Basically, these lines are written in the colloquial language, and are employed to explain the many classical allusions that appear in the arias. For instance, in the *Yuan Edition*'s scene depicting Cai Bojie at the Mid-autumn Festival, in the fifth *qupai* the following lyrics are sung by Cai's second wife, the prime minister's daughter:

Lustrous light!
I want to blow the jade panpipes till they break,
Mount on a phoenix and return to the moon,
But I wonder if the wind is cold in that immortal city?
My jade ornaments are moistened with dew,
Just like Fei-ch'iung as she returned to the moon.
And more,
With these clouds of perfumed hair,
Dazzling arms of jade,
I'm the equal of the moon goddess herself.[10]

光瑩
我欲吹斷玉蕭
驂鸞歸去
不知風露冷瑤京
環珮濕
似月下歸來飛瓊
那更
香鬟雲鬢
清輝玉臂
廣寒仙子也堪並[11]

In fact, the above translation is easier to understand than
the original Chinese verse, for Mulligan adds material only
hinted at in the original (for example, the third line of the
Chinese original does not mention the moon). Nevertheless,
the translator still found it necessary to include two footnotes
further explaining the classical allusions in the passage.[12]

In a live performance, however, the audience is not
provided with written footnotes. How, then, were these
classical allusions explained in a performance put on some
four hundred years ago? Taking the same verse in *ZJQY* as
an example, annotations in the form of spoken lines were
inserted as follows:

Lustrous light
(Once upon a time, the daughter of Mugong, the King of

Qin, whose name was Nongyu, got married to Xiaoshi.
The couple often played vertical flutes on a raised
terrace. One day, a phoenix flew down to them; the
couple mounted the phoenix and disappeared beyond the
horizon. Afterwards the terrace became known as the
'Phoenix Terrace.' ...)[13]
I want to blow the jade panpipes till they break,
Mount on a phoenix and return to the moon ...

光莹
昔有秦穆公之女名喚弄玉，後來配與蕭史為妻。夫婦二人
吹蕭於臺上。一日鳳凰自天而下，夫婦乘鸞而去。遺下一
台名曰鳳凰臺 ...
我欲吹斷玉蕭
驂鸞歸去[14]

Undoubtedly, such a spoken annotation made the verse more
intelligible to the audience.

A special device within the joined-song structure

Regarding the annotations inserted into the arias, one special
kind of device must be noted. As explained above, a *qupai*
contains a fixed number of lines which are irregular in length.
In both *CLYZ* and *ZJQY*, however, poems with lines of regular
length (usually five or seven characters)[15] were frequently
inserted into the original arias. For example, in the *Yuan
Edition*, in the second *qupai* of the scene depicting Wuniang
longing for her husband, Wuniang sings the following lyrics:

He was forced to go to the spring examination;
Our love knot had just been tied.
Alas, the sounds of 'Yang-kuan' died away,
And I saw you off from Nan-p'u.[16]

春闈催赴
同心帶綰初
歎陽關聲斷
送別南浦[17]

But in its counterpart in *CLYZ* a poem with seven-character
lines was inserted into the lyrics:

He was forced to go to the spring examination;
    (I remember when we first got married,
    The fragrant ribbon bound in a lovers' knot;
    The pair of phoenixes separated by the imperial exam)[18]
Our love knot had just been tied.
    (When I said farewell to my husband in Nanpu/Nan-p'u
    Just then[19]
    A morning rain has settled the dust in Weicheng
    Willows are green again in the tavern dooryard
    Wait till we empty one more cup –
    West of Yang Gate there'll be no old friends.)[20]
Alas, the sounds of 'Yang-kuan' died away,
And I saw you off from Nan-p'u.

春闈催赴
    奴家記得初婚之時
    香羅纔綰同心結
    又被春闈拆鳳凰
同心帶綰初
    奴家當初與丈夫在南浦分別之時
    正是
    渭城朝雨浥輕塵
    客舍青青柳色新
    勸君更盡一杯酒
    西出陽關無故人
嘆陽關聲斷
送別南浦[21]

These seven-character lines were employed to explain the sung arias, and they might enhance the effect of the performance as well.

Sometimes the character *gun* 滾 (roll) is appended to the very beginning of these annotative poems.[22] But even in the parts without the stage direction *gun*, one can easily identify the annotations according to the differing formats used in the Chinese text: the original sung arias are irregular in length and printed in large characters; the inserted annotative poems are regular in length and in middle-size characters; and the annotative spoken lines consist of double-lines in small characters. The *gun* could be either a *gunbai* 滾白 (rolling speech), a type of recitative or rhythmical speech, or a *gunchang* 滾唱 (rolling recital), a kind of chanting.

Essentially, the insertion of *gun* into an aria indicates a kind of modification of the joined-song structure. In writing a play with this kind of musical structure, a playwright selected a pre-existing *qupai* and then followed its prosodic pattern to fix the number of lines, the number of words and the tone of each word. Since experienced performers were already very familiar with the *qupai* serving as the playwright's model, they had no difficulty singing newly written arias. Of course, performers and musicians sometimes had to adjust pre-existing tunes, and they sometimes even made considerable changes to the melodies in order to have them fit the arias exactly.[23] However, making revisions to plays like *The Lute* was another matter entirely. Although performers were very proficient in singing and dancing, they were usually illiterate or semi-literate and lacked any poetic training. Furthermore, in traditional China theatre performers were widely regarded as outcasts.[24] Unlike playwrights, performers did not have the kind of literary skills required to compose or revise the sung arias of a *chuanqi* play. That is why, in *CLYZ* and *ZJQY* scenes, all the arias are almost exactly the same as those in the *Yuan Edition*. Nevertheless, it would not have been very difficult for the performers to create a poem in the colloquial language with a regular rhythm,[25] and then get someone with the requisite writing ability to insert it into the script. As a result, the whole appearance of a play was modified, but without changing the underlying framework of the play, namely the suite of songs.

Gun annotations and the grassroots theatre before 1616

The term *qingyang shidiao* 青陽時調 (fashionable Qingyang melodies) in the full title of *CLYZ*[26] indicates that the scenes included in this collection were performed in the *qingyang qiang* 青陽腔 (tunes of Qingyang) style. In fact, Tang Xianzu, the author of *Peony Pavilion* and a native of Jiangxi, once mentioned *qingyang qiang* in one of his works:

> In Jiangxi, there was a type of theatre known as *yiyang qiang* 弋陽腔 (songs of Yiyang). The songs were accompanied by boisterous drumming. During the reign of Emperor Jiajing (1522–1567), it fell out of fashion, but evolved into the theatrical style of *leping qiang* 樂平腔 (songs of Leping) and then the theatrical style of *qingyang qiang* of Anhui.[27]

Unlike *kunqu* mentioned above and also discussed in other essays in this volume, *yiyang qiang* was a kind of grassroots theatre. Geographically, Jiangxi province shares a border with Anhui province, which is to the north. Leping is in northern Jiangxi, and Qingyang is in southern Anhui. Therefore, it is easy to understand that *yiyang qiang* went north to Leping and then to Qingyang, absorbing the dialects and regional musical styles of the areas it reached, thereby evolving into new regional forms.

Similarly, the full title of *ZJQY*[28] contains the name of Anhui where grassroots theatre was very popular in the late Ming dynasty. Also, as mentioned earlier, there are many *gun* in this collection. In other words, the descendants of *yiyang qiang* inherited the folk traditions of its forerunner, and frequently added *gun* to *chuanqi* arias so as to make the literary allusions of the theatre of the elite more intelligible to the masses.

To sum up, by comparing a number of scenes from *The Lute* in *CLYZ* and *ZJQY*, two anthologies produced in the early seventeenth century, with their counterparts in the *Yuan Edition* of 1548, we can see that the insertion of spoken and chanted lines made the original plays more understandable to the audience. Moreover, adding *gun* was a common device in such grassroots theatre, as was the *qingyang qiang* in eastern China during the late Ming dynasty.

Notes

1   Wu Junda, '*Xiqu changqiang yuepu*', in *Zhongguo da baike quanshu: Xiqu quyi* (Beijing and Shanghai: Zhongguo da baike quanshu chubanshe, 1983), p. 441.

2   Miao Yonghe, *Mingdai chuban shigao* (Nanjing: Jiangsu renmin chubanshe, 2000), pp. 226–7; Zhu Chongzhi, *Zhongguo gudai xiqu xuanben yanjiu* (Shanghai: Shanghai guji chubanshe, 2004), pp. 32, 65.

3   See Guo Yingde and Wang Lijuan, '*Cilin yizhi, Baneng zoujin bianzuan niandai kao*', *Wenyi yanjiu*, 8 (2006), p. 61.

4   See Xi Zhengwo (comp.), *Zhaijin qiyin*, photolithographic reprint in Wang Chiu-kui (ed.), *Shanben xiqu congkan* (Taipei: Taiwan xuesheng shuju, 1984), vol. 3, p. 6.29b.

5   See Wang (ed.), *Shanben xiqu congkan*, vol. 12, p. 18.

6   See Ling Xuzi (comp.), *Yue lu yin*, 'Xu' (Preface), p. 4a; photolithographic reprint in *Shanben xiqu congkan*, vol. 15, p. 7.

7   This play was written at the end of the Yuan dynasty (1271–1368) and was very popular during the Ming (1368–1644) and Qing (1644–1911) dynasties; it can be regarded as a forebear and model of *chuanqi* plays.

8   Jin Ningfen, *Nanxi yanjiu bianqian* (Tianjin: Tianjin jiaoyu chubanshe, 1992), pp. 158–62.

9   Qian Nanyang, *Yuan ben pipa ji jiaozhu* (Beijing: Zhonghua

shuju, 2009), 'Preface', p. 2; Liu Nianzi, *Nanxi xinzheng* (Beijing: Zhonghua shuju, 1986), p. 360; Huang Shizhong, *Pipa ji yanjiu* (Guangzhou: Guangdong gaodeng jiaoyu chubanshe, 1996), pp. 170–3; Sun Chongtao, *Fengyue jinnang kaoshi* (Beijing: Zhonghua shuju, 2000), p. 72.

10   Jean Mulligan (trans.), *The Lute* (New York: Columbia University Press, 1980), p. 203.

11   Gao Ming, *Xinkan yuanben Cai Bojie Pipa ji*, photolithographic reprint in *Guben xiqu congkan*, 1st series (Shanghai: Shangwu yinshuguan, 1953/4), 2.10a.

12   Mulligan (trans.), *The Lute*, p. 203.

13   My translation of the original Chinese text.

14   Xi Zhengwo (comp.), *Zhaijin qiyin*, pp. 1.22b–23a.

15   Classical Chinese language is monosyllabic – usually, one syllable represents one word, which is transcribed into one Chinese character.

16   Mulligan (trans.), *The Lute*, p. 80.

17   Gao Ming, *Xinkan yuanben Cai Bojie Pipa ji*, 1.12a.

18   My translation of the original Chinese text.

19   My translation of the original Chinese text.

20   This was a very popular quatrain by Wang Wei 王維 (?–761), and the English translation here was made by Witter Bynner. For details on the translation see Lü Shuxiang (ed.), *Yingyi Tangren jueju baishou* (Changsha: Hunan renmin chubanshe, 1980), p. 15.

21   Huang Wenhua (comp.), *Cilin yizhi*, in *Shanben xiqu congkan*, (Taipei: Taiwan xuesheng shuju, 1984), vol. 4, 3.1a.

22   Xi Zhengwo (comp.), *Zhaijin qiyin*, pp. 1.20b, 1.21b, 1.22b–25b.

23   In certain ways, this work may be understood as a musical composition.

24   For example, in the early Ming performers of all types often had to wear a special style of clothing in daily life and were not allowed to walk in the middle of the road, but instead were forced to travel on the side of the road; actresses were prohibited from wearing gold or silver ornaments and from

wearing silk. See Xu Fuzuo, *Qu lun*, in *Zhongguo gudian xiqu lunzhu jicheng* series (Beijing: Zhongguo xiju chubanshe, 1959), vol. 4, p. 243.

25 That is exactly what theatre performers often did in various regional forms of Chinese theatre during the Qing dynasty, among which *jingju* 京劇 (Beijing opera) is a typical example.

26 *Xinke jingban qingyang shidiao cilin yizhi* 新刻京板青陽時調詞林一枝.

27 Tang Xianzu, *Tang Xianzu ji* (Beijing: Zhonghua shuju, 1962), p. 1128. My translation of the original Chinese text.

28 *Xinke huiban hexiang gundiao yuefu guanqiang zhaijin qiyin* 新刊徽板合像滾調樂府官腔摘錦奇音.

8.2 Music in the English theatre of 1616

David Lindley

One of the most important consequences of the King's Men taking back the Blackfriars theatre in 1608 was their acquisition of significantly greater musical resources than they previously had at the Globe. Whereas they had earlier provided music largely from within the acting resources of the company, they now employed a separate band of musicians on a regular basis. The results of that transformation extended from the provision of a wider instrumental palette to the very shaping of the drama itself, as the five-act structure was underlined by the musical interludes that filled the act breaks. The musical revolution also prompted the 'retro-fitting' of existing plays with additional opportunities for music, song and dance. This new musical richness, I will argue, also modified the nature of the relationship between the drama and the audience in important ways, prophetic of the direction theatre was to take after the Restoration. By 1616, as we shall see, that transformation was well under way.

It is often suggested that the most immediate consequence of the acquisition of an indoor theatre was the replacement of loud instruments (drums and trumpets) by quieter cornets or recorders. While it is true that these instruments only came into general use by the adult companies after the move indoors, there are a number of questions one might want to ask about using musical volume as an explanation for the change in instrumentation. In the first place, trumpets and drums were actually played indoors at court to herald the monarch's movement about the space, and to accompany meals. Paul Hentzner commented that Queen Elizabeth dined at Greenwich to the accompaniment of 'twelve trumpets and two kettledrums' which 'made the hall ring for half-an-hour together'.[1] The masque performed indoors in the Banqueting House at court in 1616, Jonson's *The Golden Age Restored*, included the stage direction: '*The antimasque and their dance, two drums, trumpets, and a confusion of martial music.*'[2] It seems odd, indeed, that modern writers who themselves happily endure the assault of electronic amplification in confined spaces should be so confident that Tudor and Stuart audiences could not have enjoyed the visceral thrill of loud noise even in an indoor theatre. Furthermore, very recent experiments in the new indoor Sam Wanamaker Playhouse at Shakespeare's Globe demonstrate unequivocally that trumpet and drum are perfectly tolerable in a space which is actually smaller than the Blackfriars.

It is surely partly the case, then, that it is the nature of the action in 'trumpet-and-drums' plays characteristically including scenes of battle, with the demands they make upon the much more limited stage space of the indoor theatres, which produced a shift in the need for these instruments, rather than the loudness of the sound in itself. Even more likely, and of rather more consequence, is the simple fact that cornets are versatile, but difficult instruments to play. They could provide the flourishes that trumpets might provide, but could equally play melodies and accompany voices.[3] The stage direction 'cornetts', then, implies most strongly 'here are expert musicians', not 'here is a quieter substitute for trumpets'. In recent years, as interest in the playing of old instruments has grown and become much more expert, cornettists have generally tended to be instrumentalists trained initially as trumpeters; in the sixteenth and seventeenth centuries, by contrast, cornettists doubled on wind instruments such as the oboe/shawm or flute. Might it not be, therefore, that once the King's Men acquired a professional band of musicians they simply no longer needed to employ trumpeters – who were in any case considered a breed apart? As Peter Holman notes: 'They were attendants rather than musicians: they played simple, monophonic music and did not belong to the section of musical society that was literate and cultivated polyphonic music.'[4] If the King's Men in their Globe days had actually employed trumpeters (though there is no real reason why actors themselves should not have mastered the relatively simple patterns that sixteenth-century trumpets, like modern bugles, were able to play), once installed in their new venue, with a fully professional ensemble, they simply had no need of such limited instrumentalists.

It is this professionalization of the musical provision that had the most important and far-reaching consequences. The transformation it brought about is evident if one considers Webster's 1604 prologue to the King's Men's appropriation of Marston's *The Malcontent* from the boys' company. There, Burbage answers Sly's question, 'what are your additions?', with the offhand: 'Sooth, not greatly needful; only as your sallet [*salad*] to your great feast, to entertain a little more time, and to abridge the not-received custom of music in our theatre.'[5]

He does not, of course, mean that there was no music in the adult theatres – far from it – but he refers to the music that the boys' companies played during the act breaks necessary for trimming candles, and perhaps primarily he alludes to the concert that preceded the play itself ('salads', it would seem, were often hors d'oeuvres – Domitia observes in Massinger's *The Roman Actor*: 'These are but salads / To sharpen appetite').[6] Webster's own 'salad' for *The Malcontent* is his newly penned induction. The implication in Webster's denigratory suggestion that music is merely an extraneous addition to the play suggests that he is engaging in the same attack on the newly fashionable rivals to the King's Men that is also evident in Rosencrantz's comments on the 'little eyases' in the 1623 text of *Hamlet* (2.2.337).

After 1608, however, Webster's dismissal of music's insubstantiality must have given way to a different attitude. It is difficult to know exactly what elements of existing practice were taken over from the boys' companies, since there is very little if any evidence as to the nature of any pre-play concert at this time. Frederic Gershow's report that, 'for an entire hour before a play one hears an exquisite instrumental concert' and his comments on a boy who 'sang beautifully in a warbling voice to a bass viol', refer to boys' company practice in 1602.[7] Clearer evidence might be provided by Bulstrode Whitelocke, who wrote that:

> I was so conversant with the musicians, and so willing to gain their favour ... that I composed an air myself, with the assistance of Mr Ives, and called it *Whitelocke's Coranto*, which being cried up, was first played publicly by the Blackfriars Music, who were then esteemed the best of the common musicians in London. Whenever I came to that house ... the musicians would presently play *Whitelocke's Coranto*, and it was so often called for that they would have played it twice or thrice in an afternoon.[8]

But this speaks of the 1630s – so neither of these witnesses gives direct testimony to King's Men practice in terms of music provided before the play began in 1616.

Nor do we know much about the length or precise musical nature of any entr'acte provision. While the stage directions in Marston's *Sophonisba* imply that he at least was interested in requiring act music that in its instrumentation seems to be tailored to the action which precedes and follows it, it is very unlikely that this was entirely typical. It is doubtful whether the crowded adult repertoire allowed for specifically composed music for each individual play. It is more probable that the musicians simply chose from their repertoire pieces that were vaguely appropriate to the action. How much attention was actually paid by audiences to the music, in any case, both before the play and during the ent'ractes, is a further unknown – one suspects it might well have been rather fitful.

But whatever, exactly, the newly assembled professional musicians played before and during the show, there is extensive evidence that, post-1610, already existing repertoire was modified by the addition of new songs or dances, and by the composition of new tunes for old songs. John Jowett and Gary Taylor have persuasively suggested that the song 'Take, O take those lips away', for example, was drafted in to *Measure for Measure* by Middleton, from Fletcher's *Rollo, Duke of Normandy*, as part of its revision around 1621.[9] Tiffany Stern has charted the ways in which Middleton himself borrowed songs from others, or else reused his own song lyrics in more than one play.[10] It has long been accepted that Act 4 of *The Winter's Tale* shows evidence of adaptation in the inclusion of a dance of satyrs, whose performers, it is claimed, have 'danced before the King' – presumably suggesting that this is the dance they had provided as the antimasque in Jonson's *Oberon*, staged at court in 1611. This dance is not necessary to the action – there has already been a dance by shepherds and shepherdesses which would seem to make the satyrs redundant (modern productions often choose between them). It does, however, witness both to the fact that King's Men actors played in court masques, and to the more frequent inclusion of masques or masque-like elements in King's Men plays post-1610. But perhaps the musical revision goes further than that. I have argued elsewhere that the three-part song which is given to Autolycus, Mopsa and Dorcas, 'Get you hence', may also be a later insertion into the play.[11] The words do not seem very like the 'merry ballad' that Autolycus promises, and, more importantly, the surviving setting by Robert Johnson, often assumed to have been used in the first performance, is nothing like a ballad tune of 'Two maids wooing a man' which Mopsa and Dorcas assert that they had the tune of a month ago. It is very much an art-song, rather than a popular air, and would be difficult indeed to memorize in the way ballad tunes were customarily learnt.

Be that as it may, Tiffany Stern has argued more generally for the fact that the texts (and the music) of songs circulated separately from the text of the play itself, becoming therefore capable of ready migration from play to play, and of easy substitution during any play's theatrical life.[12]

One example, particularly useful in attempting to assess the situation of theatrical music in 1616, is the transference of songs from Middleton's *The Witch* as part of a major revision of Shakespeare's *Macbeth*, for which Middleton seems most likely to have been responsible. *The Witch* was probably written in 1615–16, and was commenting directly both upon the Thomas Overbury murder trials, the court sensation of those years, and upon the annulment of Frances Howard's marriage to the Third Earl of Essex in 1613.[13] In the annulment hearings Essex's alleged impotence had for a while been attributed to witchcraft. Scandalized and ribald comment later reached its peak with the indictment of Frances Howard and Robert Carr for murder in 1616.[14] Middleton had been directly involved in the first movement of this scandal when he wrote, at very short notice, a 'Masque of Cupids' for the lord mayor, who, despite his objections, had been ordered by King James to celebrate this marriage of his favourite.[15]

The relationship of *The Witch* to court scandal is part of its fascination, but more significant for present purposes is the fact that two of its songs are almost certainly to be found in the Hecate sections of *Macbeth*, though indicated there only by brief *incipit*s (as is not uncommon with song lyrics in plays). These songs, and other palpable revisions to the text of *Macbeth*, have for many years been attributed to Middleton, and the Oxford editors suggest that though the revision of Shakespeare's play could theoretically have happened at any time between 1616 and 1623, 1616 itself is the most likely date.[16] Speculation as to the reasons for the revision of *Macbeth* lie outside the remit of this essay, as, indeed, do the textual arguments about the precise nature and extent of Middleton's scissors-and-paste job on his predecessor's play. I am here more interested in what the inclusion of these songs might tell us about the ways in which musical taste in the theatre was shifting in 1616.

Linda Austern, noting the conventional association of music and magic in the theatre of the sixteenth and seventeenth centuries, suggests that in *The Witch* it is a 'key ingredient in the ritual magic' that the 'grotesque, comical figures', the 'lustful, unattractive hags', practise.[17] No doubt it is in part the ambivalence of Middleton's satirical representation of the witches, and, by implication, his critique of those credulous enough to believe in their charms, which has contributed to the almost universally negative perception of the Hecate scenes when transferred to Shakespeare's play. They are almost always cut in modern performance. Shakespeare in his original text appears to be representing King James's firm belief in witchcraft, embodied in his *Demonologie* (1597), rather than siding with the scepticism of Reginald Scot's *Discoverie of Witchcraft* of 1584 to which the king had been responding. Within the culture of the time there was deep ambivalence about the very existence and practice of witchcraft. A modern audience, however, with little or no investment in the reality of witchcraft, yet a desire to find the weird sisters truly threatening, is in danger of simplifying the complex and contradictory attitudes that might have been found in a Blackfriars audience, both to witches in themselves and to any theatrical representation of their activity. Even in Jonson's *Masque of Queens*, played before King James himself, and apparently taking the witches with the utmost scholarly seriousness (Jonson almost overwhelms his text with learned commentary), there is room for humour in the antimasque of hags as they attempt to summon their master with increasingly desperate and ineffectual incantations. The juxtaposition of menace and comic undercutting characterizes *The Witch*, and is generated in Shakespeare's play by the insertion of the Hecate scenes. Far from finding them trivial, however, all the evidence points to the continued presence in *Macbeth* of Middleton's Hecate and her company, and to the long-lasting importance of the musical interludes in the witches' performance to the play's audiences. As Stephen Orgel observes: 'to judge from the play's stage history, the vaudevillian witches constituted a stroke of theatrical genius'.[18] Paul Menzer argues in more general terms that the introduction of masque-like and spectacular elements into the

Blackfriars repertory indicates that, far from succumbing to courtly and Italianate influences, 'a consistent reading of the King's servants' business acumen would find them giving the people precisely what they wanted: a show'.[19]

At the very least, then, the importation of song and dance into Shakespeare's tragedy suggests something of the theatrical expectations of the fashionable 1616 audience. But it is important to consider the nature of the music the Middletonian witches sing. No music survives for the charm 'Black spirits and white', though, as Austern observes, 'the irregularities of rhythm and metre in the song's text imply a through-composed setting with a single, unprepared repetition of the charmed refrain'.[20] A setting for 'Come away, Hecate' is still, however, extant.[21] It is generally attributed to Robert Johnson, a court lutenist who composed both for the court theatre of the masque, and for the King's Men. This is significant in a number of ways. In the first place it would seem likely that in the years before the acquisition of Blackfriars the adult companies rarely used specially commissioned settings of songs, instead simply borrowing published material, or else fitting new words to existing, popular tunes.[22] It is probable, then, that the Globe audience would often already have been familiar with the music they heard, even if the lyrics were new. Boys' companies, by contrast, had always, in their various manifestations, been able to call on the services of composers to set many of the songs which their plays demanded.[23] What they offered, then, was the distinct pleasure of the new and up to date.

Johnson's setting of 'Come away' belongs very clearly to the latter category. It is in a style sometimes known as 'declamatory', a kind of semi-recitative which eschews simple melody until the final section. It might have been ornamented in performance; its frequent octave leaps demand at the least a reasonably accomplished singer. Moreover, this style was associated with the court masque, and had been introduced by Alfonso Ferrabosco and Nicholas Lanier just a few years before. In 1617 Jonson's *Lovers Made Men*, set by Lanier, might have been the very first English example of a work through composed in '*stilo recitativo*'. There has been controversy over this claim, since it does not appear in print until the Second Folio of 1640, but Peter Walls is 'convinced that recitative was used in the masques of 1615–17'.[24] Clearly the music in the modified *Macbeth* is stylistically fashionable and up to the moment. This creates a paradox – that the wild and marginal figure of the witch should yet be singing in the elite musical vocabulary of the court. This suggests that the music as event, as performance, is becoming more significant than music as a direct expression of a 'realistic' character. Something the same is true of Johnson's expressive chromatic setting of the madman's song, 'Howl, howl' for *The Duchess of Malfi* a couple of years earlier. This is also a highly sophisticated piece of music which demands expert performance in a way that, say, Ophelia's mad songs do not. Its representation of madness, like the musical expression of demonic possession in the *Macbeth* song, looks forward to the scenes in post-Restoration mad songs, converting distraction or menace into an aesthetic object to be appreciated by the musically sophisticated.

What does all this imply for the nature of the theatrical experience in 1616? Penelope Woods is surely right to note that in the space of the Blackfriars playhouse 'music plays a crucial role in the production of affect'.[25] But the effect and affect of music is much more complicated than this. Film criticism has accustomed us to the distinction between 'diegetic' and 'non-diegetic' music – between music that is part of the action, and music that exists in the ears of the audience, but not in the consciousness of the characters on stage. I believe that there is little evidence for the existence of the latter category of music in early modern drama. What certainly exists, however, is a different kind of sound, which we might call music as part of the experience of being in a theatre, created primarily by the pre-show concert and by the entr'acte music. Not only is this music detached from the action, but its executants, too, are separable from the acting troupe. Often ensconced on a balcony, and perhaps hidden by curtains, they are no longer, as they almost certainly were in the Globe, part of the acting company and direct participants in the dramatic action. Bulstrode Whitelocke's narrative, quoted above, emphasizes the separateness of musical content from any particular play, even as it suggests a close relationship between the musicians and the audience they were apparently able to observe entering the theatre.

At the same time, the changed musical style of songs establishes a different relationship between singer, character and auditor. If, as seems likely, the Globe theatre actor-singer was largely using melodies and songs that the audience already knew, then this created a particular experiential bond between actor and audience. It offered the pleasure of familiarity, or else the piquancy that derives from hearing new words to a known tune – an effect that John Gay was to employ to its fullest in *The Beggar's Opera*. The singer performing a song setting by Robert Johnson, however, perhaps with virtuoso ornamentation, stands before the audience demanding applause for his expertise, even as the audience are patting themselves on the back for their recognition of, and response to, the latest style. It is, of course, true that the borderline between 'popular' and 'art' music was nowhere near as firmly drawn in the early modern period as (regrettably) it has become more recently. None the less there can be little doubt that the nature of the music itself reinforced the social distinction between the top and bottom end of the theatrical market.

Curiously, then, though the indoor theatres were more intimate, and spectators were closer to the action, with gallants onstage even interfering with the performance itself, yet at the same time the separation between the worlds of audience and play was gradually being reinforced. Martin White suggests that the distribution of candles in the indoor theatre 'would have resulted in a concentration of light on the main acting area',[26] and Paul Menzer suggests that 'the commercial success of indoor playhouses brought about, in short, a counterintuitive move – not the close-up drama of psychological intimacy, but

a theatre of wonder, distance, and deferral, a theatre of domes-
ticate spectacle'.[27] This may well be to overstate the case, but
yet in the effect that the importation of the songs from *The
Witch* has upon the psycho-drama of Shakespeare's *Macbeth*
it may well seem that a similar shift is taking place in the
nature of the relationship between music, drama and spectator/
auditor. While the music does not take on the highly formalized
relationship to non-musical action that seems to pertain in
Chinese theatre of the period, as essays in this volume describe
it, we are none the less on the way towards something much
more like the opera of post-Restoration theatre, with musical
items as set pieces framed within the action.

Notes

1   Peter Holman, *Four and Twenty Fiddlers: The Violin at the
     English Court* (Oxford: Clarendon Press, 1993), p. 111.

2   David Bevington, Martin Butler and Ian Donaldson (eds), *The
     Cambridge Edition of the Works of Ben Jonson* (Cambridge:
     Cambridge University Press, 2012), vol. 4, p. 455.

3   See Bruce Dickey, 'The Cornett', in Trevor Herbert and
     John Wallace (eds), *The Cambridge Companion to Brass
     Instruments* (Cambridge: Cambridge University Press, 1997),
     pp. 51–67.

4   Holman, *Four and Twenty Fiddlers*, p. 36.

5   John Marston, *The Malcontent*, ed. George K. Hunter
     (Manchester: Manchester University Press, 1975), 'Induction',
     pp. 81–4.

6   Philip Massinger, *The Roman Actor*, ed. Martin White
     (Manchester: Manchester University Press, 2007), 4.2.107–8.

7   Linda Phyllis Austern, *Music in English Children's Drama of
     the Later Renaissance* (London: Routledge, 1992), p. 311.

8   Andrew Gurr, *Playgoing in Shakespeare's London*, 3rd edn
     (Cambridge: Cambridge University Press, 2004), p. 244.

9   John Jowett and Gary Taylor, *Shakespeare Reshaped*

1606–1623 (Oxford: Clarendon Press, 1993), pp. 468–75; Gary Taylor and John Lavagnino (eds), *Thomas Middleton and Early Modern Culture* (Oxford: Clarendon Press, 2007), pp. 417–21, 681–3.

10 Tiffany Stern, 'Middleton's Collaborators in Music and Song', in Gary Taylor and Trish Thomas Henley (eds), *The Oxford Handbook of Thomas Middleton* (Oxford: Clarendon Press, 2012), pp. 64–79.

11 David Lindley, 'Music and Shakespearean Revision', *Archiv*, 164 (2012), pp. 50–64.

12 Tiffany Stern, *Documents of Performance in Early Modern England* (Cambridge: Cambridge University Press, 2009), pp. 119–73.

13 Marion O'Connor (ed.), *The Witch*, in Gary Taylor and John Lavagnino (eds), *Thomas Middleton: The Collected Works* (Oxford: Oxford University Press, 2007), pp. 1124–6.

14 See David Lindley, *The Trials of Frances Howard* (London: Routledge, 1993), and Alastair Bellany, *The Politics of Court Scandal in Early Modern England* (Cambridge: Cambridge University Press, 2002).

15 See Taylor and Lavagnino (eds), *Middleton, The Collected Works*, pp. 1027–33.

16 Gary Taylor and John Lavagnino (eds), *Thomas Middleton and Early Modern Textual Culture* (Oxford: Clarendon Press, 2007), p. 385.

17 Linda Phyllis Austern, '"Art to Enchant": Musical Magic and Its Practitioners in English Renaissance Drama', *Journal of the Royal Musical Association*, 115 (1990), p. 202.

18 Stephen Orgel, '*Macbeth* and the Antic Round', *Shakespeare Survey 52*, Stanley Wells (ed.) (Cambridge: Cambridge University Press, 1999) p. 147.

19 Paul Menzer, 'In Event of Fire', in Andrew Gurr and Farah Karim Cooper (eds), *Moving Shakespeare Indoors: Performance and Repertoire in the Jacobean Playhouse* (Cambridge: Cambridge University Press, 2014), p. 180.

20 Austern, 'Musical Magic', p. 202.

21 Printed in Waller and Lavagnino, *Textual Culture*, pp. 153–5.

22 See Ross Duffin, *Shakespeare's Songbook* (New York: W. W. Norton, 2004), 'Prologue'.

23 Austern, *Children's Drama*.

24 Peter Walls, *Music in the English Courtly Masque* (Oxford: Clarendon Press, 1995), pp. 89–103.

25 Penelope Woods, 'The Audience of the Indoor Theatre', in Gurr and Karim-Cooper (eds), *Moving Shakespeare Indoors*, p. 167.

26 Martin White, 'Light and Darkness in the Indoor Jacobean Theatre', in Gurr and Karim-Cooper (eds), *Moving Shakespeare Indoors*, p. 118.

27 Menzer, 'In Event of Fire', p. 175.

9

Theatre in theory and practice

How differently was theatre conceptualized across the two cultures? Regina Llamas's discussion of language and music helps to illustrate a dominant form of Chinese dramatic criticism. Will Tosh's emphasis on stage design and theatrical architecture reminds us of the practicalities of performance and the difference these make.

9.1 Xu Wei's *A Record of Southern Drama*: The idea of a theatre at the turn of seventeenth-century China

Regina Llamas

Introduction

Xu Wei 徐渭 (1521–93) was not the first to write about theatre: before him, others had written about the life of actors, the playwrights and their works, about music and prosody, singing methods, the function and style of drama and the composition of plays. The birth of drama was already understood as a by-product of leisure, and so was its potential as a popular instrument for improving, expounding and disseminating social values. But Xu Wei's essay, *A Record of Southern Drama* (*Nanci xulu* 南詞敘錄, hereafter *Record*), written in 1559, is the first and only 'defence' of southern drama (*nanxi*) we have.[1] It is also an apology that reflects and responds to current concerns with the genre and how this genre had to be understood. This essay will explore how Xu Wei attempted to establish the reputation of southern theatre on the basis of contemporary values of naturalness and authenticity, and how he modified and honed these values to fit his defence. It will show that Xu's advocacy of natural language and authentic music in southern drama implied standards that had long since departed the popular milieu he claimed conceived them and became instead the dominant aesthetic values of an educated class and of *chuanqi*, the leading southern dramatic form of the age. At the turn of the seventeenth century, Xu Wei's fundamental concern with the linguistic and musical prerequisites for theatre, while partially preserved by critics like Lü Tiancheng (1580–1618) as a means to evaluate what was 'authentic' in the language of individual works, had become largely polarized. This polarization, however, was no longer concerned with the linguistic register of the play or the authenticity and freedom of musical categories, but more generally with the primacy of language over music or music over language. This is exemplified in dramatic history by the debate between Tang Xianzu versus Shen Jing, where Shen, a musicology expert and troupe owner, made textual emendations to Tang Xianzu's *Peony Pavilion* in order to better adapt it to performance requirements. Tang was not happy with these changes and famously countered that as long as he could transmit his ideas he did not mind 'twisting everyone's throats'.[2] The concern with language and music prevailed, but southern drama found its new aesthetic in musical and prosodic norms, and its linguistic register further removed from what was immediately aurally comprehensible.

The context

As a defence of southern drama, the *Record* appears very late, 150 years after the first manuscripts of southern plays were included in the imperial *Yongle Collectanea*, and a century after plays like *White Rabbit* (*Baitu ji* 白兔記), written by the so-called Yongjia Academy, and the anonymous *Golden Hairpin* (*Jinchai ji* 金釵記) were printed and buried with aficionados to be enjoyed in the afterlife. It also appears at a time when Gao Ming's celebrated *The Lute* had already been canonized as one of the representative works of the southern tradition. Further, the *Record* was produced when the gentle southern kunshan musical style reformed by Wei Liangfu 魏良輔 (1522–66) was in full swing; the Suzhou native, Liang Chenyu 梁辰魚 (1519–91) had already set his play *Washing Silk* (*Huansha ji* 浣紗記, 1558) to this musical style, much to the acclaim of the urban and educated elite,[3] and the first prosodic manual for southern songs, by Jiang Xiao 蔣孝 (*jinshi* 1544), had already been composed. Even northerners like the Shandong official and drama enthusiast Li Kaixian

李開先 (1502–68) were attempting to write in the southern style. In short, in the second half of the sixteenth century, when Xu Wei set out to defend southern theatre, an evolution of the form had already captured the interest and appreciation of the literati.

Xu Wei's *Record* also appeared at a time when a heated debate raged on the merits of one northern play – *The Western Wing* (*Xixiang ji* 西廂記) – and two southern plays, *The Lute* and *The Pavilion for Praying to the Moon* (*Baiyue ting* 拜月亭). This debate, initiated by He Liangjun 何良俊 (1506–73), and focusing on the language, contents, prosody and music of these plays, divided authors into two camps: those in favour of *The Lute*, and those in favour of the other two plays. In his very short critical text, He compared the three plays, and observed that *Western Wing* was a romance that followed in a long tradition of love poetry, easy to compose and easy to listen to. *The Lute*, on the other hand, was a play with a clear moral message, but so suffused with erudition that it had effaced all trace of 'natural language', one of the essential ingredients of a good play.[4] He's critique directly addressed the shortcomings of both plays, noting that *Western Wing* was easy to understand but bereft of moral meaning, while *The Lute* carried moral significance, but lacked the correct language, thus underlining two essential and interrelated functions of drama: to communicate and disseminate orthodox values and improve society. For He, it was the third play in the debate, *Praying to the Moon*, that retained the core element of theatre: its capacity to convey meaning through simple and lucid language. Wang Shizhen (1526–90) expanded the terms of dramatic criticism to include the assessment of the craft of the poet and the aims of theatre, while contesting He's preferences. Wang argued that *Praying to the Moon* did not manifest the proficiency of the poet, engage in romance, expound moral teachings or ultimately succeed in moving people, and championed *The Lute* instead. In response to He and Wang's exchange, Xu Fuzuo 徐復祚 (1560–1630), yet again expanding the critical boundaries, dismissed the need for poetic erudition and conversely praised the prosodic and musical perfection of *Praying to the Moon*, observing that the play displayed, in addition to the correct linguistic register, great musical skill. In Xu Fuzuo's discussion, *Praying to the Moon* was the preferred play not just for its language and meaning, but because it showed the expertise of the master musician, whose final aim was the entertainment of his audience through the beauty of the music. Thus, in the framework for the critical evaluation of drama during Xu Wei's time, critics and playwrights were concerned with both the literary and the performing aspects of drama, they discussed language as a poetic medium and aural medium, they addressed the function of theatre as means of instruction and as entertainment, they considered the aims of theatre as a means to elicit an emotional response from the audience and they underlined the importance of the poet as aesthete and of the musician as entertainer.

Language

In the emergence of dramatic criticism, *bense* 本色 (literally, 'natural colour') became a standard of critical evaluation, often linked to 'natural aptitude' (*danghang* 當行) referring to the poet's profound insight into all aspects of the genre. Thus, a playwright came to be qualified as possessing aptitude when his poetry possessed the quality of *bense*; conversely, if a piece of drama displayed the quality of *bense*, the playwright was bound to be *danghang*. The critical concept of *bense* inherited from Song dynasty (907–1279) poetic criticism, was first applied to the 'original' lyrical language[5] – and by extension to the form – of a genre, but eventually was expanded to express critical appreciation of other parts of dramatic composition including the spoken language (a balance between crudeness and truth), prosody and music, finesse in plot construction or more generally the excellence of a play. *Danghang* too was expanded from a focus on the creative capacity of the poet to the troupes of actors and the audience. The greatest challenge in understanding these concepts, however, is accepting their indeterminateness. Just what a given critic meant by 'natural colour' or 'natural aptitude' is often as elusive as it is central.

According to Xu Wei, southern drama was undervalued on two accounts: because drama aficionados considered the language of the plays 'vulgar' and because the songs of plays possessed no prosodic (or musical) rules. It is not that southern drama did not have its own circle of aficionados, but the language of their plays remained unrefined. Xu Wei concedes that their criticism is not entirely off the mark when he writes: 'Southern [songs] are easy to compose, yet there are few excellent ones; northern [songs] are hard to write, yet there are some exquisite ones. Why is this so? It is because during Song times, prominent men were not willing to turn their attention to [southern songs]'.[6]

The partiality of men of letters for northern theatre and their assiduous endeavours to transform this genre into a legitimate and respectable literary form had, for Xu, led to neglect of the southern tradition. Thus Xu began his campaign to elevate the status of southern theatre by empha- sizing the aesthetic qualities that he believed distinguished 'good' southern theatre not from its northern rival, but from current practices by men of letters in the south: unlike the work of inferior writers, southern theatre possessed the quality of *bense*. In order to limn this quality in a piece of dramatic work, Xu began by demonstrating what was not *bense* through the contrived and elaborate work *The Perfume Satchel* (*Xiangnang ji* 香囊記) by the erudite scholar Shao Can (d. ca. 1495). This work, Xu grumbled, was everything that went counter to *bense* standards: it utilized very obscure language, made extensive use of parallelism and employed classical allusions to excess.[7] Like most of his contemporaries, Xu dismissed *The Perfume Satchel* as too philosophical, a desiccated discussion of the classics among erudite scholars. Drama was a popular genre and had to use language that could be popularly understood. Thus, the terse language of the classics and reliance on allusion demanded cultivated listeners steeped in classical lore, and was not *authentic* to the nature of the form. Pieces like *The Perfume Satchel*, while learned and even quite popular among the elite for their advocacy of orthodox Confucian morality, were the works of pretentious erudites attempting to mask their lack of creative talent. In fact, so popular was the work of Shao Can and so often copied by others, that Xu Wei remarked: 'As for the making of the poor imitations of *The Perfume Satchel*, they diligently and avidly [pursue them], but there is not a line that does not come from a former [work], there is not a place where there is not a literary allusion, and they cannot recover even the smallest hair of the Song and Yuan drama.'[8] That which was not genuine, Xu called 'likeness' or imitation (*xiangse* 相色). In his preface to the *Western Wing*, Xu wrote: 'The matters of this world have natural colour (*bense*) and they have a likeness colour (*xiangse*). *Bense* is what in common language is called the main body, *xiangse* is the substitute body.' Xu explains that what he calls the 'substitute body' is the equivalent of 'the maid servant taking on the appearance of a lady', referring to imitations.[9] The display of erudition disguised the dramatist's lack of creative talent, and those that imitated these already mediocre plays were even further removed from fulfilling any of the requirements for a good piece of dramatic literature. Most damning of all, they lacked *bense*.

At the other end of the spectrum, Xu placed the already canonical work of southern drama, *The Lute*. This play was instrumental in formulating the principles underlying the function of drama as a moral paradigm designed to influence social popular customs. It established that a good play should expound moral teachings and 'move' the audience.[10] Xu, following Gao, insisted that the ultimate aim of a play was to stir the audience: 'Drama-songs at root are supposed to move the heart, and only when they can be understood by slaves, children, women, and young girls do they find their proper form.'[11] The means to carry out this task was through language: if the language was unintelligible, theatre could not perform its highest function. As an example of this language, Xu presented the *Eighteen Replies* (*shiba da* 十八答) in Scene 30 of *The Lute*, where in a dialogue full of popular expressions on the duty of a wife, Mistress Niu, the daughter of the doting prime minister, rebukes her father for not allowing her to travel to her husband's village to fulfil her wifely obligations to her parents-in-law. Of these exchanges, Xu gushes: 'every line is everyday common language turned into song, like touching iron and turning it into gold'.[12] In other words, it was not just the choice of words, but the meaning language generated that was also *bense*. In sum, a song that was *bense* possessed just the right measure of artifice, close enough to colloquial language so as to be understood without effort. Neither vulgar (*su* 俗) nor base (*lou* 陋), the quasi-vernacular language of effective drama must convey its subject matter in a way that is accessible yet learned, stripped of allusion and excessive erudition and poetic enough to move the heart.[13]

Half a century after Xu, his preference for *The Lute* as the canonical early southern play and the exigency of *bense* in dramatic language were as apparent as ever in the work of Lü Tiancheng. Lü followed Xu's preference for the superiority of *The Lute*, highlighted Xu's idea of *bense* as referring only to language composition, and further underlined the fact that *bense* should not be imitation: 'Naturalness (*bense*) does not imitate everyday language. [The work that possesses *bense*] is clever and conveys natural pleasure; it cannot tolerate the least fakery. As for imitation, it really harms *bense*.'[14]

By Lü's time, the two concepts of *bense* and *danghang* had become alienated in the timeless struggle to avoid both the overly embellished and the excessively simple and unadorned: 'One denigrating the other for its lack of literary value; the other ridiculing the former for forsaking substance.'[15] Lü, however, showed that in the critique of any play, these two concepts were deeply intertwined, thus restoring Xu's former ideal: 'Moreover, they do not know that in what is really *danghang*, the tones of the language must be natural (*bense*), and in that [i.e. the language] which is really natural (*bense*), the ambience of the play has to be *danghang*.'[16] Xu had availed himself of a critical term as a means to establish the value of a genre. Half a century later, however, this same critical term had become established as a means of determining the value of a given play.

Music

When Xu Wei wrote his essay in defence of southern drama, although over two and a half centuries had elapsed since southern drama was first recorded, the lack of musical norms and tonal rules remained an obstacle to the acceptance of the genre as a legitimate literati pursuit. Zhu Yunming 祝允明 (1460–1526) noted with irritation that the music of southern drama had become so popular that its singing style and musical rules had 'already lost all tonal norms or musical modes'.[17] Exactly what norms Zhu refers to we do not know, but for Xu, the opposite was true. Xu claimed that what made southern music compelling was precisely its lack of modal norms: '[It was] made up of small songs from the villages; it did not make use of modes and had almost no regular rhythmic pattern. The songs were merely gathered from what the peasants remaining in the fields or the girls in the market could sing offhand, that is all.'[18] Establishing the origins of southern drama in popular song allowed Xu to legitimize this new tradition within the parameters of traditional Chinese poetic song-lore (like, for example, the canonical *Book of Songs*) as its generating source, and at the same time underlined its genuine and uncorrupted nature.

Xu repeatedly criticized the various attempts by the music academy to force a modal structure onto southern dramatic music in an attempt to show that this was not 'of its nature' or authentic: 'I do not know who conceived the nine modes. I expect it must have been someone from the Music Bureau at the beginning of this dynasty; they are most nonsensical and ridiculous.'[19] But just as in the concept of *bense*, dramatic perfection lay not in a *raw* natural form, but in a 'poetic' balance between the vulgar and the overly elaborate, in prosody and music. To avoid the charge of vulgarity, Xu required that the music of theatre possess some modal organization, and underlined that southern music had a 'kind of harmony', but this was not the same as fitting it into modes. A mode is a musical term that indicates the pitch on which a basic scale is constructed. Modes were considered important in determining the emotional context of a piece of music, and may originally have been instrumental for musicians in clarifying pitch (in wind and string instruments) and perhaps also for singers.[20] But by Xu's time, modes had lost their musical function and become a category under which tune titles were classified, the matrixes of these tunes, including tones and rhymes, and possibly the moods. This meant that part of the charm of southern music lay in its freedom of musical organization and, by extension, its potential for innovation.

Xu's position on musical norms can perhaps be better illustrated through two anecdotes. In his *Record*, Xu describes how Gao Ming, author of *The Lute*, retired to a tower for three years where he devoted his time to measuring the rhythm of his songs by tapping the beat with his foot until he made a 'hole on the wooden board where his foot beat the rhythm'.[21] The sole purpose of this possibly spurious anecdote was to highlight Gao's musical knowledge and the rhythm inherent in southern drama. In a later anecdote, Xu described a scene in which the first Ming emperor, Hongwu (1328–98), after seeing a performance of *The Lute* for the first time, compared it to the classics and praised its singularity: 'Gao Ming's *The Lute* is like the most exquisite delicacies from the mountains or the sea, that the noble and rich households cannot do without.'[22] However, the emperor, apparently not favouring the sound of southern music, ordered the Music Bureau to set it to strings.[23] Anyone reading this anecdote at the time would have immediately noticed the exceptional request of the emperor to set southern music to strings, and some must have lamented the emperor's ignorance. Shen Defu, writing in the early decades of the seventeenth century, disapproved of this practice as it showed the lack of concern for the authentic nature of the form, a practice he likened to 'putting a straw rain cape over a brocade gown'.[24] That the Ming emperor was incapable of appreciating the music without setting it to strings is best understood as a form of indirect criticism, not just of the emperor's oafish lack of understanding of musical propriety but also of the stubborn preference of the elite for northern music. Xu himself was not entirely against the practice of adding strings to southern drama, but he accepted these modifications in an attempt to search for a balance between the authentic nature of southern music and his own refined aesthetic experience.

Xu Wei's praise of the music after its adaptation to strings reflects the same search for balance he employs when using the term *bense* with regard to the linguistic register of plays. While adaptations to strings were appropriate reforms, the idea of fitting southern tunes to the prosodic strictures of 'modes' was a step too far, risking the loss of the natural quality that made southern theatre compelling.[25] Xu's efforts to maintain the relative freedom of phonology and music in southern drama were not as successful as he would have liked. As Lü Tiancheng shows, by the turn of the seventeenth century keys and modes became a categorization system of sounds and tunes to be followed, as was the correct positioning of tones and rhymes. Lü considered this sort of formal organization fundamental to good theatre: 'Further, there is the studying of the keys and modes (*gongdiao* 宮調), which are grouped into similar categories, and segments of fast and slow music. If they are disorderly when produced, then the words will contain many dissonant sounds.'[26] Never again, to my knowledge, was the freedom of southern music defended as Xu Wei had done. Thereafter, the composition of drama-song followed the norms established in manuals. Setting aside composition, what actors did in their performances is, of course, another matter.

Conclusion

Undoubtedly, for the late sixteenth-century champion of *bense*, Xu Wei, there was a discrepancy between text and performance. In order to establish drama as a reputable genre of literati endeavour, he was limited by the conventionally accepted cultural domains of poetry and music. Thus, while trying to institute the literary value of drama, he focused on the language of the text, and this language had to *reflect* the oral requirements of the stage. But whether these requirements underscored the practice of theatre or simply referred to the language on the page, we cannot know. The final aim of establishing *bense* as a critical standard, however, went beyond the demands of drama whether creative, receptive or critical; it was a means of establishing a value for a neglected but bourgeoning genre in order to position it in the larger framework of Chinese literary practice. In a similar manner, Xu insisted on the unstructured nature of the music of southern drama, singling out for praise what many aficionados had identified as flaws. Whether this musical freedom was ultimately desirable was questioned even by Xu, but it was certainly proof of the genesis of the form and of its authenticity.

By 1616, a little over two decades after Xu's death, the terms of the debate that were to establish southern drama as a legitimate vehicle of elite expression were firmly in place. Theatre was evaluated for what it had been, as critics speculated on the origins of southern theatre, and for what it was. They continued to defend the nature of drama through references to an earlier, nobler pedigree, claiming that at its origins southern theatre was unaffected and natural, and related to these issues the aspects of theatre they valued most, music and language; but by this time, the terms of this debate had been expanded to include not just the language and the music, but also narrative, comedy and dialogue. But that is another story.

Notes

1   Xu's essay is short, consisting of the essay proper, a list of key terms and a valuable register of plays. Xu Wei, *Nanci xulu*, *Zhongguo gudian xiqu lunzhu jicheng* (hereafter LZJC) series (Beijing: Zhongguo xiqu chubanshe, 1959), vol. 3. The attribution of authorship to Xu Wei has been questioned by Luo Yuming and Dong Rulong in the article '*Nanci xulu* fei Xu Wei zuo', *Fudan xuebao (shehui kexue ban)*, 6 (1987), pp. 71–8. Their thesis has been refuted by Zheng Zhiliang in 'Guanyu *Nanci xulu* de banben wenti', *Xiqu yanjiu* 80.1 (2010), pp. 340–71.

2   Wang Jide, *Qulü*, in LZJC, vol. 4, p. 165.

3   Shen Chongsui (fl.1639), *Duqu xuzhi*, LZJC, vol. 5, p. 198.

4   He Liangjun, *Qulun*, LZJC, vol. 4, p. 6.

5   The question of the 'original' language relates to when the form was first established, but this issue becomes increasingly complex as 'original' is exemplified by a collection of texts which are not the original texts.

6   Xu Wei, *Nanci xulu*, pp. 242–3.

7   Ibid., p. 243.

8   Ibid., pp. 242–3.

9   Xu Wei, Preface to *Xixiang ji*, in Cai Yi (ed.), *Zhongguo gudian xiqu xuba huibian* (Jinan: Qi Lu shushe, 1989), vol. 1. pp. 647–8.

10 *The Lute*, Scene 1. Qian Nanyang, *Yuan ben pipa ji jiaozhu*, p. 1.

11 Xu Wei, *Nanci xulu*, p. 243.

12 Ibid.

13 Ibid.

14 Lü Tiancheng, *Qupin*, in LZJC, vol. 6, p. 211.

15 Ibid.

16 Ibid.

17 Zhu Yunming, '*Gequ*', in *Wei Tan*, in Feng Kebin (comp.), *Guang baichuan xuehai* (c. 1642 edition, reprint Taipei: Xinxing shuju, 1970), pp. 1353–4.

18 Xu Wei, *Nanci xulu*, p. 240.

19 Ibid.

20 Rulan Chao Pian, *Sonq Dynasty Musical Sources and Their Interpretation* (Hong Kong: The Chinese University Press, 2003), pp. 43–50; Yang Yingliu, *Zhongguo gudai yinyue shigao* (Taipei: Dahong, 1997), section 3, pp. 117ff.

21 Xu Wei, *Nanci xulu*, p. 239.

22 Ibid., p. 240.

23 Ibid. For the significance of this anecdote in the Chinese dramatic canon formation see Patricia Sieber's essay in this volume (Section 6.1).

24 Shen Defu, *Wanli yehuo bian*, p. 641. Some scholars argue that the practice marked the beginning of the 'northification' of southern music. An emphasis on the tonal composition of words, and the use of strings in marking the rhythm, are two aspects of this phenomenon. Once the music of *Kun* drama was established, it became the predominant musical style of southern drama.

25 Yu Weimin, *Nanxi tonglun* (Zhejing renmin chubanshe, 2008), pp. 102, 254.

26 Lü Tiancheng, *Qupin*, p. 212.

9.2 Taking cover: 1616 and the move indoors

Will Tosh

In 1699 a lawyer and antiquary called James Wright set out to prove that the theatre, currently under attack for the allegedly impious farces then in fashion, had a history that was worthy of academic note. Wright's *Historia Histrionica* is one of the first scholarly examinations of the English theatrical tradition, presented as a pedagogic exchange between Lovewit, a gallant whose taste for the forgotten plays of Ben Jonson we would now term 'retro', and Truman, an 'honest old cavalier' whose memory stretches back to the pre-war days of the Jacobean and Caroline stage. Wright's argument is that the vulgarity displayed upon London's Restoration stages is a reflection of the decay of the state of dramatic art, not an indictment of theatre itself. For the heights of playwriting and acting skill, one had to cast one's mind back to 'the last age' – the time before the Civil War – and the theatre of John Lowin, Joseph Taylor and Richard Robinson, when artful plays were produced before 'men of grave and sober behaviour' in the candle-lit civility of the Blackfriars, the Cockpit and the Salisbury Court.[1] James Wright did not use the term 'Renaissance' (still less 'early modern') but he unquestionably regarded this period as the golden age of English drama, a judgement that few modern scholars contest. The impact of the Jacobean and Caroline stage on the modern theatrical tradition is the subject of this essay.

Whatever other reasons we have to celebrate 1616, and the essays in this volume have found many, the year does not mark the beginning of indoor performance in England. That tradition was very much older. Drama in guildhalls, church naves and private houses developed alongside the processional street performance of medieval mystery plays, and the habits of touring actors who set up a scaffold in the market square. By the 1570s, London was home to four distinct types of theatrical spaces: outdoor inn-yards, and the public chambers within; small indoor theatres known as 'private' playhouses in which boy-choristers performed for a monied audience; and large roofless amphitheatres that attracted a more heterogeneous crowd.[2] As early as 1596, the tenants of one such 'public' amphitheatre, Shakespeare's company the Lord Chamberlain's Men, attempted to move their operation into an adapted hall in what had been the Blackfriars monastery. Thwarted by local opposition, the Lord Chamberlain's Men eventually leased their indoor theatre to a children's company. Shakespeare's fellows, by now the King's Men, reclaimed their indoor space in 1609, and from this point on they performed both inside and out, playing a winter season at Blackfriars and a summer season at the Globe on Bankside.[3] Two other indoor theatres, Whitefriars and the very short-lived Porter's Hall, endeavoured to establish a hold on the market in the years before 1616.

The year is none the less significant in the development of English theatre. 1616 saw the establishment of the Cockpit playhouse (later known as the Phoenix) near Drury Lane as London's second dedicated indoor space that staged commercially successful plays performed by adult actors. From then on, London's theatre fashions were determined by the output of its elite indoor theatres, the Cockpit, Blackfriars and, from 1629, the Salisbury Court. After 1642, when commercial theatre lay dormant, it was the Cockpit that served as the locus for covert stage-playing. It hosted the first large-scale public performances in the closing years of the Interregnum, and when professional playing resumed in 1660, the Cockpit was the first Restoration playhouse. Its significance goes further: the men who re-established the theatre in the 1660s emulated the management structure of the Cockpit, which had been run for almost all of its pre-war existence by the impresario Christopher Beeston. More than any other London playhouse, it was the Cockpit that served as the model for theatre culture in England from the late seventeenth century until well into the twentieth.[4]

First, some context. When the King's Men established themselves at the Blackfriars in 1609, they demonstrated that an adult commercial theatre company, running a daily repertory, could make a profit in a smaller, more expensive indoor venue. This had not previously been apparent: the indoor theatres at Blackfriars and Paul's (which operated until 1606) had until this time been used for performances by boys, drawn either from the royal chapel choirs or run as commercial entertainment companies. The boys had not performed daily, and their repertories were not as wide as those of the adult companies, professionals who occupied the large amphitheatres in the suburbs. The King's Men proved that the habits of an adult company were suited to the different playing conditions and audience composition of an indoor venue, where the cheapest seat in the upper gallery cost sixpence – the price of a seat in a box at the Globe. Christopher Beeston, then the manager of Queen Anne's Men at the Red Bull in Clerkenwell, took note. In 1616 he invested some £400 of company money in the leasing and conversion of the 'edifices or building called the cockpits and the cock houses and the sheds thereunto adjoining' in the newly developing neighbourhood of Covent Garden. Beeston's company had just started playing in the new indoor theatre in March 1617, when an apprentice riot caused serious damage, but by July 1617 the playhouse was up and running.[5] After a slow start and some major changes of personnel – of which more later – Beeston's Cockpit became London's premier new-writing venue, offering work by Thomas Heywood, John Ford and James Shirley among many others, and, in Herbert Berry's view, achieved an artistic standard 'second only' to that of the King's Men at the Blackfriars and Globe.[6] If the King's Men offered ongoing indoor playing by adult companies as an innovation, Christopher Beeston turned it into a convention.

The conventions of indoor performance were to prove longer lasting than those of the suburban amphitheatres. The most obvious characteristic of indoor playing to be carried through the seventeenth century was the design and layout of the private playhouses, which differed substantially from the large amphitheatres. Wright's *Historia Histrionica* asserts that all three major Jacobean and Caroline indoor theatres were 'built almost exactly alike, for Form and Bigness'.[7] In fact, the Blackfriars, at about 66 feet by 46 feet, was larger than the other two (both approximately 40 square feet), and the number and arrangement of galleries in all three is open to question. But the configuration of the Cockpit was undoubtedly based on the Blackfriars: a bare stage wider than it was deep; a stage wall with two or three entrances and a musicians' gallery above; boxes lining both sides of the stage as far as the stage wall; a pit furnished with benches; and two or three levels of galleries arranged in a rectangle or half-polygon. All the audience was seated, and performances took place under a combination of candlelight and daylight (night-time performances which were wholly lit by candles were not unknown).[8] The Salisbury Court was almost certainly a close copy of the Cockpit. It was these two structures that survived into the Restoration (the Blackfriars had by this point been converted into tenements). The Salisbury Court suffered at the hands of Interregnum soldiers who, as the records of a lawsuit reveal, 'by force of arms entered the said playhouse, cut down the seats, broke down the stage, and utterly defaced the whole building'. This damage was repaired in 1659 to return 'the said theatre and all the seats and boxes and viewing rooms thereto belonging' to their original state.[9] The Cockpit, after similar vandalism in 1647 and 1648, when a group of former King's Men actors were arrested during a production of John Fletcher's *Rollo, Duke of Normandy*, was refitted in time for William Davenant's opera *The Siege of Rhodes*, staged there in 1658.[10] It is possible that this refit equipped the small playhouse with the sort of scenic flats and stage machinery that had become popular. By spring 1660, playing had resumed full-time at the Cockpit: on 18 April the civil servant and diarist Samuel Pepys was taken to see Fletcher's *The Loyal Subject*, 'the first that I have had time to see since my coming from the sea', in which Edward Kynaston played the leading female role: a Jacobean play performed in a Jacobean playhouse under the pre-war conditions of transvestite theatre, but overlaid with embryonic signs of proscenium-arch performance.[11] The new West End theatres that followed in the 1660s and 1670s were close cousins of their Jacobean and Caroline antecedents: the playhouses that spearheaded the revival of professional theatre in England were therefore the Cockpit, and its sister-space the Salisbury Court.

Perhaps more significantly, Christopher Beeston's management style was to have an enormous impact on the Restoration and modern stage. Christopher Beeston had taken out the lease on the Cockpit in 1616 in his role as senior member of Queen Anne's Men where he was, technically at least, *primus inter pares* in a company of men who worked for the good of the group. The object of this property deal was presumably to emulate the King's Men and their two houses, the Globe and the Blackfriars: Queen Anne's would now have the Red Bull for summer, and the Cockpit for winter. But the company struggled. In Thomas Middleton's *Inner Temple Masque*, a character remarks that the 'poor players ne'er thrived' in the new playhouse.[12] Low profits prompted a bold move by Beeston. Taking advantage of the death of their patron in 1619, he unilaterally dissolved Queen Anne's Men (apparently seizing the company's 'furniture and apparel'), ejected the patron-less players back to the Red Bull and hired in their stead Prince Charles' Men. Beeston repeated this manoeuvre in 1622 when Prince Charles' Men were dispatched to a suburban amphitheatre and the Lady Elizabeth's Men placed at the Cockpit. In 1625 it happened again: he formed a new company for the Cockpit, partly out of the existing troupes, called Queen Henrietta's Men in honour of the new French queen, which was to thrive for the next decade, the period of the Cockpit's greatest success.[13] Beeston was emerging as a new breed of showman: a business-minded impresario who could take up and drop theatre companies as he saw fit. This approach was very different to the joint-stock principles which prevailed at the King's Men. Beeston's high-handedness generated grievance and legal action, but it came to be seen as the model most likely to succeed: when the Salisbury Court theatre was established in 1629, its founders William Blagrave and Richard Gunnell did exactly the same thing as Beeston, hiring a group of actors who had no investment or involvement in the building and company themselves.[14]

It was also the form of management that survived into the Restoration and beyond. Beeston's playhouse in its heyday was the inspiration behind the theatres established by the most significant impresarios of the 1660s, William Davenant and Thomas Killigrew, even as the Cockpit itself – the venerable theatrical survivor – was stifled in the first years of Charles II's reign. Davenant had in fact briefly been in charge of the Cockpit, during the period that followed Christopher Beeston's death in 1639 before the closure of the theatres in 1642, and, as we have seen, the Cockpit was the venue for Davenant's first operas in 1658 and 1659.[15] When Davenant and Killigrew appealed to the king for duopoly rights to the staging of plays in London, they had Beeston's example in mind: their licence of August 1660 did

> give & Grante unto the said Thomas Killigrew and Sir William Davenant full power & authority to Erect two Companies of Players ... And to purchase builde and Erect or Hire at their Charge, As they shall thinke fit, two Houses or theatres, with all Convenient Roomes and other Necessaries thereunto appertaining for the Representation of Tragydies, Comedyes, Playes, Operas & all other Entertainments of that Nature.[16]

Their next move was to deal with the competition: they persuaded the elderly Master of the Revels, Henry Herbert, to send an intimidating letter to the company then resident at the Cockpit warning them that 'severall complaints have been made against you to the Kings most excellent Majesty by Mr Killigrew and Sir William Davenant concerning the unusuall and unreasonable rates taken by your play house doores' and hinting at the 'restrainte' that was to come their way under the new legislative dispensation (the Cockpit did not survive long).[17] For all that the target was the Cockpit, Christopher Beeston (now dead) would have recognized this commercially minded assertiveness as his own. It was Beeston's style of impresarioism, born of his property deals in 1616, that came to dominate London's theatre culture and is still with us today.

The most important result of Beeston's decision in 1616 to set up a new indoor playhouse was to embed the cultural shift to indoor playing that had been initiated by the King's Men in 1609. The nature of the artistic and social changes produced by this move has been debated for many years. In the 1950s, Alfred Harbage argued that the late Elizabethan and Jacobean years saw the development of rival stage traditions, represented by the popular culture of the suburban amphitheatres (which hosted plays noted for 'robustness and clear-eyed moral vigour') and the more courtly fare of the indoor 'private' playhouses, where playwrights pandered to a decadent coterie audience.[18] Harbage's view was supported by a historiography of pre-Civil War England that insisted on a widening gulf between court (characterized as royalist, flattering, supine) and country (populist, oppositional, engaged).[19] Both of these views have been challenged, and it is no longer considered at all clear that the repertories of the indoor and outdoor playhouses were so distinct.[20] But the fact remains that the trend from 1616 was for a form of theatre that took place under cover, artificially lit, with a fully-seated audience of between 500 and 1,000. Inevitably, this drew artistic investment and talent from the big outdoor venues, where up to 3,000 spectators (half of them standing in the unroofed yard) could watch a play for as little as a penny.

The story of the decline of the amphitheatres and the

dominance of the more elite indoor playhouses is complicated. The most powerful figures in Jacobean and Caroline
theatre-land managed portfolios of real estate that were made
up of both indoor and outdoor venues. The King's Men
enjoyed the use of the Blackfriars and the Globe. Christopher
Beeston, landlord of the Cockpit and the Red Bull, was
similarly invested in both forms of playhouse. If the indoor
theatres were the driving forces of fashion and reputation,
the amphitheatres still pulled their weight when it came
to profitability: the King's Men spent lavishly when they
rebuilt the Globe after a fire in 1613. But the very obvious
differences in admission price, audience composition and
geographical location between the two sorts of theatre (the
indoor playhouses were on the more fashionable west side of
the city) encouraged the development of a simplistic dyadism
that presented the amphitheatre fare as brash, old-fashioned
and unchallenging, and the plays at the 'private' houses as
modern, literary and expressly intended to appeal to the
beau-monde. As early as 1601, the child company of Paul's
were said to attract a 'good gentle Audience' compared to
the 'Beer-brewers' elsewhere; in the late 1630s James Shirley
explained that his modish tragi-comedy *The Doubtful Heir*,
first performed in Dublin, was wholly unsuitable for 'this
Meridian; the Banckside' when it received its London staging
at the Globe rather than the Blackfriars.[21] This became more
than a matter of reputation after the closure of the theatres by
Parliament in 1642. The difference between the alleged drum-
and-trumpet populism of the amphitheatres and the genteel
artistry of the private theatres was held up as a reason to permit
the indoor theatres to operate. *The Actors Remonstrance*, a
petition published in 1643, explained that 'it is not unknown
to all the audience that have frequented the private houses
of Blackfriars, the Cockpit and Salisbury-Court, without
austerity we have purged our stages from all obscene and
scurrilous jests, such as might either be guilty of corrupting
the manners, or the defaming the persons of any men of note
in the City or Kingdome'. The authors of the *Remonstrance*

promised to endeavour to 'repress bawling and railing' – code for the more vocally energetic style of delivery demanded by the outdoor playhouses.[22] Attempts such as these, unsuccessful as they were, reinforced the idea that 'proper' theatre was to be found inside; the amphitheatres were for the unthinking crowds. Only one outdoor theatre, the Red Bull, reopened for a short period after the Restoration. When Pepys visited, in March 1661, he found the place in a sad state:

> I was led ... up to the tireing-room, where strange the confusion and disorder that there is among them in fitting themselves, especially here, where the clothes are very poor, and the actors but common fellows. At last into the pit [yard], where I think there was not above ten more then myself, and not one hundred in the whole house. And the play, which is called *All's Lost by Love*, poorly done; and with so much disorder, among others, that in the music room the boy that was to sing a song, not singing it right, his master fell about his ears and beat him, so that it put the whole house in an uproar.[23]

The depredations of the Civil War and the Interregnum had combined to make real what had been a largely imaginary convention in the pre-war era: that serious theatre was only to be found inside, under candlelight.

The decay of the amphitheatre tradition meant that commercial theatre, as it was reconceived in the 1660s, followed the precedents established at the Blackfriars and embedded at the Cockpit and the Salisbury Court. The most privileged and expensive seats were those nearest the stage, in the pit and the boxes. Less well off patrons sat higher up and further back, their view of the stage often obscured by the rake of the galleries, and by the glare of low-hanging candles. These drawbacks did not greatly signify; just as important was the fact that an audience-member was engaged in a sociable pastime that allowed him or her to be numbered among the elite (or at least among those who sat in the same room as the elite). The social range of indoor audiences comprised the well off and the demi-monde chancers who followed in their wake, but excluded the greater part of London's working populace who could not afford (or had no wish) to sit in the obscure cheap seats. The idea that indoor theatres were the raffish playgrounds of high society took root remarkably early. In 1617, the year Beeston's Cockpit opened for business, Henry Fitzgeoffrey's 'Notes from BlackFriars' took the reader on a spatial and ethnographic tour of that playhouse, pointing out the braggart officers, gentlemen travellers, upwardly mobile citizens' wives and – inevitably – whores ranged in the galleries.[24] Nearly seventy years later, Robert Gould sketched out a similar terrain in his poem 'The Playhouse: A Satyr' (1685), although his tone was more scabrous: the middle section of the auditorium (or 'bitch-gallery') was the home of masked court ladies, rich citizens and their wives (again) and 'playhouse punks' (again).[25]

1616 was not the year in which England's theatre changed for good. The development of playhouse design, repertory and audience was evolutionary, not revolutionary. Historical and literary scholarship is rarely well served by the insistence on false nativities or teleologies. The other essays in this volume have illuminated ways in which theatre culture can be sustained in a variety of forms and modes, including print, performance, elite and popular. But I have suggested that a corner was turned when Beeston developed the indoor Cockpit in Drury Lane, and if the slow decline of the suburban amphitheatre is to be assigned an origin, then 1616 is as good as any.

Notes

1   James Wright, *Historia Histrionica. An Historical Account of the English Stage* (London: G. Croom for William Haws, 1699), sigs B2r and B3r.

2   For the development of English theatre under Elizabeth I,

see Glynne Wickham, *Early English Stages 1300 to 1600* (London: Routledge, 1959–81), vol. 1; Glynne Wickham, Herbert Berry and William Ingram (eds), *English Professional Theatre, 1530–1660* (Cambridge: Cambridge University Press, 2000), pp. 17–120 and 287–329; and W. R. Streitberger, 'Adult Playing Companies to 1583', in Richard Dutton (ed.), *The Oxford Handbook of Early Modern Theatre* (Oxford: Oxford University Press, 2009), pp. 19–38. English theatre offers a contrast to Chinese theatre of the same era, which took place at public festivals or in private homes.

3   Gurr, *The Shakespeare Company*, pp. 4–12.

4   Material relating to the Cockpit/Phoenix is to be found in G. E. Bentley, *The Jacobean and Caroline Stage* (Oxford: Clarendon Press, 1941–68), vol. 1, pp. 158–75, 218–59 and 324–42, and vol. 2, pp. 366–7; Wickham, Berry and Ingram (eds), *English Professional Theatre*, pp. 623–37; and Francis Teague, 'The Phoenix and the Cockpit-in-Court Playhouses', in Dutton (ed.), *Oxford Handbook*, pp. 240–59.

5   See John Chamberlain's letter to Dudley Carleton, 8 March 1617, in which he describes how the 'unruly people of the suburbs' stormed the new playhouse, in Norman Egbert McClure (ed.), *The Letters of John Chamberlain* (Philadelphia: American Philosophical Society, 1939), vol. 2, pp. 59–60.

6   Wickham, Berry and Ingram (eds), *English Professional Theatre*, p. 623.

7   Wright, *Historia Histrionica*, sig. B4r.

8   Keith Sturgess, *Jacobean Private Theatre* (London: Routledge, 1987), pp. 38–46.

9   The National Archives (TNA), C10/53/7 and C10/80/15, cited in Wickham, Berry and Ingram (eds), *English Professional Theatre*, pp. 655 and 671.

10   Teague, 'The Phoenix and Cockpit-in-Court Playhouses' in Dutton (ed.), *Handbook*, p. 258; Leslie Hotson, *The Commonwealth and Restoration Stage* (Cambridge, MA: Harvard University Press, 1928), p. 147.

11   Henry B. Wheatley (ed.), *The Diary of Samuel Pepys, 1659–1663* (London: G. Bell, 1946), pp. 207–8.

12   Thomas Middleton, *The Inner Temple Masque, or Masque of Heroes* (London: John Browne, 1619), sig. B3v.

13   Beeston's manoeuvrings are well documented in Eva Griffith, 'Christopher Beeston: His Property and Properties', in Dutton (ed.), *Oxford Handbook*, pp. 607–22.

14   Wickham, Berry and Ingram (eds), *English Professional Theatre*, pp. 649–51.

15   Mary Edmond, 'Davenant, Sir William', and Andrew Gurr, 'Beeston [Hutchinson], William', *Oxford Dictionary of National Biography* (online edition) [accessed 23 May 2014].

16   BL Additional MS 19256 (Master of the Revels MSS), fol. 47r.

17   Henry Herbert to Michael Mohun and the actors at the Cockpit, Drury Lane, 13 October 1660, BL Reserved Photocopy (RP) MS 6063.

18   Alfred Harbage, *Shakespeare and the Rival Traditions* (New York: Macmillan, 1952); the quoted characterization (exaggeration?) of Harbage's views is Sturgess, *Jacobean Private Theatre*, p. 4.

19   The most influential exponent of this view was Perez Zagorin, *The Court and the Country: The Beginning of the English Revolution* (London: Routledge, 1969).

20   See, for example, Martin Butler, *Theatre and Crisis 1632–1642* (Cambridge: Cambridge University Press, 1984); Kevin Sharpe, *Criticism and Compliment: The Politics of Literature in the England of Charles I* (Cambridge: Cambridge University Press, 1990); Roslyn Lander Knutson, 'What If There Wasn't a "Blackfriars Repertory"?', in Paul Menzer (ed.), *Inside Shakespeare: Essays on the Blackfriars Stage* (Selinsgrove: Susquehanna University Press, 2006), pp. 54–60; and Mariko Ichikawa, 'Continuities and Innovations in Staging', in Andrew Gurr and Farah Karim-Cooper (eds), *Moving Shakespeare Indoors: Performance and Repertoire in the Jacobean Playhouse* (Cambridge: Cambridge University Press, 2014), pp. 79–94.

21   John Marston, *Jacke Drums Entertainment* (London: Richard Olive, 1601), sig. H3v; James Shirley, *The Doubtful Heir. A Tragi-comedy* (London: Humphrey Robinson and Humphrey Moseley, 1653), sig. A3r.

22   W. C. Hazlitt (ed.), *The English Drama and Stage Under the Tudor and Stuart Princes, 1543–1664. Illustrated by a Series of Documents, Treatises and Poems* (Roxburghe Library, 1869), pp. 259–65.

23   Wheatley (ed.), *The Diary of Samuel Pepys*, p. 338.

24   H.[enry] F.[itzgeoffrey], *Satyres and Satyricall Epigrams* (London: Edward Allde for Miles Patrich, 1617), sigs E7r-F8v.

25   Robert Gould, *Poems Chiefly Consisting of Satyrs and Satyrical Epistles* (London: no printer's information, 1689), sigs L6r-N5r.

10

Theatre across genres and cultures

In what ways can Chinese and English theatres in 1616 connect to the broader literary landscapes of their respective cultures? The circulation of texts and the meanings of literary drama are evident in Xiaoqiao Ling's example of citing and reading drama in fiction, and also in Kate McLuskie's reading across two cultures and theatrical systems.

10.1 Elite drama readership staged in vernacular fiction: *The Western Wing* and *The Retrieved History of Hailing*

Xiaoqiao Ling

Commercial woodblock printing in China flourished from the last quarter of the sixteenth century throughout the seventeenth century. Catering to an emerging reading public, commercial publishers produced imprints that were beautiful objects adorned with exquisitely executed illustrations. As carefully crafted reading matter, these books promised to enhance the overall experience for the reader by also including accompanying commentary by renowned cultural figures. To give just a few examples of the most common (and often spurious) attributions, these include the iconoclastic thinker Li Zhi 李贄 (1527–1602), the eccentric writer Xu Wei and the acclaimed playwright Tang Xianzu. The year 1616 in particular is significant for the study of how drama was being presented to readers. As Stephen H. West shows in his essay in this volume (Section 5.1), Zang Maoxun published his monumental anthology of northern *zaju* plays to teach the anticipated reader how to become a drama specialist. The year also witnessed one of the many printed editions of Wang Shifu's (fl. thirteenth century) tremendously popular romantic play *The Western Wing*. Historically, 1616 was the year when Nurhaci (1559–1626) established the Latter Jin dynasty, an event that marked the rise of the Manchus. In the following decades, the Manchus were to pose an increasingly serious threat to the northern border of China until the fall of the Ming and the founding of the Qing dynasty in 1644.

The Retrieved History of Hailing (*Hailing yishi* 海陵佚史)[1] is a late Ming vernacular novella that provides a unique prism through which to assess both the historical significance of the year 1616 and the dynamics of elite drama readership in this period. The novella focuses on the despotic Jurchen ruler King Hailing (r. 1149–61) of the Jin dynasty (1115–1234), who had murdered his own mother and allegedly seized by force more than ten thousand women from his subjects. Since '[t]he Manchus were descended from the same Tungusic tribal people who had founded the Jin dynasty',[2] the novella is first and foremost a product of imagining the ultimate barbarian *other* as a response to the historical event in 1616. The preface to the novella, for example, carries a particular sense of historical urgency as it addresses those who 'collude with barbarians':

> For those who [have the mission to] wipe out all the clans of barbarians, do they also know of those of the northern barbarians who, being atrocious and cruel, bestial and perverse, observe nothing of the [cardinal] relationships between the ruler and the subject, father and son, husband and wife, elder and younger brothers? Why do they not look at the deposed emperor of the Jin [Dynasty] Wanyan Liang (King Hailing) for a lesson? ... Overcome with indignation, the Daoist Master [of No Hindrance] thereupon composed *The Retrieved History of Hailing*. What were retrieved were [acts of] debauchery, and how can debauchery admonish? The Daoist Master has compiled [those stories into a] book and provided illustrations for them – is [the book] not supposed to bring out how outrageous are the northern barbarian's depravity and cruelty in order to caution those who collude with those slaves?[3]

The novella in its printed form is a beautiful object that is emblematic of what the blossoming print culture had to offer. But most pertinent to our interest are the ways in which the text informs us of the reading practice of the seventeenth century. The story proper is copied verbatim from the *Official History of the Jin Dynasty* and lays out the framework of the narrative: Hailing and his consorts' ignominious behaviours. Fleshing out the historical narrative are anecdotes in the storyteller's voice interspersed with textual fragments drawn from all levels of textual traditions, from Confucian classics and Taoist canon to witty repartee, ditties and popular songs. In its active engagement with different modes of the contemporary cultural production, *The Retrieved History of Hailing* exemplifies what Yuming He has termed the 'book conversancy' that characterized the print culture and its targeted reading public.[4]

What is singular about *The Retrieved History of Hailing* as a printing endeavour is its innovative use of marginal commentary. Following the convention of vernacular fiction, the novella eschews explicit authorial attribution,[5] and instead designates one Daoist Master of No Hindrance (Wuzhe daoren) to be the compiler,[6] whose authority over the text is equally shared with that of the commentator, The Drunk and Crazy Layman (Zuihan jushi). The Drunk and Crazy Layman, however, did not write his own comments. Instead, he enlisted a total of 122 lines from arias in Wang Shifu's northern *zaju* play *The Western Wing* and 36 lines from Li Rihua's (1565–1635) *chuanqi* adaptation titled *Southern Western Wing* (*Nan Xixiang* 南西廂). This, to my knowledge, is the only case of marginal commentary that comprises nothing but direct quotations from a play. Such a highly unusual use of the marginal space of the page pushes to the fore the act of reading as the deciding source that produces meaning. By citing exclusively from *The Western Wing* as an established cultural icon, the marginal commentary functions very much as a mediating figure that engages the novella in its discursive reading of the play, so much so that the hierarchy of the book page in its spatial layout may be fully reversed, as the text proper presents itself to be a commentary on the play. This is an ingeniously conceived literary game that probably targeted a very exclusive group of readers such as drama connoisseurs in the Jiangnan area.[7] In what follows, I will examine in detail how elite drama readership is enlisted to foster the fictional imagination of the barbaric *other*, as well as to explore the hidden possibilities of understanding *The Western Wing*.

Celebrating subversive readings of *The Western Wing* to construct the barbaric *other*

The fictional construction of King Hailing as the ultimate barbaric *other* is enabled by the marginal commentary which shows how the Jurchen king upsets the Confucian ethical codes in fundamental ways. One of the earlier episodes employs the trope of voyeurism common in erotic fiction by having King Hailing stage an orgy in front of a peeping virgin, Chongjie, the fifteen-year-old daughter of Hailing's consort Alihu, in order to seduce the young maiden: he has the ground covered with fabric and orders that everyone strips naked. He then chases after his consorts to force them into copulation. Chongjie is indeed aroused, and allows herself to be deflowered. Enchanted by his new possession, Hailing casts Alihu aside for days. When the forlorn mother confronts her daughter for having stolen the monarch away from her, the marginal commentary reads: 'She'll turn you into a loving, a caring, a handsome husband, / So why fear a mother who now has the power to restrict her?'[8] The original aria dramatizes the tension between a mother who is eager to keep the family's honour and a daughter who desires a romantic tryst. Against this established reading of the lines from *The Western Wing*, the novella presents a mother jealously guarding her lord from her own daughter – a dramatic scene that must have been unsettling for a traditional reader well tuned to Confucian teachings such as the Five Principal Relationships mentioned in the preface.

To a large extent, the grotesque body of the barbaric *other* also capitalizes on the stark contrast between the original meaning of the aria and the new, subversive reading of the lines as a comment on the novella. In *The Western Wing*, the male protagonist Student Zhang (Zhang sheng) travels to the capital to take the civil service examination. Having successfully attained the degree as the top candidate, he finally receives the much anticipated letter from his beloved Oriole (Yingying). Admiring her elegant handwriting, the Student sings:

> This could serve as a history of characters
> Or should be a monumental inscription.
> It has Liu's [Gongquan's] bones, Yan's [Zhenqing's] force.[9]

The last line, 'Liu's bones, Yan's force', which refers to the way Oriole writes with panache, appears in *The Retrieved History of Hailing* to comment instead on King Hailing's enormous sexual organ. One of the women Hailing has sexually conquered is Shigu, whose deceased husband sported an organ that was 'extremely strong and robust, meaty and stout. From the root to its tip, there was a vein protruding like an earthworm.'[10] Having encountered Hailing, Shigu told a youngster, whose lack of sexual potency had earlier left her unsatisfied, that 'The Emperor's sexual intercourse indeed has profound skill, not some messing around for nothing.'[11] At this point, the marginal comment chimes in: 'Indeed, "it has Liu's bones, Yan's force."'[12] The word 'force' (*jin* 筋) here is deliberately misread to refer to the protruding vein (*jin* 筋) on Hailing's sexual organ (which may have reminded Shigu fondly of her deceased husband), thereby appropriating what was initially a quality of significant cultural implications (Liu's bone and Yan's force as signs of virtuosity in calligraphy) in *The Western Wing* to describe instead a grotesque body part.

Clearly it is a self-conscious attempt on the novella's part to celebrate the liberating power of subversive (mis)reading in its capacity to produce new meaning. Earlier in this anecdote, Hailing hears of Shigu's sexual adventures and sends her the following note:

> Your romantic flair is bold and uninhibited, unsurpassed in your own time. Yet you have sunk low to fondle dicks of inferior kinds, and for all your indulgence you have not met with the Grand Marshal of Romance. Have you not lived your life in vain? (Marginal comment: *'The fame of the Flying Tiger General has spread everywhere south of the Dipper'*.) Your lord's revered *yang* force is Nine in the fifth place,[13] an official of supreme status. If you could truly

work up the gust of wind from your vagina, and get your water-mill in full operation to flood the big dick until it cringes, such that the *yang* force is hidden in the depths[14] – only then shall I acknowledge your prowess.[15]

The original aria from *The Western Wing* cited by the commentator reads: 'The fame of the Flying Tiger General has spread everywhere south of the Dipper. / But that lout is capable only of lust and desire, competent only in avarice and greed. / He's not worth a thing.'[16] The Flying Tiger General in the play is a bandit who threatened to abduct Oriole as his wife,[17] and in the original dramatic context, his fame as a ferocious warrior is undercut by his lust and greed as the arch villain. The novella, by contrast, cites the dramatic line to comment on Hailing's sexual prowess. Here the language of war in *yin–yang* terminology, which is the stock metaphor in vernacular fiction to describe sexual encounters, converges seamlessly with the language of statecraft, with the word *liao* 膫 (penis) used interchangeably with its homophone *liao* 僚 (bureaucrat): in a state governed by the ultimate barbaric *other*, King Hailing as the Grand Marshal of Romance, political success is contingent upon sexual potency. To be mired down in lower-level bureaucracy (*chenni xiaoliao* 沈溺下僚), which is the common fate of a frustrated Confucian scholar, is identical to Shigu's wallowing in pleasure provided by subpar organs (*chenni xiaoliao* 沈溺下膫).

Alternative, new theatre: productive consumption of *The Western Wing*

In its discursive (mis-)reading of *The Western Wing* evoked by marginal commentary, *The Retrieved History of Hailing* has interpreted the play in such a way as to remind us of Pierre Bourdieu's concept of consumption as 'the manner of consuming which creates the object of consumption'.[18] The arias from the play are juxtaposed against passages in the novella that shock and intrigue by creating meaning against the 'horizon of expectations'[19] promulgated by the original play, so much so that the fictional world of *The Retrieved History of Hailing* stages an alternative theatre that is brave and new not so much with the novelty of writing as by merit of unearthing buried possibilities of reading the play.[20]

One example in which the novella stages a drama that brings out the full potential of *The Western Wing* as reading matter is in the aforementioned scene of orgy arranged by Hailing to seduce the young maiden Chongjie. The marginal commentary provides three entries on this scene: 1) 'The old ones and the young ones, / The boorish and the clever – / All are turned topsy-turvy'[21]; 2) 'It makes me wild and crazy; / My itching heart cannot be scratched'[22]; 3) 'This good affair is concluded too soon'.[23]

All the three comments come from the same scene (1.4) in *The Western Wing,* in which Student Zhang and a group of Buddhist monks gasp at Oriole's charm at a deliverance ritual. While the play stages this farcical scene as a comic intervention that at once underscores Oriole's rapturous beauty and pokes fun at the Buddhist monastery as paradoxically an ideal place for a romantic tryst, the marginal commentary in *The Retrieved History of Hailing* brings out the full potential for reading debauchery into this scene by referring to the lustful longing of the peeping virgin. Watching a bevy of imperial consorts being chased by their naked monarch (described by the first comment) makes the fifteen-year-old Chongjie burn with sexual desire (second comment), until, as the third comment indicates, the farce ends prematurely from the virgin's point of view, no doubt because she was not able to participate. The dramatic energy held in the mildly titillating scene in *The Western Wing* is fully unleashed in the novella, as the farce transmutes into a disturbing psychological drama that highlights the absolute lack of shame of the barbarian *other* – the king, his consorts and the young virgin.

The alternative, new theatre that is premised on creative and subversive consumption of *The Western Wing* finds its fullest expression in the novella's evocation of Li Rihua's *Southern Western Wing*, which is itself a reading of Wang Shifu's northern play. When we examine the marginal commentary's citation of the southern play, it becomes clear that the novella is aiming to further develop the character of Crimson (Hongniang 紅娘), Oriole's bright maid who acts as an intermediary figure to bring the romantic couple together.

Let us first look at Li Rihua's revision of the aria in the scene when the romantic couple consummate their love affair. While the first part of the aria is very much a faithful translation of the northern song into a southern tune, the second part departs from Wang Shifu's northern play to dramatize instead Crimson's inner world:

[CRIMSON *speaks*]
Student Zhang promised earlier that once the affair was arranged, he would thank me by 'having an altar erected to pay tribute to the general.' Now the two of them just retreated into the inner chamber holding hands.
[CRIMSON *sings*]
They heed nothing about the fact that Crimson is waiting outside the door.
My rootless amorous feelings – to whom can I plead to give vent to them?
All I can do is to endure, gritting my teeth with my gauze shirt between them.
Yet I am afraid that the Old Lady will wake up.
That will turn the serendipitous affair into disaster …
Now look, the moon has climbed on top of the painted wall,
Please do not blame me for rushing you.[24]

What Li Rihua has added in his revision is Crimson's repressed sexual frustration, a development that *The Retrieved History of Hailing* further pursues in the episode featuring Hailing's seduction of Dingge (Oriole's counterpart in the novella) through the help of the latter's maid Guige (Crimson's counterpart). The novella goes to great lengths to impress the reader with the maid's quick wit and persuasive power that allows her to successfully bring Hailing into the inner quarters of her mistress. At this point, Crimson's repressed sexual frustration in the *Southern Western Wing* ('My rootless amorous feelings – to whom can I plead to give vent to them?') is amplified in the novella into Guige's surging desire: 'They left Guige all by herself to listen to them for a while, then get up to peek for a while. Hearing and witnessing all this merry-making rendered her even more desolate, as she tossed and turned, not being able to keep her eyes shut.'[25]

Li Rihua falls short of having Crimson fulfil her unrequited desire, and no redaction of the northern play has ever allowed Crimson to have sexual intercourse with Student Zhang – such a design would certainly compromise the highly aestheticized romantic story. By contrast, in the novella Guige indeed receives her physical reward from Hailing after the latter consummated his affair with her mistress. At this point the marginal commentary appropriates Crimson's worry that the Old Lady may find out about the tryst in *Southern Western Wing* to refer instead to Guige's fear lest her own lady finds out about her transgression ('Yet I am afraid that the Lady will wake up'). The novella then proceeds to turn Guige into a most disturbing version of Crimson who eventually supersedes her own mistress to become Hailing's consort, producing an altogether new theatre of lust and betrayal.

The Retrieved History of Hailing therefore makes a compelling case for us to understand how the prolificacy of imprints helped to cultivate reading as a creative energy, as the novella is as much about the act of writing as it is about the act of reading. Although it is not clear who are the compiler and commentator, their assumed personae (a religious figure who has perfected his cultivation to the point of having no hindrance, and a free-spirited figure celebrating himself for being drunk and crazy) resonate with the late Ming literati sensibility that revered eccentricity and religious knowledge in addition to book learning. The novella's skilful deployment of marginal commentary was clearly meant to appeal to a very prestigious group of readers from the late Wanli period who, being writers and connoisseurs on their own accounts, were fully aware of the productive power of reading. And for these elite consumers to relish an essentially xenophobic narrative, the reading experience must entail not only a Confucian moral underpinning, but also moments of pleasant surprise that can whet the appetite of blasé scholars.[26] Here is where reading against the grain contributes much to the fictional imaginary of the non-Chinese *other* as a response to the historical event in 1616, and adding more to the value of *The Retrieved History of Hailing* as an elite cultural product is the novella's creative consumption of *The Western Wing*.

Notes

1   The text survived in a woodblock edition titled *The Retrieved History of Hailing with Illustrations and Commentary* (*Chuxiang piping Hailing yishi*) that is dated no earlier than 1606. All the citations in this essay are to the modern typeset edition in the *Collected Treasures of 'In Thoughts, There is Nothing Deviant'* (*Siwuxie huibao*) series, comps Chan Hing-ho and Wang Chiu-kuei (Taipei: Encyclopedia Britannica, 1995).

2   Frederic Wakeman, *The Great Enterprise: The Manchu Reconstruction of Imperial Order in Seventeenth-century China* (Berkeley: University of California Press, 1985), p. 55.

3   'Preface' in *The Retrieved History of Hailing*, pp. 29–30.

4   See Yuming He, *Home and the World: Editing the 'Glorious Ming' in Woodblock-printed Books of the Sixteenth and Seventeenth Centuries* (Cambridge, MA: Harvard University Asia Center, 2013), pp. 1–16.

5   Traditional Chinese writers did not sign their own names for fiction and drama, as both forms were excluded from the four-pronged traditional bibliography: Confucian classics

(*jing*), writings by important thinkers designated as Masters (*zi*), History (*shi*) and *Belles-Lettres* (*ji*).

6   The rhetoric of compiling rather than composing harks back to Confucius' claim regarding his compilation of the classics: 'I transmit; I do not compose' (*shu er bu zuo*).

7   For a discussion of printed plays as a public space for the self-expression and community-building of the literati, see Katherine Carlitz, 'Printing as Performance: Literati Playwright-publishers of the Late Ming', in Cynthia Brokaw and Kai-wing Chow (eds), *Printing and Book Culture in Late Imperial China* (Berkeley: University of California Press, 2005), pp. 267–303.

8   *The Retrieved History of Hailing*, A.40 (in this essay I use A to designate *juan shang* 卷上 and B to designate *juan xia* 卷下). For the aria, see Wang Shifu, *Xixiang ji* 1.2 (in this essay, I use the book number before the period and act number after the period), 'Wu sha' (fifth from coda), photographic reproduction of the 1498 editiõn (Shijiazhuang: Hebei jiaoyu chubanshe, 2006), 47a. For the translation, see Stephen H. West and Wilt L. Idema (eds and trans), *The Story of the Western Wing* (Berkeley: University of California Press, 1995), p. 134.

9   Both Liu Gongquan (778–865) and Yan Zhenqing (709–85) were paragons of calligraphic skill. *Xixiang ji*, 5.2, 'Shang xiaolou'; *Western Wing*, p. 261.

10   *The Retrieved History of Hailing*, B.106.

11   Ibid., B.109.

12   Ibid.

13   Nine in the fifth place refers to the fifth position of the first hexagram *qian* in *The Book of Changes* (*Yijing*). The line statement reads: 'When a flying dragon is in the sky, it is fitting to see the great man.' See Richard Lynn (trans.), *The Classic of Changes: A New Translation of the* I Ching *as Interpreted By Wang Bi* (New York: Columbia University Press, 1994), p. 137. This is traditionally interpreted to be the monarch's position, as the *yang* force (nine, as opposed to six that designates the *yin* force) resides at the proper *yang* line at the centre of the upper trigram (the fifth position of the hexagram).

14 This is a commentary on the line statement of the first position of the *qian* hexagram, which reads: 'A submerged dragon does not act.' Lynn, *The Classic of Changes*, p. 132. This is traditionally interpreted to mean that the *yang* force is not at its proper place, and therefore must not assert itself.

15 *The Retrieved History of Hailing*, B.106–7.

16 *Xixiang ji*, 2.2, 'Tang xiucai', 64b; *Western Wing*, p. 160.

17 Seized by fear, the Old Lady (Oriole's mother) offers her daughter's hand to anyone who can save them from the bandit. The male protagonist, Student Zhang, thereupon seeks help to defeat the bandit only to find, later, that the Old Lady does not intend to keep her word.

18 Pierre Bourdieu, *Distinction: A Social Critique of the Judgement of Taste* (Cambridge, MA: Harvard University Press, 1984), p. 282.

19 Hans Robert Jauss, *Toward an Aesthetic*, cited from Richard Wang, *Ming Erotic Novellas: Genre, Consumption and Religiosity in Cultural Practice* (Hong Kong: The Chinese University Press, 2011), p. 38.

20 Pierre Bourdieu notes in *Outline of a Theory of Practice* that 'If witticisms surprise their author no less than their audience, and impress as much by their retrospective necessity as by their novelty, the reason is that the *trouvaille* appears as the simple unearthing, at once accidental and irresistible, of a buried possibility.' Bourdieu, *Outline of a Theory of Practice* (Cambridge: Cambridge University Press, 1977), p. 79.

21 *The Retrieved History of Hailing*, A.37. For the aria, see *Xixiang ji*, 1.4, 'Tianshui ling', 55a; *Western Wing*, p. 146.

22 *The Retrieved History of Hailing*, A.37. For the aria, see *Xixiang ji*, 1.4, 'Zhegui ling', 55a; *Western Wing*, p. 146.

23 *The Retrieved History of Hailing*, A.37. For the aria, see *Xixiang ji*, 1.4, 'Yuanyang sha', 56a; *Western Wing*, p. 148.

24 *Southern Western Wing*, in Mao Jin (comp.), *Liushi zhong qu* (Beijing: Zhonghua shuju, 1958), 3.27, 'Shier hong', p. 78.

25 *The Retrieved History of Hailing*, B.87.

26 For a discussion of literati drama playwright-publishers in the late Wanli period who were jaded connoisseurs seeking

stimulation in unconventional writing, see Wilt L. Idema,
' "Blasé Literati": Lü T'ien-ch'eng and the Lifestyle of the
Chiang-nan Elite in the Final Decades of the Wan-li', in
Robert van Gulik, *Erotic Colour Prints of the Ming Period
with an Essay on Chinese Sex Life from the Han to the
Ch'ing Dynasty, B.C. 206–A.D. 1644* (Leiden: Brill, 2004),
pp. xxxi–lix.

10.2 'There be salmons in both': Models of connection for seventeenth-century English and Chinese drama

Kate McLuskie

The task of exploring the 'Brave new theatres' of China and England in 1616 presents a number of intractable methodological questions. We are not dealing here with the established analytical methods applied to contemporary intercultural performance or cultural exchange but with the much more difficult task of identifying synergies between different forms of theatre from quite distinct and geographically distant cultural and literary formations. Those distinctions of geography and culture impose severe limits on the direct connections that characterize a 'diffusion model' of cultural exchange, though identifying those limits also helps us to define the terms in which the enquiry can usefully take place.

It is clear, for example, that by 1616, England and China were part of the same imaginative world. As David Markley observes:

> No literate man or woman in western Europe could plead ignorance of the relative size, wealth and natural resources of, say, England and China. By the middle of the seventeenth century, China had become a crucial site of contention and speculation in a variety of fields ... and, most significantly, the wealth of the nation whetted a seemingly insatiable desire (among Europeans) for Chinese goods and what seemed, for many merchants, an infinitely profitable trade.

Markley's analysis deals with the economic basis for this imaginative link that allows him to map the 'complex network of ports, agricultural regions and trading opportunities' known to international traders onto the travel narratives that envisioned 'an almost ritualistic praise of the country's natural wealth and the industry of its people'.[1]

The heroic dimensions of this early modern vision of China's potential for economic exploitation depended, however, on the mediating interests and knowledge of those who imagined them. Unlike the travellers and merchants who saw China as a source of wealth and adventure, most early modern writers had no direct experience of the world beyond England. Instead, the world outside England was always seen in relation to the one they knew. 'China' existed as a defining by-word for the exotic and the strange. Recording Shane O'Neil's 1562 visit to England, the antiquarian William Camden described his 'Guard of Ax-bearing Galloglasses, bare-headed, with curled Hair hanging down, ... whom the English people gazed at with no less admiration than now-adays they do them of China and America'.[2] The strangeness of an Irish aristocrat from within the British archipelago could be bracketed with those from the far east and far west of the known world. The comparison only provided a means of establishing Englishness as the central norm from which to judge the literal 'outland-ishness' of other cultures.

A similar Anglo-centric parochialism was evident in the discourse of the early modern stage. On the rare occasions when China – as opposed to a more generic 'east' – is mentioned in plays of the time, the exotic and essentially strange character of Chinese practices has become assimi-lated into a commonplace location for a joke. In Marston's *Parasitaster*, for example, Dulcimella, 3.1. uses hearsay about China to elaborate a standard anti-misogynist joke: 'They say in China, when women are past child-bearing, they are all burnt to make gun-powder. I wonder what men should bee done withal, when they are past child-getting' (3.1.198–201).[3] Dulcimella's prattle, of course, tells us nothing with any authority about the perceptions of or connection to China in early modern England. She is as unreliable a witness as most characters in plays. The connection between characters' perceptions of any feature of early modern culture is mediated by literary and theatrical demands made by dramatic narratives that condition their existence. The characters exist in an imagined world that includes commonplace, casual references to exotic objects but those references are fully assimilated into the idiosyncratic speech of a particular character in a particular situation.

In Shakespeare's *Measure for Measure*, for example, the bawd, Pompey, examined by the patient magistrate, Escalus, explains how the constable's wife came into his tavern in search of stewed prunes for his pregnant wife. He launches into a rambling, complicated story: 'Sir, she came in great with child; and longing, saving your honour's reverence, for stewed prunes; sir, we had but two in the house, which at that very distant time stood as it were, in a fruit-dish, a dish of some three-pence, your honours have seen such dishes; they are not china dishes, but very good dishes' (*Measure for Measure*, 2.1.88–94). 'China', in Pompey's speech, is a synecdoche for the high status trade goods that constituted the main material connection to the exotic imagined land of travellers and merchants. The delicious, self important irrelevance of his reference to 'China' dishes demonstrates his desire for the authenticating detail that might impress an examining magistrate.

Pompey's reference to china dishes is quite different from the kind of cultural exchange that takes place in what Ian Watson has called 'sites of discussion, conflict, eruption, compromise, debate and above all negotiation'.[4] Those sites of conflict do exist in Shakespeare's plays where the dynamics of difference are the subject of the plays themselves but they are fully assimilated into character and narrative. Othello's or Caliban's or Shylock's senses of their differences from the cultures in which they function are developed into eloquent poetic and narrative representations of their psychic and political implications. Foreign travel and trade are constructed as part of the lived experience that shapes their relation to the world in which they find themselves and the articulation of difference is central to the emotional structure of the plays in which they appear.

As theorists of cultural exchange have shown, the process of cultural exchange needs to pay close attention to the discursive locations of the centre, periphery and direction of travel, not merely in material terms but in terms of the needs and impulses of those who engage with it. As the bathos of passing references to China shows, the fact that early modern England and early modern China were part of the same trading world is far from creating the conditions for being part of the same cultural world.

Since the intervening effects of character and situation complicate the cultural exchange effected by contact and diffusion, it may be more appropriate to identify cultural synergies by working through models of 'parallel development': the analogies between practices that seem to evolve in similar ways even when there is limited identifiable contact involved between the cultures concerned. Here, too, we must be alert to the tension between parallels and false analogies, wittily dramatized in Fluellen's comic attempt to insist on the greatness of his king, Henry V, born at Monmouth, by a comparison with Alexander the Great, born in Macedon:

> I tell you, captain, if you look in the maps of the 'orld, I warrant you sall find, in the comparisons between Macedon and Monmouth, that the situations, look you, is both alike. There is a river in Macedon; and there is also moreover a river at Monmouth: it is called Wye at Monmouth; but it is out of my prains what is the name of the other river; but 'tis all one, 'tis alike as my fingers is to my fingers, and there is salmons in both. (*Henry V*, 4.7. 23–31)

As Fluellen indicates, the argument from parallel development depends upon finding common features by abstraction that will create a meta-analysis that can include multiple cases.

Addressing the remarkable symbiosis between Spanish and

English drama in the Renaissance, Walter Cohen cites a note from Leonard Digges, author of commendatory verses on the 1640 edition of Shakespeare's poems, to Will Baker on the flyleaf of a copy of Lope de Vega's 1613 *Rimas*: 'Knowing that Mr Mab: was to send you this booke of sonnets, wch with Spaniards here is accounted of their lope de Vega as in England wee sholde of our Will Shakespeare.'[5] This shared taste among two well-read, cosmopolitan gentlemen could not itself create a paradigm for a comparison of different literary and theatrical practices. For Cohen, however, it can provide a telling starting point for an attempt 'to discover why the drama of the two countries took the course it did'.[6] His analysis usefully connects the formal characteristics of English and Spanish drama that arise from their analogous synthesis of native popular and neoclassical learned traditions and the larger historical coincidence of the development of early modern capitalism and the rise of particular forms of 'public theatre' in England and Spain.

This connection between systemic factors and formal analysis provides a useful set of checks and balances for a robust analysis of the remarkable coincidence that the cultures of Ming-dynasty China and English Jacobean theatre both produced a literary drama: a drama in written form that was able to be reproduced and sustained beyond its originary cultural moment through the technology of print. In the case of Jacobean theatre, it was the literary, scripted and printed texts that came to constitute the 'backlist' that provided the content for the revival of theatre after the 1642–60 closure. The domination of that backlist by work that had been reproduced in Folio – the work of Shakespeare, Jonson and, belatedly, Beaumont and Fletcher – laid the foundations for an author-centred, aesthetic criticism of the drama of the previous age and began the process of critical analysis that created the canon of early modern theatre.

Because critical responses to that drama were informed by printed texts as much as by audition in a restricted court theatre, their literary qualities were addressed alongside their theatrical characteristics. A number of critics have suggested that the 'literary' quality perceived in plays of the early modern period and Shakespeare in particular may have been the product of a printing industry that addressed a readerly audience rather than a theatrical one. Lukas Erne and others have demonstrated the extent to which the multiple printed texts of Shakespeare's plays provide additional, more extended, poetic speeches in later editions such as the prologues to *Henry V* or speech additions to *Othello* and *King Lear*.[7] Although late twentieth- and early twenty-first-century criticism has tended to emphasize the theatrical origins of Shakespeare's plays, it is their literary qualities of narrative consistency, individualized characters and an eloquent metaphorical poetics that constitute their claims to value and the potential to be compared with other literary works distant in place and time.

In the Jacobean period, the literary characteristics of new dramatic output were certainly used to establish a hierarchy between competing theatrical organizations. It was not enough that attendance at more financially exclusive hall theatres ensured that its clientele would not be 'pasted to the barmy jacket of a beer brewer';[8] the superior experience of the hall theatres was often connected to their literary qualities, invoked to establish the alignment of taste with wealth.

The differentiation between literary appreciation and theatrical pleasure was as much a matter of theatrical organization as particular architectural form. Though Shakespeare's and Fletcher's *Henry VIII* was performed at the open-air Globe theatre in 1613, it was produced by the King's Men whose plays dominated the repertory of court entertainment and controlled the distribution of theatrical productions by virtue of their unique possession of two theatre outlets. Their old and new writers, Shakespeare and Fletcher, demanded from their audience a commitment to serious literary appreciation based on the neoclassical preference for empathy over comedy. Their prologue announced:

I come no more to make you laugh: things now
That bear a weighty and a serious brow
Sad, high and working, full of state and woe,
Such noble scenes as draw the eye to flow,
We now present. Those that can pity here
May, if they think it well, let fall a tear:
The subject will deserve it. Such as give
Their money out of hope they may believe
May here find truth, too. Those that come to see
Only a show or two and so agree
The play may pass, if they be still and willing
I'll undertake may see away their shilling
Richly in two short hours.

That desired audience were clearly distinguished from the spectators

That come to hear a merry, bawdy play,
A noise of targets, or to see a fellow
In a long motley coat guarded with yellow ...
          For, gentle hearers, know
To rank our chosen truth with such a show
As fool and fight is, beside forfeiting
Our own brains, and the opinion that we bring
To make that only true we now intend,
Will leave us never an understanding friend.

(*Henry VIII*, Prologue, 1–22.)[9]

This emphasis on the literary qualities of the Jacobean repertory may have helped to establish the dominance of the King's Men, the company that had produced Shakespeare's plays. In 1616, their performances dominated entertainments at court. From November 1615 to April 16 they presented 'fourteen unnamed plays' before the king and queen; and between 31 October 1616 and 5 March 1617 they offered thirteen plays (unnamed) before the king and queen.

Though the literary drama provided the canon for subsequent criticism, this formal repertory of court theatre and printed texts was seen by fewer people than the quasi-dramatic activity associated with festivities to celebrate the creation of lord mayors of London. It is there that we are likely to find the most explicit celebration of the global reach and ambition of early modern culture. The livery companies, whose leaders were likely to become lord mayor, also dominated the international trade that became a major source of wealth and prosperity. In 1617, for example, the show of the 'Triumphs of Honour and Industry', written by Shakespeare's young contemporary, Thomas Middleton, celebrated the mayoralty of Sir George Bowles, a grocer. It presented a Ship drawn by beasts; Pageant of Nations, the Indian Chariot, the Castle of Fame. Bowles's triumph offered tangible treats for the city audience as the company 'payd for 50 sugar loaves, 36 li of nutmegge, 14li of dates and 114li of ginger wch were thrown about the streetes by those wch sate on the Griffyns and Camells 005 07 8d'.[10]

The direct pleasures of communal feasting may have been an equally significant aspect of the lord mayor's shows as their highly patterned, symbolic iconography that connected the livery company to its exotic trading locations.

This range of literary and theatrical activity not only provides a deep context for the year of Shakespeare's death: it also indicates the extent to which he left a theatre world that was in strong form, characterized not only by great literary drama but by a creative and artistic diversity that included, as David McInnes has shown, 'more than 550 plays (that) have been lost, or exist only in manuscript fragments'.[11] This plethora of dramatic and quasi-dramatic output, performed at court, in the purpose-built theatres, on tour throughout England and in the streets of early modern London, calls into question the dominance of the literary drama in our account of the dramatic output of the early modern theatres and complicates the possibility of any connection to Ming-dynasty Chinese theatres.

I have been intrigued to find in my elementary reading on Chinese theatre that questions of the specific formal literary characteristics appear not to have dominated discussion. Rather the marked characteristics of Chinese theatre, noted in Faye Chunfang Fei's collection of *Chinese Theories of Theatre and Performance*, seem to have been a much more direct and unmediated capacity of skilled performers for communication of essential truths about human experience. Faye Chunfang Fei quotes Pan Zhiheng, commenting on a performance of Tang's *Peony Pavilion*:

> Jiang and Chang, the two young performers from Wuchang are not only capable of becoming emotionally possessed by their characters' love, but they are also capable of physically enacting their love – one dreamy and ethereal, the other bold and romantic – in a completely natural and unaffected manner. Through training the performers' voices are smooth and supple like pearl strings, and their movements are elegant and graceful like divine beings.[12]

This account seems to provide no space for specifically literary analysis since the mimetic connection between performance and perception is seamless and pays no attention to narrative or aesthetic form: 'The performer/dancer does not know where his feelings come from, and the enraptured spectator does not know where his own mind has gone.'[13]

I have no way of knowing how authoritative or representative Faye Chunfang Fei's selections are, but I am nevertheless struck by the way in which the evidence she presents gives no suggestion of a theatrical community interacting in systems of literary exchange. Other essays in this volume indicate how far this celebration of an already significant dramatist such as Tang Xianzu addresses the critical preoccupations of a small subset of the audience for theatre and how far it characterizes the sense of the theatre output as a whole.

In the literary remains of the early modern English theatre on the other hand, particularly as late in its development as

1616, it is possible to discern a shared access to deep structures of narrative and theatricality. Those structures are most evident in Shakespeare's work but they can be examined, perhaps more dispassionately, in the work of the much less well-established playwrights whose work surrounded the canonical output of the Folio published playwrights. One such text – not entirely a random example – is a play called *The Love-sick King*. It was written possibly by an actor, Anthony Brewer,[14] possibly in 1615–17 (which makes it relevant for our comparison point).[15] It was not printed until 1655 in the printers' exploitation of the backlist of early modern drama during the opportunity provided by the brief freedom of the press. Without that development, *The Love-sick King* might have disappeared into the abyss of the 'lost' plays that are so hard to identify in literary, thematic or theatrical terms. Unlike Shakespeare's plays, *The Love-sick King* has not been the subject of thematic connections made to plays from other times and places: rather it is interesting to the extent it shows a competent dramatist, drawing on the literary materials available to him in the printed histories of pre-Norman England that also attracted Middleton in *Hengist King of Kent*, Fletcher in *Bonduca* and Shakespeare in *King Lear* and *Cymbeline*. The rhetorical tropes and dramatic devices that its author uses to construct its dramatic narrative show the common stock of literary material which contemporary dramatists contributed as content for the brave new theatres of early modern England.

Brewer's play is chronologically confused: he draws on two different phases of the Danish invasions of Britain and includes a subplot that deals with Thornton, a historical Mayor of Newcastle from the fifteenth century. It is also generically unstable, not only in combining the conflict of Dane and Anglo Saxon with the comic scenes in Newcastle but in bringing together the battle narratives with a double melodrama of disastrous love stories. The play never achieves the stable arc that links the narrative to an emotional movement in a Shakespeare play. Yet in literary terms, and at the level of individual scenes, its management of narrative and the rhetoric of high emotion, it is remarkably accomplished.

The play is clearly a product of a literary culture, not only in its use of literary sources such as John Speed's *History of the Empire of Great Britaine* and its adaptation of the plot of William Barksted's *Hiren, or, The Faire Greeke* (1611) but in its attention to irony and suspense. Its rhetoric turns on the familiar trope of the contrast between love and war as the victorious Danish King Canutus is unmanned by his (ultimately successful) passion for the chaste nun Cartesmunda and his loyal soldiers' despair of the loss of all the victories he has gained. The war scenes move from foreground to background as the seduction narrative develops, and then come to the foreground again as the English forces are rallied with support from the Scots. The resolution of the narrative takes precedence over that of the love stories. Both Cartesmunda and the parallel love plot of the Danish Elgina and her English lover, Alured, are killed accidentally, caught by their opponents' sword play, and the newly triumphant English king graciously offers a model of kingly victory by extending mercy to Canutus, rescinding the Danish tribute and extending Scottish lands from the Tyne to the Tweed.

The play's literary aspirations are clear from the beginning. The opening battle takes place off stage and the horror of impending defeat is created by the retreating soldiers' cries:

1. Captain
The breach is made, the Danes rush o'er the walls,
And like the pent up ocean 'bove his banks
Falls from his height with roaring violence, and drowns us all in blood.

Edmond
The Danes are in the streets, slaughter begins,
And execution is their soldiers' words.
Your houses will be prey to fire and theft.

Ethelred
Your wives and daughters slaves to Danish lust.

Alured
Your children in their mothers' arms struck dead.

Edmond
The names of English torn from memory. (1.1.10–22)

These simple rhetorical effects are elaborated into an extended poetic soliloquy when the triumphant Danish king is overcome by seeing the nun Cartesmunda:

What power unknown
By magic thus transforms me to a stone,
Senseless of all the faculties of life
My blood runs back, I have no power to strike.
Call in our guards, and bid them all give o'er.
Sheath up your swords with me, and kill no more;
Her angel-beauty cries, she must not die
Nor live but mine. (1.3.25–32)

King Canutus's speeches as he grapples with his passion for Cartesmunda freeze the action so as to focus on his high emotion and ethical dilemma when his beloved calls for death rather than dishonour:

Death would die for thee, if he even saw thee,
And for thy sake make blunt his ebon dart;
Pray weep no more. He prays that might command;
We will not force the jewel thou so prizest
Till thou bequeath it freely to my youth.
We are o'th' eagles kind, and scorn to stoop
To an ignoble thought. Sweet will you hear me;
'Twas King *Canutus* fetched that sigh you heard.
Still turn aside! Well, if you loathe me, leave me;
There lies your way: Yet be advised, fond maid:
No sooner shalt thou pass from forth my sight,

> But the base soldiers will lay hold on thee,
> And what I value 'bove religion,
> Will not be thus much there. They'll ravish thee,
> And therefore prithee stay, with tears I pray thee.
> Thou frosty *April,* woo't not love for love?
> Doo't then for honour, pleasure, majesty.
> Ungentle still? Then get thee from my sight.
> Go to the woods, and learn of wilder beasts
> A little pity. You preserve chastity
> With a foul sin: ingratitude. Goodnight. (1.3.165–85)

Though the 1655 edition[16] prints all the speeches as prose, the modern editor can easily identify competent, regular blank verse. The rhetorical oppositions between love and honour, chastity and ingratitude, majesty and wildness are also part of a lexicon of abstractions and iconography found everywhere in the drama of the period.

In the subplot of the opportunist entrepreneur, Thornton, the dramatist is, moreover, comically self-conscious about the effects he is using. When Thornton soliloquizes his plans to fulfil the prophecy that he will become rich in Newcastle, the other figures on stage comment on the curiosity of his speaking to himself (2.1.68–85) and when Grim, the collier, uses a rhetorical flourish to dedicate his colliers to the works to embellish Newcastle, Thornton responds with 'This speech I think was penned on purpose' (4.3.31).

These literary effects can be found in the work of the canonical dramatists. Canutus's soldiers' anxiety about his passion for Cartesmunda echoes the opening dialogue of *Antony and Cleopatra* and both plays rehearse the familiar opposition between lovers and soldiers that finds different rhetorical and dramatic form in plays as diverse as Shakespeare's *Much Ado About Nothing* and *Richard III,* Thomas Heywood's *Edward IV,* the anonymous *Edward III* or, comically, in the final scenes of *Henry V.* Brewer's play also includes direct verbal echoes: Canutus's threat to Cartesmunda – 'I'll rip thy bosom now to see that wonder, a constant woman's heart' – echoes

King Lear's wish to 'anatomize Regan' (*King Lear* 3.6.34) and the startling literalizing of that image from the finale of Ford's *'Tis Pity she's a Whore*.

In the Elgina/Alured plot, the lovers' scenes not only reverse the pattern of the Canutus/Cartesmunda seduction with the chaste Danish woman unaccountably falling for the English prisoner, they include Elgina's lines 'For thy sake, Ile teach women what to do / And spight of custom to begin to wooe' (1.3.289–90). Both the situation and its expression of unconventional women's behaviour present another version of both situation and expression in *The Duchess of Malfi* and *Women Beware Women*.

The congruences of situation and expression between Brewer's play and the canonical Jacobean drama present a small-scale version of the theoretical problems that attend the connection between Ming-dynasty and Jacobean theatres. Complications of date and provenance make it impossible to be confident about their direction of travel and it is safest to identify them through the 'parallel development' methodology: to acknowledge that all the playwrights of the age, including the canonical literary figures, undertook the complex business of turning narrative into drama by taking scenic situations and ironic reversals both from historical sources and from preceding playwrights. By 1616 the literary and theatrical world had created an extensive resource bank of scenes and expressions that constituted the literary material for early modern drama.[17]

The 'diffusion method' might be more securely applied to the Thornton plot. *The Love-sick King*'s most recent editor identifies the play's explicit references to the earlier story of *Grim the Collier of Croydon* and its use of the song 'Be gone, be gone, my juggy my puggy' (2.1.1–4) from Old Merrythought's version in *The Knight of the Burning Pestle* (1608) and its origins in Heywood's *Rape of Lucrece* (1607).[18] The Thornton story also follows the standard Dick Whittington narrative of the simple fellow destined to make his fortune in the city; a story that occurs in various guises in the action of Heywood's *If You Know Not Me You Know Nobody* and Dekker's *The Shoemaker's Holiday*. However, this tradition follows the mythologization of history and narrative that occurs in a number of places in the print culture of early modern England, making the 'parallel development' method a more effective route into understanding and analysing its cultural significance.

Both of these methods will require us to abandon older, author-centred ideas of the literary and above all the continuing urge to place Shakespeare at the centre of the period. In *The Shakespeare Apocrypha*, Tucker Brooke analysed a group of plays that seemed to echo Shakespeare's characteristic literary style but which, in his view, did not match his individual marks of genius. These plays, he suggested, 'possess an attractiveness of their own by very virtue of their dull impersonality, because they display so little of the individual author and so much of the vulgar dramatic taste. Such literary phenomena evolve themselves, they are not created; the writer does no more than drift down the current of theatrical convention.'[19] Tucker Brooke, of course, was attempting two distinct literary tasks: to identify connections, however circumstantial, between the apocrypha and Shakespeare's work *and* to halt the drift of the remaining flotsam of individual plays by snagging them on a possible connection to Shakespeare. My interest is more in the implications for literary analysis that reveals the way that *The Love-sick King*, like the plays that it echoes, builds on the dramatic scenes taken from the literary drama in order to turn narrative into drama. It does so by structuring the narrative around individual tropes, scenes that have a familiar thematic resonance, and so can be relied upon to offer a familiar set of possibilities for developments with their ironies and rhetorical pleasures built in. These literary skills arguably facilitated the development of a wide-ranging and robust theatre industry that may provide a more secure basis for examining parallel developments in other parts of the world. By focusing on the literary characteristics of the dramatic output of the Jacobean theatre as a whole, we can pay attention to the difference between the two literary systems rather than forcing similarity. We might thus identify their two greatest playwrights not as 'the Chinese Shakespeare' or the 'English Tang Xianzu' but as the products of distinctive and equally complex literary and theatrical cultures.

Notes

1   David Markley, *The Far East and the English Imagination 1600–1730* (Cambridge: Cambridge University Press, 2006), p. 3.

2   William Camden, *The History of the Most Renowned and Victorious Princess Elizabeth*, 4th edn (1688; reprint New York, 1970), p. 62, quoted in Jim Ellis, 'Kenilworth, King Arthur, and the Memory of Empire', *English Literary Renaissance*, 43 (2013), p. 25.

3   John Marston, *Parasitaster, or The Fawn*, ed. David A. Blostein. The Revels Plays (Manchester: Manchester University Press, 1978).

4   Ian Watson, *Negotiating Cultures: Eugenio Barba and the Intercultural Debate* (Manchester: Manchester University Press, 2002), p. 3.

5   Quoted in Paul Morgan, '"Our Will Shakespeare" and Lope de Vega: An Unrecorded Contemporary Document', *Shakespeare Survey* 16, ed. Allardyce Nicoll (Cambridge: Cambridge University Press, 1963), p. 118.

6   Walter Cohen, *Drama of a Nation: Public Theater in Renaissance England and Spain* (Ithaca: Cornell University Press, 1985), p. 17.

7   Erne, *Shakespeare as Literary Dramatist*.

8   John Marston, *Jack Drum's Entertainment*, Act V in *The Plays of John Marston*, H. Harvey Wood (ed.), vol. 3, p. 234.

9   I have addressed the process by which audience taste was constructed in relation to literary characteristics in 'Figuring the Consumer for Early Modern Drama', in Bryan Reynolds and William N. West (eds), *Rematerializing Shakespeare* (Basingstoke: Macmillan Palgrave, 2005).

10   *Malone Society Collections, Vol. 3, A Calendar of Dramatic*

Records in the Books of the Livery Companies of London, 1485–1640 (Oxford: Oxford University Press for the Malone Society, 1954), p. 92.

11   David McInnes, 'Lost Plays from Early Modern England: Voyage Drama, A Case Study', *Literature Compass*, 8(8) (2011) (doi: 10.1111/j.1741-4113.2011.00817.x), p. 534.

12   Fei, *Chinese Theories of Theatre and Performance*, p. 59.

13   Ibid., p. 57.

14   See David Kathman, 'Anthony Brewer fl. 1607–17', in the *Oxford Dictionary of National Biography*, http://www. oxforddnb.com.ezproxyd.bham.ac.uk/view/article/3359 [accessed 11 May 2014].

15   The dating of the play at 1617 depends upon assuming that the Thornton plot, set in Newcastle, may be connected to King James's visit to the town in 1617 on his journey to Scotland. See M. Hope Dodds, '"Edmond Ironside" and "The Love-sick King"', *The Modern Language Review*, 19(2) (1924), pp. 158–68. The dating is also discussed in *Edmond Ironside and Anthony Brewer's The Love-sick King,* ed. Randall Martin (New York: Garland, 1991), pp. 200–6.

16   Identified in the Stationers' Register for 1655 as 'Robert Pollard at the Ben Jonson head behind the exchange' as 'a booke called The Love-sick King, an English tragicall history with the life & death of Cartis Mundy the faire Nunne of Winchester. Written by Anthony Brewer, gent. Vjd.'

17   The seduced, raped or violated nun is another core trope that follows material dramatized from John Foxe's *Book of Martyrs* onwards, is significant in the period and is analysed in Mami Adachi's forthcoming Shakespeare Institute thesis on 'Nuns in Early Modern Drama'.

18   Randall Martin, *Edmond Ironside*, p. 309.

19   Tucker Brooke, *The Shakespeare Apocrypha* (Oxford: Clarendon Press, 1908), 'Introduction', p. vi.

AFTERWORD

On the morning of Sunday 26 June 2011, His Excellency Mr Wen Jiabao, Premier of the State Council of the People's Republic of China, chose, as a preliminary first event of his state visit to Great Britain, to make a pilgrimage, along with his entire retinue, to Shakespeare's Birthplace in Stratford-upon-Avon. As Honorary President of the Shakespeare Birthplace Trust I had the honour, along with the Trust's Director, Dr Diana Owen, and the British Culture Secretary, Jeremy Hunt, of receiving him. After speeches of welcome, during which His Excellency heard of the Trust's growing links with China, he inspected an exhibition of relevant items selected from our extensive collections which included one of our three copies of the Shakespeare First Folio, the first collected edition of Shakespeare's works translated into Chinese, published in 1978, and an album of photographs of the Chinese Drama Shakespeare Festival of 1986. The premier became one of the numerous distinguished persons who over the centuries have signed our visitors' book, and inscribed in it a brief poem of his own composition. Translated, it reads: 'Shakespeare brings sunshine to your life and gives your dreams wings to fly.'

After His Excellency had been shown round the Birthplace, we sat on a bench in the garden for a short performance by a resident company of actors of excerpts from *Hamlet*, following which I rose preparatory to saying farewell. But the Premier turned, placed a hand on my arm, and asked if he might say something. We sat again, and for close on half an hour he spoke eloquently (as was clear from the simultaneous translation) about how literature and culture in general can build bridges between nations. Not only Shakespeare, he said, but also Daniel Defoe and Charles Dickens were

'household names in China'. Referring to his own experience
of studying Shakespeare as a young man, and of reading
Goethe's comments on Shakespeare, he stressed the need for
reading and rereading the works in order to deepen one's
appreciation of them. Politicians and statesmen, he said,
need to respect history and the creativity of the people they
represent if they are to build lasting foundations for international friendship and understanding.

Premier Wen's visit was an event of immense symbolic significance in relations between China and Great Britain, followed
up some eighteen months later by the Royal Shakespeare
Company's production of the Chinese classic, *The Orphan
of Zhao*, by Ji Junxiang. More significant in scholarly terms,
however, was the subsequent conference co-hosted by the
School of Oriental and African Studies of the University of
London, the Shakespeare Birthplace Trust and the National
Chung Cheng University of Taiwan which is recorded in the
preceding pages. It took as its point of departure the coincidence that two of the greatest playwrights of England and
China, William Shakespeare and Tang Xianzu, both died in
the same year, 1616. This year, as Wilt L. Idema points out in
his Foreword, also saw the publication of the first collected
edition of an English dramatist's works, those of Ben Jonson
– without which we might well not have had the Shakespeare
First Folio of 1623 – as well as, in China, the deluxe edition
of 100 plays from the Yuan dynasty.

To read the essays in the preceding pages is to be made
aware of both the many resemblances and the many differences between the theatrical cultures of both nations, and of
the immense amount of dedicated and ongoing scholarship
that is currently being brought to bear upon them. Royal court
performances were common in both countries, but England
appears to have had a more flourishing popular tradition. In
both countries collective authorship was common and many
plays challenged scholars of the future by appearing without
attribution. Political censorship was exercised, in China
through the Office of Music Instruction and in England

through the office of the Master of the Revels. The drama in both countries was highly conventionalized in both language and presentation, creating problems of understanding and interpretation. Music was important in both Chinese and English theatre but too little of the original music survives and the printed texts of plays are far more informative about the words spoken than about what audiences heard. Theatre is nothing without an audience, which both reflects and helps to shape taste, so we need to know as much as we can about those who saw plays in both countries. Scholars of early drama in both China and England labour under the handicap of inadequate survival of evidence, and the research that lies behind this volume demonstrates the energy and imagination with which scholars of both cultures, independently and in collaboration, are labouring to fill the gaps.

Contributors to this volume have not been content simply to summarize the current state of knowledge about their respective subjects. Each of them presents the product of original research. They have, moreover, both before and after the conference itself, been willing to engage with each other's arguments and findings. Their essays represent significant new interventions in cultural studies.

It was fitting that this conference concerned with the performative arts came to a conclusion with an extract from 'The Interrupted Dream', part of one of the most famous and most popular masterpieces of early Chinese drama, *Peony Pavilion*, by Tang Xianzu. And the collaboration in this performance between one Chinese and one British actor – Ouyang Biqing (SOAS) and Kim Hunter Gordon (Royal Holloway), both of whom are PhD students from the University of London Chinese Opera Network – exemplified the spirit of international collaboration that infused the whole of this delightful and historically significant conference.

Stanley Wells, Shakespeare Birthplace Trust

WORKS CITED

Anon., *The Second Maiden's Tragedy*, ed. Anne Lancashire, Manchester: Manchester University Press, 1978.

Austern, Linda Phyllis, '"Art to Enchant": Musical Magic and Its Practitioners in English Renaissance Drama', *Journal of the Royal Musical Association*, 115 (1990), pp. 191–206.

Austern, Linda Phyllis, *Music in English Children's Drama of the Later Renaissance*, London: Routledge, 1992.

Bacon, Francis, *The Historie of the Raigne of King Henry the Seventh*, ed. Michael Kiernan, The Oxford Francis Bacon Series, Oxford: Clarendon Press, 2012, vol. 8.

Barish, Jonas, *The Antitheatrical Prejudice*, Berkeley: University of California Press, 1981.

Bate, Jonathan, *Soul of the Age: The Life, Mind and World of William Shakespeare*, London: Viking, 2008.

Bellany, Alastair, *The Politics of Court Scandal in Early Modern England*, Cambridge: Cambridge University Press, 2002.

Bentley, G. E., *The Jacobean and Caroline Stage*, 7 vols. Oxford: Clarendon Press, 1941–68.

Bevington, David, Lars Engle, Katharine Eisaman Maus and Eric Rasmussen (eds), *English Renaissance Drama: A Norton Anthology*, London: W. W. Norton & Co., Inc., 2002.

Bevington, David, Martin Butler and Ian Donaldson (eds), *The Cambridge Edition of the Works of Ben Jonson*, Cambridge: Cambridge University Press, 2012.

Birch, Cyril, 'A Comparative View of Dramatic Romance: *The Winter's Tale* and *The Peony Pavilion*', in Roger T. Ames et al. (eds), *Interpreting Culture through Translation*, Hong Kong: The Chinese University Press, 1991, pp. 55–77.

Birch, Cyril, *Scenes for Mandarins: The Elite Theater of the* Ming, New York: Columbia University Press, 1995.

Birch, Cyril (trans.), *The Peony Pavilion: Mudan Ting*, 2nd edn, Bloomington: Indiana University Press, 2002.

Blayney, Peter W. M., 'The Publication of Playbooks', in John D. Cox and David Scott Kastan (eds), *A New History of Early English Drama*, New York: Columbia University Press, 1997, pp. 383–422.

Bourdieu, Pierre, *Outline of a Theory of Practice*, Cambridge: Cambridge University Press, 1977.

Bourdieu, Pierre, *Distinction: A Social Critique of the Judgement of Taste*, Cambridge, MA: Harvard University Press, 1984.

Brooke, C. F. Tucker (ed.), *The Shakespeare Apocrypha*, Oxford: Clarendon Press, 1908.

Brooks, Douglas, *From Playhouse to Printing House: Drama and Authorship in Early Modern England*, Cambridge: Cambridge University Press, 2000.

Butler, Martin, *Theatre and Crisis 1632–1642*, Cambridge: Cambridge University Press, 1984.

Cai Yi 蔡毅, *Zhongguo gudian xiqu xuba huibian* 中國古典戲曲序跋彙編, Jinan: Qi Lu shushe, 1989.

Carlitz, Katherine, 'Printing as Performance: Literati Playwright-publishers of the Late Ming', in Cynthia Brokaw and Kai-wing Chow (eds), *Printing and Book Culture in Late Imperial China*, Berkeley: University of California Press, 2005, pp. 267–303.

Chambers, E. K., *Notes on the History of the Revels Office under the Tudors*, London: A. H. Bullen, 1906.

Chambers, E. K., *The Elizabethan Stage*, Oxford: Clarendon Press, 1923.

Chen Duo 陳多, '*Xilouji* jiqi zuozhe Yuan Yuling' 《西樓記》及其作者袁于令, *Xuzhou jiaoyu xueyuan xuebao* 徐州教育學院學報, 1998.4, pp. 38–44.

Chen Jiru 陳繼儒, 'Ti *Xilouji*' 題西樓記, *Jianxiaoge ziding Xiloumeng chuanqi* 劍嘯閣自訂西樓夢傳奇, in *Guben xiqu congkan* 古本戲曲叢刊, 2nd series, Shanghai: Shangwu yinshuguan, 1955, vol. 102.

Chester, Robert, *Loves Martyr: Or Rosalins Complaint*, London: Edward Blount, 1601.

Chonghe Jushi 沖和居士 (comp.), *Yichun jin* 怡春錦, photolithographic reprint in *Shanben xiqu congkan* 善本戲曲叢刊, Taipei: Taiwan xuesheng shuju, 1984, vols 19–20.

Chow, Kai-wing, *Publishing, Culture and Power in Early Modern China*, Stanford: Stanford University Press, 2004.

Christensen, Thomas, *1616: The World in Motion*, Berkeley: Counterpoint, 2013.

Chuxiang piping Hailing yishi 出像批評海陵佚史, in *Siwuxie huibao* 思無邪匯寶 series, comps Chan Hing-ho 陳慶浩 and Wang Chiu-kui 王秋桂, Taipei: Encyclopedia Britannica, 1995.

C. J., *The Two Merry Milkmaids. Or, The Best Words Weare The Garland*, ed. George Harold Metz, New York: Garland, 1979.

Clare, Janet, *'Art made tongue-tied by authority': Elizabethan and Jacobean Dramatic Censorship*, Manchester: Manchester University Press, 1999.

Clare, Janet, *Shakespeare's Stage Traffic: Imitation, Borrowing and Competition in Renaissance Theatre*, Cambridge: Cambridge University Press, 2014.

Cohen, Walter, *Drama of a Nation: Public Theater in Renaissance England and Spain*, Ithaca: Cornell University Press, 1985.

Cornwallis, William, *Essayes*, London: Edmund Mattes, 1600.

Cromwell: The Life and Death of the Lord Cromwell, in *The Shakespeare Apocrypha*, C. F. Tucker Brooke (ed.), Oxford: Clarendon Press, 1908.

Da Ming lü jijie fuli 大明律集解附例, Wanli edn. Reprint, Taipei: Xuesheng shuju, 1970.

Day, John, *John Day's Isle of Gulls: A Critical Edition*, ed. Raymond S. Burns, New York: Garland, 1980.

Dekker, Thomas, *The Dramatic Works of Thomas Dekker*, Fredson Bowers (ed.), Cambridge: Cambridge University Press: vol. 1, 1953: *Sir Thomas Wyatt*; vol. 2, 1955: *The Whore of Babylon*.

Dickey, Bruce, 'The Cornett', in Trevor Herbert and John Wallace (eds), *The Cambridge Companion to Brass Instruments*, Cambridge: Cambridge University Press, 1997.

Dodds, M. Hope, '"Edmond Ironside" and "The Love-sick King"', *The Modern Language Review*, 19(2) (1924), pp. 158–68.

Donaldson, Ian, *Jonson's Magic Houses: Essays in Interpretation*, Oxford: Oxford University Press, 1997.

Donaldson, Ian, *Ben Jonson: A Life*, Oxford: Oxford University Press, 2011.

Draper, John W., 'The Occasion of *King Lear*', *Studies in Philology*, 34(2) (1937), pp. 176–85.

Drue, Thomas, *The Life of the Dutches of Suffolke*, London, 1631.

Drue, Thomas, 'Thomas Drue's *The Duchess of Suffolk*: A Critical

Old-spelling Edition', Robert Anthony Raines (ed.), unpublished PhD dissertation, University of Delaware, 1968.

Duffin, Ross, *Shakespeare's Songbook*, New York: W.W. Norton, 2004.

Duncan-Jones, Katherine, *Shakespeare: Upstart Crow to Sweet Swan 1592–1623*, London: Bloomsbury, 2011.

Dutton, Richard, 'Jonson's satiric styles', in Richard Harp and Stanley Stewart (eds), *The Cambridge Guide to Ben Jonson*, Cambridge: Cambridge University Press, 2000.

Dutton, Richard (ed.), *The Oxford Handbook of Early Modern Theatre*, Oxford: Oxford University Press, 2009.

Ellis, Jim, 'Kenilworth, King Arthur, and the Memory of Empire', *English Literary Renaissance*, 43 (2013), pp. 3–29.

Erne, Lukas, *Shakespeare as Literary Dramatist*, Cambridge: Cambridge University Press, 2003.

Erne, Lukas, *Shakespeare and the Book Trade*, Cambridge: Cambridge University Press, 2013.

Falaschi, Isabella, 'Tang Xianzu, *The Peony Pavilion*, and *Qing*', in Tian Yuan Tan and Paolo Santangelo (eds), *Passion, Romance, and Qing: The World of Emotions and States of Mind in Peony Pavilion*, Leiden: Brill, 2014, vol. 1, pp. 1–43.

Farmer, Alan B. and Zachary Lesser (eds), *DEEP: Database of Early English Playbooks* (2007). Available online: http://deep.sas.upenn.edu/cite.html (accessed 6 February 2015).

Fei, Faye Chunfang (ed. and trans.), *Chinese Theories of Theatre and Performance from Confucius to the Present*, Ann Arbor: University of Michigan Press, 1999.

Feng Menglong 馮夢龍, *Feng Menglong quanji* 馮夢龍全集, Wei Tongxian 魏同賢 (ed.), Nanjing: Jiangsu guji chubanshe, 1993.

Feuillerat, A., *Documents Relating to the Office of the Revels in the Time of Queen Elizabeth*, Leuven: Uystpruyst, 1908.

F.[itzgeoffrey], H.[enry], *Satyres and Satyricall Epigrams*, London: Edward Allde for Miles Patrich, 1617.

Ford, John, *The Chronicle History of Perkin Warbeck*, Peter Ure (ed.), London: Methuen, 1968.

Foucault, M., 'What Is An Author?' (1969), trans. Josué V. Harari, in P. Rabinow (ed.), *The Foucault Reader*, London: Penguin, 1984.

Gants, David L. and Tom Lockwood, 'The Printing and Publishing of Ben Jonson's Works', in David Bevington, Martin Butler and

Ian Donaldson (eds), *The Cambridge Edition of the Works of Ben Jonson*, Cambridge: Cambridge University Press, 2012.

Gao Ming 高明, *Xinkan yuanben Cai Bojie Pipa ji* 新刊元本蔡伯喈琵琶記, photolithographic reprint in *Guben xiqu congkan* 古本戲曲叢刊, 1st series, Shanghai: Shangwu yinshuguan, 1953/4.

Gould, Robert, *Poems Chiefly Consisting of Satyrs and Satyrical Epistles*, London: no printer's information, 1689.

Griffith, Eva, 'Christopher Beeston: His Property and Properties', in Richard Dutton (ed.), *The Oxford Handbook of Early Modern Theatre*, Oxford: Oxford University Press, 2009.

Gu, Ming Dong, *Chinese Theories of Reading and Writing: A Route to Hermeneutics and Open Poetics*, Albany: SUNY Press, 2005.

Guo Qitao, *Ritual Opera and Mercantile Lineage: The Confucian Transformation of Popular Culture in Late Imperial Huizhou*, Stanford: Stanford University Press, 2005.

Guo Yingde 郭英德 and Wang Lijuan 王麗娟, 'Cilin yizhi, Baneng zoujin bianzuan niandai kao' 詞林一枝、八能奏錦編纂年代考, *Wenyi yanjiu* 文藝研究, 8 (2006), pp. 55–62.

Gurr, Andrew, *Playgoing in Shakespeare's London*, 3rd edn, Cambridge: Cambridge University Press, 2004.

Gurr, Andrew, *The Shakespeare Company, 1594–1642*, Cambridge: Cambridge University Press, 2004.

Gurr, Andrew and Farah Karim-Cooper (eds), *Moving Shakespeare Indoors: Performance and Repertoire in the Jacobean Playhouse*, Cambridge: Cambridge University Press, 2014.

Harbage, Alfred, *Shakespeare and the Rival Traditions*, New York: Macmillan, 1952.

Hazlitt, W. C. (ed.), *The English Drama and Stage Under the Tudor and Stuart Princes, 1543–1664. Illustrated by a Series of Documents, Treatises and Poems*, Roxburghe Library, 1869.

He Liangjun 何良俊, *Qulun* 曲論, in *Zhongguo gudian xiqu lunzhu jicheng* 中國古典戲曲論著集成 series, Beijing: Zhongguo xiqu chubanshe, 1959, vol. 4.

He, Yuming, *Home and the World: Editing the 'Glorious Ming' in Woodblock-Printed Books of the Sixteenth and Seventeenth Centuries*, Cambridge: Harvard University Asia Center, 2013.

Heywood, Thomas, *If You Know Not Me, You Know Nobody I*, (ed.) Madeleine Doran, Oxford: Malone Society, 1934.

Heywood, Thomas, *If You Know Not Me, You Know Nobody II*, ed. Madeleine Doran, Oxford: Malone Society, 1934.

Hill, T., *Anthony Munday and Civic Culture*, Manchester: Manchester University Press, 2004.

Holman, Peter, *Four and Twenty Fiddlers: The Violin at the English Court*, Oxford: Clarendon Press, 1993.

Homer, *The Iliad*, trans. Robert Fagles, London: Penguin, 1991.

Hooks, Adam G., 'Shakespeare at the White Greyhound', *Shakespeare Survey* 64, Peter Holland (ed.), Cambridge: Cambridge University Press, 2011, pp. 260–75.

Hotson, Leslie, *The Commonwealth and Restoration Stage*, Cambridge, MA: Harvard University Press, 1928.

Hoy, Cyrus, *Introductions, Notes and Commentaries to Texts in 'The Dramatic Works of Thomas Dekker'*, Fredson Bowers (ed.), Cambridge: Cambridge University Press, 1980.

Huang Shizhong 黃仕忠, *Pipa ji yanjiu* 琵琶記研究. Guangzhou: Guangdong gaodeng jiaoyu chubanshe, 1996.

Huang Wenhua 黃文華 (comp.), *Cilin yizhi* 詞林一枝, photolithographic reprint in *Shanben xiqu congkan* 善本戲曲叢刊, Taipei: Taiwan xuesheng shuju, 1984, vol. 4.

Huang Zhushan 黃竹三 and Feng Junjie 馮俊傑 (eds), *Mingfeng ji pingzhu* 鳴鳳記評注, in *Liushizhong qu pingzhu* 六十種曲評注, Changchun: Jilin renmin chubanshe, 2001, vol. 4, pp. 245–659.

Hucker, Charles O., *A Dictionary of Official Titles in Imperial China*, Stanford: Stanford University Press, 1985.

Hunt, Arnold, 'Libraries in the Archives: Researching Provenance in the British Library', in Giles Mandelbrote and Barry Taylor (eds), *Libraries within the Library: Aspects of the British Library's Early Printed Collections*, London: British Library, 2009, pp. 363–84.

Ichikawa, Mariko, 'Continuities and Innovations in Staging', in Andrew Gurr and Farah Karim-Cooper (eds), *Moving Shakespeare Indoors: Performance and Repertoire in the Jacobean Playhouse* (Cambridge: Cambridge University Press, 2014).

Idema, Wilt L., 'Stage and Court in China: The Case of Hung-wu's Imperial Theatre', *Oriens Extremus* 23(2) (1976), pp. 175–89.

Idema, Wilt L., 'Why You Never Have Read a Yuan Drama: The Transformation of *Zaju* at the Ming Court', in S. M. Carletti, M. Sacchetti and P. Santangelo (eds), *Studi in onore di Lanciello*

Lanciotti, Naples: Istituto Universitario Orientale, 1996, pp. 765–91.

Idema, Wilt L., '"Blasé Literati": Lü T'ien-ch'eng and the Lifestyle of the Chiang-nan Elite in the Final Decades of the Wan-li Period', in Robert van Gulik, *Erotic Colour Prints of the Ming Period with an Essay on Chinese Sex Life from the Han to the Ch'ing Dynasty, B.C. 206–A.D. 1644*, Leiden: Brill, 2004, pp. xxxi–lix.

Idema, Wilt L. and Stephen H. West, *Chinese Theater, 1100–1450: A Source Book*, Wiesbaden: Franz Steiner, 1982.

Ioppolo, G., 'Hengist, King of Kent; Or, The Mayor of Queenborough', in Gary Taylor and John Lavagnino (eds), *Thomas Middleton: The Collected Works*, Oxford: Oxford University Press, 2007.

Iwaki Hideo 岩城秀夫, 'Min no kyūtei to engeki' 明の宮廷と演劇, in idem, *Chūgoku gikyokyu engeki kenkyū* 中國戲曲演劇研究, Tokyo: Sōbunsha, 1972.

Jiang, Yonglin (trans.), *The Great Ming Code*, Seattle: University of Washington Press, 2004.

Jiao Xun 焦循, *Jushuo* 劇說, in *Zhongguo gudian xiqu lunzhu jicheng* 中國古典戲曲論著集成 series, Beijing: Zhongguo xiju chubanshe, 1959, vol. 8.

Jin Ningfen 金寧芬, *Nanxi yanjiu bianqian* 南戲研究變遷. Tianjin: Tianjin jiaoyu chubanshe, 1992.

Jonson, Ben, *Sejanus, His Fall*, London, 1605.

Jonson, Ben, *The Workes of Beniamin Ionson*, London, 1616.

Jowett, John and Gary Taylor, *Shakespeare Reshaped 1606–1623*, Oxford: Clarendon Press, 1993.

Kathman, David, 'Shakespeare and Warwickshire', in Paul Edmondson and Stanley Wells (eds), *Shakespeare Beyond Doubt: Evidence, Argument, Controversy*, Cambridge: Cambridge University Press, 2013, pp. 121–32.

Keats, John, *Selected Letters*, ed. Robert Gittings, rev. John Mee, Oxford: Oxford University Press, 2002.

Kernan, Alvin, *Shakespeare, the King's Playwright: Theatre in the Stuart Court, 1603–1613*, New Haven: Yale University Press, 1995.

Kidnie, M. J. (ed.), *The Devil is an Ass: And Other Plays*, Oxford: Oxford University Press, 2001.

Kinney, Arthur (ed.), *The Oxford Handbook to Shakespeare*, Oxford: Oxford University Press, 2012.

Knapp, J., 'Shakespeare as Coauthor', *Shakespeare Studies*, 36 (2008): 49–59.

Knutson, Roslyn Lander, *Playing Companies and Commerce in Shakespeare's Time*, Cambridge: Cambridge University Press, 2001.

Knutson, Roslyn Lander, 'What If There Wasn't a "Blackfriars Repertory"?', in Paul Menzer (ed.), *Inside Shakespeare: Essays on the Blackfriars Stage*, Selinsgrove: Susquehanna University Press, 2006.

Komatsu Ken 小松謙, 'Naifuhon-kei shohon kō' 內府本系諸本考, in *Tanaka Kenji hakushi shōju kinen Chūgoku koten gikyoku ronshū* 田中謙二博士頌壽記念中國古典戲曲論集, Tokyo: Kyūko Shoin, 1991, pp. 125–59.

Komatsu Ken, *Chūgoku koten engeki kenkyū* 中國古典演劇研究, Tokyo: Kyūko Shoin, 2001.

Leggatt, Alexander, *Jacobean Public Theatre*, Abingdon: Routledge, 1992.

Lesser, Zachary and Alan B. Farmer, 'The Popularity of Playbooks Revisited', *Shakespeare Quarterly*, 56 (2005), pp. 1–32.

Levine, Laura, *Men in Women's Clothing: Anti-Theatricality and Effeminization, 1579–1642*, Cambridge: Cambridge University Press, 1994.

Li, Wai-yee, *Enchantment and Disenchantment: Love and Illusion in Chinese Literature*, Princeton: Princeton University Press, 1993.

Li Yu 李漁, *Xianqing ouji* 閒情偶寄, in *Li Yu quanji* 李漁全集, Hangzhou: Zhejiang guji chubanshe, 1992, vol. 3.

Li Zengpo 李增坡 (ed.), Zhang Qingji 張清吉 coll., *Ding Yaokang quanji* 丁耀亢全集. Zhengzhou: Zhongzhou guji chubanshe, 1999.

Li Zhanpeng 李占鵬, '*Maiwangguan chaojiaoben gujin zaju* zhengli yanjiu shuping' 《脈望館鈔校本古今雜劇》整理研究述評, *Mianyang shifan xueyuan xuebao* 綿陽師範學院學報, vol. 31, No 3 (2012), pp. 72–6.

Li Zhenyu 李真瑜, *Mingdai gongting xiju shi* 明代宮廷戲劇史. Beijing: Zijincheng chubanshe, 2010.

Limon, Jerzy, *Dangerous Matter: English Drama and Politics in 1623/24*, Cambridge: Cambridge University Press, 1986.

Lindley, David, *The Trials of Frances Howard*, London: Routledge, 1993.

Lindley, David, *Shakespeare and Music*, London: Arden Shakespeare, 2006.

Lindley, David, 'Music and Shakespearean Revision', *Archiv,* 164 (2012), pp. 50–64.

Ling Xuzi 淩虛子 (comp.), *Yue lu yin* 月露音, photolithographic reprint in *Shanben xiqu congkan* 善本戲曲叢刊, Taipei: Taiwan xuesheng shuju, 1984, vols 15–16.

Liu Nianzi 劉念茲, *Nanxi xin zheng* 南戲新證. Beijing: Zhonghua shuju, 1986.

Liu Ruoyu 劉若愚, *Zhuozhong zhi* 酌中志, Beijing: Beijing guji chubanshe, 1994.

Liu Shiheng 劉士珩 (ed.), *Nuanhongshi Huike Linchuan Simeng* 暖紅室彙刻臨川夢, Yangzhou: Guangling guji keyinshe, 1981.

Liu Shiheng 劉士珩 *Nuanhongshi Huike Canhuazhai Wuzhong* 暖紅室彙刻粲花齋五種, Yangzhou: Guangling guji keyinshe, 1982.

Lu Eting 陸萼庭, *Qingdai xiqujia congkao* 清代戲曲家叢考, Shanghai: Xuelin chubanshe, 1995.

Lu Eting 陸萼庭, '"Youyuan jingmeng" jishuo' 〈遊園驚夢〉集說, in Hua Wei (ed), *Tang Xianzu yu Mudanting* 湯顯祖與牡丹亭, Taipei: Zhongyang yanjiuyuan Zhongguo wenzhe yanjiusuo, 2005, vol. 2.

Luo Yuming 駱玉明 and Dong Rulong 董如龍, '*Nanci xulu* fei Xu Wei zuo' 《南詞敍錄》非徐渭作, *Fudan xuebao (shehui kexue ban)* 復旦學報（社會科學版）1987. 6.

Lü Shuxiang 呂叔湘 (ed.), *Yingyi Tangren jueju baishou* 英譯唐人絕句百首, Changsha: Hunan renmin chubanshe, 1980.

Lü Tiancheng 呂天成, *Qupin* 曲品, in *Zhongguo gudian xiqu lunzhu jicheng* 中國古典戲曲論著集成 series, Beijing: Zhongguo xiqu chubanshe, 1959, vol. 6.

Lü Tiancheng 呂天成, *Qupin jiaozhu* 曲品校註, Beijing: Zhonghua shuju, 1990.

Lynn, Richard (trans.), *The Classic of Changes: A New Translation of the* I Ching *as Interpreted By Wang Bi*, New York: Columbia University Press, 1994.

Ma Xiaoni 馬曉霓, 'Yuan zaju *Shuzhe xiachuan* de banben wenti' 元雜劇《疏者下船》的版本問題, *Dongnan daxue xuebao (zhexue shehui kexue ban)* 東南大學學報（哲學社會科學版）, Vol. 10, No.3 (2008): pp. 81–5.

Macdonald, Mairi, '"Not a Memorial to Shakespeare, but a Place for Divine Worship": The Vicars of Stratford-upon-Avon and the

Shakespeare Phenomenon, 1616–1964', *Warwickshire History*, 11 (2001–2), pp. 207–26.

Maiwangguan chaojiaoben gujin zaju 脈望館鈔校本古今雜劇, *Guben xiqu congkan* 古本戲曲叢刊, 4th series, Shanghai: Shangwu yinshu guan, 1958.

Malone Society Collections, Vol. 3, A Calendar of Dramatic Records in the Books of the Livery Companies of London, 1485–1640, Oxford: Oxford University Press for the Malone Society, 1954.

Manningham, John, *The Diary of John Manningham*, Robert Parker Sorlien (ed.), Hanover: University Press of New England, 1976.

Mao Jin 毛晉 (comp.), *Liushi zhong qu* 六十種曲, Beijing: Zhonghua shuju, 1982.

Markley, David, *The Far East and the English Imagination 1600–1730*, Cambridge: Cambridge University Press, 2006.

Marston, John, *Jacke Drum's Entertainment*, in *The Plays of John Marston*, London: Richard Olive, 1601.

Marston, John, *The Malcontent*, ed. George K. Hunter, Manchester: Manchester University Press, 1975.

Marston, John, *Parasitaster or The Fawn*, ed. David A. Blostein, Manchester: Manchester University Press, 1978.

Martin, Randall (ed.), *Edmond Ironside and Anthony Brewer's The Love-sick King*, New York: Garland, 1991.

Massinger, Philip, *The Roman Actor*, ed. Martin White, Manchester: Manchester University Press, 2007.

Masten, J., *Textual Intercourse*, Cambridge: Cambridge University Press, 1997.

McClure, Norman Egbert (ed.), *The Letters of John Chamberlain*, Philadelphia: American Philosophical Society, 1939.

McInnes, David, 'Lost Plays from Early Modern England: Voyage Drama, A Case Study', *Literature Compass*, 8(8) (2011), pp. 534–42.

McLuskie, Kate, 'Figuring the Consumer for Early Modern Drama', in Bryan Reynolds and William N. West (eds), *Rematerializing Shakespeare*, Basingstoke: Macmillan Palgrave, 2005.

McMillin, Scott and Sally-Beth MacLean, *The Queen's Men and Their Plays*, Cambridge: Cambridge University Press, 1998.

Mei Dingzuo 梅鼎祚, *Luqiu shishi ji* 鹿裘石室集, *wenji* 文集. *Xuxiu Siku quanshu* 續修四庫全書, Shanghai: Shanghai guji chubanshe, 1995.

Menzer, Paul (ed.), *Inside Shakespeare: Essays on the Blackfriars Stage*, Selinsgrove: Susquehanna University Press, 2006.

Miao Yonghe 繆咏禾, *Mingdai chuban shigao* 明代出版史稿, Nanjing: Jiangsu renmin chubanshe, 2000.

Middleton, Thomas, *The Inner Temple Masque, or Masque of Heroes*, London: John Browne, 1619.

Milling, Jane and Peter Thomson (eds), *The Cambridge History of British Theatre, Vol. 1: Origins to 1660*, Cambridge: Cambridge University Press, 2004.

Morgan, Paul, '"Our Will Shakespeare" and Lope de Vega: An Unrecorded Contemporary Document', *Shakespeare Survey* 16, ed. Allardyce Nicoll, Cambridge: Cambridge University Press, 1963, pp. 118–20.

Morgan, Paul, 'Frances Wolfreston and "Hor Bouks": A Seventeenth-Century Woman Book-Collector', *The Library*, 6th series, 11 (1989), pp. 197–219.

Mullaney, Steven, *The Place of the Stage: License, Play and Power in Renaissance England*, Chicago: University of Chicago Press, 1988.

Mulligan, Jean (trans.), *The Lute*, New York: Columbia University Press, 1980.

Munday, Anthony et al., *Sir Thomas More*, ed. J. Jowett, London: Arden Shakespeare, 2011.

Murray, Timothy, *Theatrical Legitimation: Allegories of Genius in Seventeenth-Century England and France*, New York: Oxford University Press, 1987.

Nagamatsu Junko 長松純子, 'Mingdai neifuben zaju yanjiu' 明代内府本雜劇研究, PhD dissertation, Sun Yat-sen University, 2009.

Nicol, D., *Middleton & Rowley*, Toronto: University of Toronto Press, 2012.

O'Connor, M., *The Witch*, in Gary Taylor and John Lavagnino (eds), *Thomas Middleton: The Collected Works*, Oxford: Oxford University Press, 2007.

Orgel, Stephen, '*Macbeth* and the Antic Round', *Shakespeare Survey 52*, Stanley Wells (ed.), Cambridge: Cambridge University Press, 1999, pp. 143–53.

Oxford Dictionary of National Biography (online edition), http://www.oxforddnb.com.

Perry, Curtis, *The Making of Jacobean Literary Culture*, Cambridge: Cambridge University Press, 1997.

Pian, Rulan Chao, *Song Dynasty Musical Sources and Their Interpretation*, Hong Kong: The Chinese University Press, 2003.

Pollard, A. W., *Shakespeare Folios and Quartos: A Study in the Bibliography of Shakespeare's Plays, 1593–1685*, London: Methuen, 1909.

Puttenham, George, *The Arte of English Poesie*, A Facsimile of the Edition of 1589, Menston: Scolar Press, 1968.

Qi Biaojia 祁彪佳. *Yuanshantang qupin* 遠山堂曲品, in *Zhongguo gudian xiqu lunzhu jicheng* 中國古典戲曲論著集成 series, Beijing: Zhongguo xiju chubanshe, 1959, vol. 6.

Qian Nanyang 錢南揚, *Yuan ben pipa ji jiaozhu* 元本琵琶記校註, Beijing: Zhonghua shuju, 2009.

Rizvi, Pervez, 'The Bibliographic Relationship between the Texts of *Troilus and Cressida*', *The Library*, 14 (2013), pp. 271–312.

Robinson, Marsha S., *Writing the Reformation: Actes and Monuments and the Jacobean History Play*, Aldershot: Ashgate, 2002.

Robson, M. (2011), 'The Ethics of Anonymity' in J. Starner and B. Traister (eds), *Anonymity in Early Modern England*, Farnham: Ashgate, pp. 159–75.

Rowe, Nicholas, *Some Account of the Life of Mr William Shakespeare*, London: Jacob Tonson, 1709.

Rowley, Samuel, *When You See Me, You Know Me*, ed. F. P. Wilson, Oxford: Malone Society, 1952.

Scott, Walter, *The Journal of Sir Walter Scott*, ed. W. E. K. Anderson, Edinburgh: Canongate Books, 1998.

Scott Kastan, David, *Shakespeare and the Book*, Cambridge: Cambridge University Press, 2001.

Shakespeare, William, *Measure for Measure*, Bloomsbury Arden Shakespeare, ed. J. W. Lever, London: Methuen, 1965.

Shakespeare, William, *Richard II*, ed. Andrew Gurr, Cambridge: Cambridge University Press, 1984.

Shakespeare, William, *The First Quarto of King Lear*, ed. Jay L. Halio, Cambridge: Cambridge University Press, 1994.

Shakespeare, William, *King Henry V*, Bloomsbury Arden Shakespeare, ed. T. W. Craik, London and New York: Routledge, 1995.

Shakespeare, William, *King Henry VIII*, ed. Gordon McMullan, 3rd edn, London: Bloomsbury Arden Shakespeare, 2000.

Shakespeare, William, *The Complete Works*, eds Stanley Wells,
    Gary Taylor, John Jowett and William Montgomery, 2nd edn,
    Oxford: Oxford University Press, 2005.

Sharpe, Kevin, *Criticism and Compliment: The Politics of
    Literature in the England of Charles I*, Cambridge: Cambridge
    University Press, 1990.

Sharpe, W., 'Authorship and Attribution', in J. Bate and
    E. Rasmussen (eds), *William Shakespeare and Others:
    Collaborative Plays*, Basingstoke: Palgrave, 2013, pp. 643–747.

Shen Chongsui 沈崇綏, *Duqu xuzhi* 度曲須知, *Zhongguo gudian
    xiqu lunzhu jicheng* 中國古典戲曲論著集成 series, Beijing:
    Zhongguo xiqu chubanshe, 1959, vol. 5.

Shen Defu 沈德符, *Wanli yehuo bian* 萬曆野獲編, Beijing:
    Zhonghua shuju, 1997.

Shirley, James, *The Doubtful Heir. A Tragi-comedy*, London:
    Humphrey Robinson and Humphrey Moseley, 1653.

Sieber, Patricia, 'Seeing the World through *Xianqing ouji* (1671)',
    Modern Chinese Literature and Culture, 12 (2000), pp. 1–42.

Sieber, Patricia, *Theaters of Desire: Authors, Readers, and the
    Reproduction of Early Chinese Song-Drama, 1300–2000*, New
    York: Palgrave Macmillan, 2003.

Sieber, Patricia, 'Nobody's Genre, Everybody's Song: *Sanqu* Songs
    and the Expansion of the Literary Sphere in Yuan China',
    Journal of Chinese Literature, 1 (2014), pp. 29–64.

Sima Qian 司馬遷, *Shiji* 史記, Beijing: Zhonghua shuju, 1959.

Song Maocheng 宋懋澄, *Jiuyueji* 九籥集, Beijing: Zhongguo shehui
    kexue chubanshe, 1984.

Stallybrass, Peter and Roger Chartier, 'Reading and Authorship:
    The Circulation of Shakespeare 1590–1619', in Andrew Murphy
    (ed.), *A Concise Companion to Shakespeare and the Text*,
    Oxford: Blackwell, 2007, pp. 35–56.

Stern, Tiffany, *Documents of Performance in Early Modern
    England*, Cambridge: Cambridge University Press, 2009.

Stern, Tiffany, 'Middleton's Collaborators in Music and Song',
    in Gary Taylor and Trish Thomas Henley (eds), *The Oxford
    Handbook of Thomas Middleton*, Oxford: Clarendon Press,
    2012, pp. 64–79.

Straznicky, Marta (ed.), *The Book of the Play: Playwrights,
    Stationers, and Readers in Early Modern England*, Amherst:
    University of Massachusetts Press, 2006.

Straznicky, Marta (ed.), *Shakespeare's Stationers: Studies in Cultural Bibliography*, Philadelphia: University of Pennsylvania Press, 2013.

Streitberger, W. R., 'Adult Playing Companies to 1583', in Richard Dutton (ed.), *The Oxford Handbook of Early Modern Theatre*, Oxford: Oxford University Press, 2009.

Sturgess, Keith, *Jacobean Private Theatre*, London: Routledge, 1987.

Sun Chongtao 孫崇濤, *Fengyue jinnang kaoshi* 風月錦囊考釋, Beijing: Zhonghua shuju, 2000.

Sun Kaidi 孫楷第, *Yeshiyuan gujin zaju kao* 也是園古今雜劇考, Shanghai: Shangza chubanshe, 1953.

Swatek, Catherine C. *Peony Pavilion Onstage: Four Centuries in the Career of a Chinese Drama*, Ann Arbor: Center for Chinese Studies, University of Michigan, 2002.

Syme, Holger Schott, 'Thomas Creede, William Barley, and the Venture of Printing Plays', in Straznicky (ed.), *Shakespeare's Stationers*.

Tang Xianzu 湯顯祖, *Tang Xianzu ji* 湯顯祖集, Beijing: Zhonghua shuju, 1962.

Tan, Tian Yuan, 'The Sovereign and the Theater: Reconsidering the Impact of Ming Taizu's Prohibitions', in Sarah Schneewind (ed.), *Long Live the Emperor: Uses of the Ming Founder across Six Centuries of East Asian History*, Minneapolis: Society for Ming Studies, 2008, pp. 149–69.

Tan, Tian Yuan, *Songs of Transgression and Contentment: Discharged Officials and Literati Communities in Sixteenth-Century North China*. Cambridge, MA: Harvard University Asia Center, 2010.

Tan, Tian Yuan and Paolo Santangelo (eds), *Passion, Romance, and Qing: The World of Emotions and States of Mind in Peony Pavilion*, Leiden: Brill, 2014.

Tang Xianzu 湯顯祖, *Tang Xianzu ji* 湯顯祖集, Beijing: Zhonghua shuju, 1962.

Taylor, Gary, 'Shakespeare Plays on Renaissance Stages', in Stanley Wells and Sarah Stanton (eds), *The Cambridge Companion to Shakespeare on Stage*, Cambridge: Cambridge University Press, 2002, pp. 1–20.

Taylor, Gary, 'Lives and Afterlives', in Gary Taylor and John Lavagnino (eds), *Thomas Middleton: The Collected Works*, Oxford: Oxford University Press, 2007.

Taylor, Gary and John Lavagnino (eds), *Thomas Middleton and Early Modern Textual Culture*, Oxford: Clarendon Press, 2007.

Teague, Francis, 'The Phoenix and the Cockpit-in-Court Playhouses' in Richard Dutton (ed.), *The Oxford Handbook of Early Modern Theatre*, Oxford: Oxford University Press, 2009.

Tillotson, Geoffrey, '*Othello* and *The Alchemist* at Oxford', *Times Literary Supplement* (20 July 1933), p. 494.

Tschanz, Dietrich. 'History and Meaning in the Late Ming Drama *Ming fengji*', *Ming Studies*, 35 (1995), pp. 1–31.

Tseng Yong-yih 曾永義, 'Mingdai diwang yu xiqu' 明代帝王與戲曲, *Wenshizhe xuebao* 文史哲學報, 40 (1993), pp. 1–23.

Vickers, B., *Shakespeare, Co-Author*, Oxford: Oxford University Press, 2002.

Volpp, Sophie, *Worldly Stage: Theatricality in Seventeenth-Century China*, Cambridge, MA: Harvard University Asia Center, 2011.

Wakeman, Frederic, *The Great Enterprise: The Manchu Reconstruction of Imperial Order in Seventeenth-century China*, Berkeley: University of California Press, 1985.

Wall, W., 'Early Modern Authorship in 2007', *Shakespeare Studies*, 36 (2008), pp. 60–6.

Walls, Peter, *Music in the English Courtly Masque*, Oxford: Clarendon Press, 1995.

Wang Chiu-kui 王秋桂 et al. (eds), *Shanben xiqu congkan* 善本戲曲叢刊, Taipei: Taiwan xuesheng shuju, 1984–7.

Wang Jide 王驥德, *Qulü* 曲律, in *Zhongguo gudian xiqu lunzhu jicheng* 中國古典戲曲論著集成 series, Beijing: Zhongguo xiqu chubanshe, 1959, vol. 4.

Wang Liqi 王利器 (comp.), *Yuan Ming Qing sandai jinhui xiaoshuo xiqu shiliao* 元明清三代禁毀小說戲曲史料, rev. edn, Shanghai: Shanghai guji chubanshe, 1981.

Wang, Richard, *Ming Erotic Novellas: Genre, Consumption and Religiosity in Cultural Practice*, Hong Kong: The Chinese University Press, 2011.

Wang Shifu 王實甫, *Xixiang ji* 西廂記, photographic reproduction of the 1498 edition, Shijiazhuang: Hebei jiaoyu chubanshe, 2006.

Wang Shih-pe 汪詩珮, 'Cong Yuankanben chongtan Yuan zaju: yi banben, tizhi, juchang san'ge mianxiang wei fanchou' 從元刊本重探元雜劇—以版本、體製、劇場三個面向為範疇, PhD dissertation, National Tsing Hua University, 2006.

Wang Shizhen 王世貞, *Quzao* 曲藻, in *Zhongguo gudian xiqu*

lunzhu jicheng 中國古典戲曲論著集成, Beijing: Zhongguo xiju chubanshe, 1959, vol. 4.

Wang Xiaoyi 汪效倚 (comp. and annot.), *Pan Zhiheng quhua* 潘之恒曲話, Beijing: Zhongguo xiju chubanshe, 1988.

Wang Yongjian 王永健, 'Guanyu *Mingfeng ji* de zuozhe wenti' 關於《鳴鳳記》的作者問題, in idem, *Tang Xianzu yu Ming Qing chuanqi yanjiu* 湯顯祖與明清傳奇研究, Taipei: Zhiyi chubanshe, 1995, pp. 119–33.

Watson, Ian, *Negotiating Cultures: Eugenio Barba and the Intercultural Debate*, Manchester: Manchester University Press, 2002.

Wells, S., *Shakespeare & Co.: Christopher Marlowe, Thomas Dekker, Ben Jonson, Thomas Middleton, John Fletcher and the Other Players in His Story*, New York: Pantheon Books, 2006.

West, Stephen H., 'Text and Ideology: Ming Editors and Northern Drama', in P. J. Smith and R. Von Glahn (eds), *The Song-Yuan-Ming Transition in Chinese History*, Cambridge, MA: Harvard University Asia Center, 2003, pp. 329–73.

West, Stephen H. and Wilt L. Idema (eds and trans), *The Story of the Western Wing*, Berkeley: University of California Press, 1995.

West, Stephen H. and Wilt L. Idema, *The Orphan of Zhao and Other Yuan Plays: The Earliest Known Versions*, New York: Columbia University Press, 2014.

Wheatley, Henry B. (ed.), *The Diary of Samuel Pepys, 1659–1663*, London: G. Bell, 1946.

Wheler, R. B., *History and Antiquities of Stratford-upon-Avon*, London: J. Ward, 1806.

Wickham, Glynne, *Early English Stages 1300 to 1600*, London: Routledge, 1959–81.

Wickham, Glynne, Herbert Berry and William Ingram (eds), *English Professional Theatre, 1530–1660*, Cambridge: Cambridge University Press, 2000.

Wiggins, M., *Shakespeare and the Drama of His Time*, Oxford: Oxford University Press, 2000.

Wilkerson, D., 'Shih and Historical Consciousness in Ming Drama', PhD dissertation, Yale University, 1992.

Williams, G. W. and G. Blakemore Evans (eds), *The History*

of King Henry IV; As Revised by Sir Edward Dering, Bart, Charlottesville: University Press of Virginia, 1974.

Wright, James, *Historia Histrionica. An Historical Account of the English Stage*, London: G. Croom for William Haws, 1699.

Wu Bin 吳炳, 'Tiqu' 題曲, in *Liaodu Geng*, 療妒羹, in Liu Shiheng (ed.), *Nuanhongshi huike Canhuazhai wuzhong*, Yangzhou: Guangling guji keyinshe, 1982, pp. 33a–37a.

Wu Junda 武俊達, '*Xiqu changqiang yuepu* 戲曲唱腔樂譜', in *Zhongguo da baike quanshu: Xiqu quyi* 中國大百科全書·戲曲曲藝, Beijing and Shanghai: Zhongguo da baike quanshu chubanshe, 1983, pp. 440–2.

Wu Mei 吳梅, *Zhongguo xiqu gailun* 中國戲曲概論, Shanghai: Shanghai shudian, 1989.

Wu Mengyang 吳夢暘, *Shetang shichao* 射堂詩抄 (undated Ming dynasty edn) 1.16b–17a, in *Siku quanshu cunmu congshu* 四庫全書存目叢書, vol. 194, Jinan: Qi Lu shushe, 1997.

Xi Zhengwo 襲正我 (comp.), *Zhaijin qiyin* 摘錦奇音, photolithographic reprint, in Wang Chiu-kui (ed.), *Shanben xiqu congkan* 善本戲曲叢刊, Taipei: Taiwan xuesheng shuju, 1984, vol. 3.

Xie Zhaozhe 謝肇淛, *Wu zazu* 五雜組, Beijing: Zhonghua shuju, 1959.

Xu Fuzuo 徐復祚, *Qu lun* 曲論, in *Zhongguo gudian xiqu lunzhu jicheng* 中國古典戲曲論著集成 series, Beijing: Zhongguo xiju chubanshe, 1959, vol. 4.

Xu Shuofang 徐朔方, *Lun Tang Xianzu ji qita* 論湯顯祖及其他, Shanghai: Shanghai guji chubanshe, 1983.

Xu Shuofang 徐朔方, *Tang Xianzu pingzhuan* 湯顯祖評傳, Nanjing: Nanjing daxue chubanshe, 1993.

Xu Shuofang 徐朔方, *Wan Ming qujia nianpu* 晚明曲家年譜, Hangzhou: Zhejiang guji chubanshe, 1993.

Xu Shuofang 徐朔方, *Xu Shuofang Ji* 徐朔方集, Hangzhou: Zhejiang guji chubanshe, 1993.

Xu Shuofang 徐朔方 (ed.), *Tang Xianzu quanji* 湯顯祖全集, Beijing: Beijing guji chubanshe, 1999.

Xu Wei 徐渭, *Nanci xulu* 南詞敘錄, *Zhongguo gudian xiqu lunzhu jicheng* 中國古典戲曲論著集成 series, Beijing: Zhongguo xiqu chubanshe, 1959, vol. 3.

Xu Yu 許宇 (comp.), *Cilin Yixiang* 詞林逸響, photolithographic reprint in *Shanben xiqu congkan* 善本戲曲叢刊, Taipei: Taiwan xuesheng shuju, 1984, vols 17–18.

Xu Zifang 徐子方, *Ming zaju shi* 明雜劇史, Beijing: Zhonghua shuju, 2003.

Yan Baoquan 延保全, '*Mingfeng ji* de zuozhe ji juzuo sixiang neirong he yishu chengjiu' 《鳴鳳記》的作者及劇作思想內容和藝術成就, in Huang Zhushan and Feng Junjie (eds), *Mingfeng ji pingzhu* 鳴鳳記評注 in *Liushizhong qu pingzhu* 六十種曲評注, Changchun: Jilin renmin chubanshe, 2001, pp. 759–78.

Yan Dunyi 嚴敦易, *Yuanju zhengyi* 元劇斟疑, Beijing: Zhonghua shuju, 1960.

Yang Yingliu 楊蔭瀏, *Zhongguo gudai yinyue shigao* 中國古代音樂史稿, Taipei: Dahong, 1997.

Yeandle, Laetitia (ed.), 'Sir Edward Dering, 1st bart., of Surrenden Dering and his "Booke of Expences" 1617–1628' (online at www. kentarchaeology.ac/authors/020.pdf, accessed 4 July 2015).

Yeandle, Laetitia, 'Sir Edward Dering of Surrenden Dering and his "Booke of Expences", 1617–1628', *Archaeologia Cantiana*, 125 (2005), pp. 323–44.

Ye Tang 葉堂, *Nashuying simeng quanpu* 納書楹四夢全譜, in *Xuxiu Siku Quanshu* edn, Shanghai: Shanghai guji chubanshe, 2002.

Ye Yongfang 葉永芳, '*Mingfeng ji yanjiu*' 鳴鳳記研究. MA thesis, Dongwu University, 1982.

Yu Weimin 俞為民, *Nanxi tonglun* 南戲通論, Zhejiang: Zhejiang renmin chubanshe, 2008.

Yuan Yuling 袁于令, *Xilouji* 西樓記, in Mao Jin 毛晉 (comp.), *Liushizhongqu* 六十種曲, Beijing: Zhonghuashuju, 1982, vol. 8.

Yuan Yuling 袁于令, *Xilouji pingzhu* 西樓記評注, annot. Chen Duo 陳多, in *Liushizhong qu pingzhu* 六十種曲評注, Changchun: Jilin renminchubanshe, 2001, vol. 15.

Yuan Yuling 袁于令, *Jianxiaoge ziding Xiloumeng chuanqi* 劍嘯閣自訂西樓夢傳奇, in *Guben xiqu congkan* 古本戲曲叢刊, 2nd series, Shanghai: Shangwu yinshuguan, 1955, vols 102–3.

Yung, Sai-shing, 'A Critical Study of *Han-Tan Chi*', PhD dissertation, Princeton University, 1992.

Zagorin, Perez, *The Court and the Country: The Beginning of the English Revolution*, London: Routledge, 1969.

Zang Maoxun 臧懋循, revised, *Linchuan simeng* 臨川四夢, Suzhou: Wujun Shuyetang 吳郡書業堂, late Ming edition kept in the National Central Library in Taiwan.

Zang Maoxun 臧懋循, *Zang Maoxun ji* 臧懋循集, ed. Zhao Hongjuan 趙紅娟, Hangzhou: Zhejiang guji chubanshe, 2012.

Zhang Dafu 張大復, *Meihua caotang bitan quanshu* 梅花草堂筆談全書, Beijing: Quanguo tushuguan wenxian suowei fuzhi zhongxin, 2006.

Zhang Tingyu 張廷玉 et al., *Mingshi* 明史, Beijing: Zhonghua shuju, 1974.

Zhang Ying 張影, *Lidai jiaofang yu yanju* 歷代教坊與演劇, Jinan: Qi Lu shushe, 2007.

Zheng Qian 鄭騫, 'Yuan *zaju* yiben bijiao (di'er zu)' 元雜劇異本比較（第二組）, in *Guoli Bianyiguan guankan* 國立編譯館館刊, II(3) (1973), pp. 91–138.

Zheng Zhiliang 鄭志良, 'Guanyu *Nanci xulu* de banben wenti' 關於《南詞敍錄》的版本問題, *Xiqu yanjiu* 戲曲研究, 80(1) (2010), pp. 340–71.

Zheng Zhiliang 鄭志良, 'Yuan Yuling yu Liulangguan pingdian "Linchuan simeng"' 袁于令與柳浪館評點「臨川四夢, *Wenxian* 文獻, 3 (July 2007), pp. 51–8.

Zhou Yude 周育德, *Tang Xianzu lungao* 湯顯祖論稿, Beijing: Wenhua yishu chubanshe, 1991.

Zhou Zhibiao 周之標 (comp.), *Shanshan ji* 珊珊集, photolithographic reprint in *Shanben xiqu congkan* 善本戲曲叢刊, Taipei: Taiwan xuesheng shuju, 1984, vol. 14.

Zhu Chongzhi 朱崇志, *Zhongguo gudai xiqu xuanben yanjiu* 中國古代戲曲選本研究, Shanghai: Shanghai guji chubanshe, 2004.

Zhu Hengfu 朱恆夫, 'Lun Diaochongguan ben Zang Maoxun pinggai *Mudanting*' 論雕蟲館本臧懋循評改牡丹亭, *Xiju yishu* 戲劇藝術, 16 (2006), pp. 40–8.

Zhu Yunming 祝允明, *Wei Tan* 猥談, in *Guang baichuan xuehai* 廣百川學海, comp. Feng Kebin 馮可賓, ca. 1642 edition, reprint Taipei: Xinxing shuju, 1970.

INDEX